W9-COO-111

WITH EYES TOWARD ZION

Scholars Colloquium on America-Holy Land Studies

WITH EYES TOWARD ZION

Scholars Colloquium on America-Holy Land Studies

Edited by

MOSHE DAVIS

Arno Press
A New York Times Company
New York 1977

Library of Congress Cataloging in Publication Data
Main entry under title:
With eyes toward Zion.

Expanded version of papers presented at the colloquium held at the National Archives, Washington, September 1975, with additional material.
Bibliography: p.
1. United States—Relations (general) with Palestine—Congresses. 2. Palestine—Relations (general) with the United States—Congresses. I. Davis, Moshe. II. Scholars Colloquium on America-Holy Land Studies, National Archives, 1975

E183.8I7W57 301.29'73'05694 77-2493
ISBN 0-405-10312-3

Book design by Carol Claar

Manufactured in the United States of America

To Shmuel Zaretski
זכרונו לברכה

master teacher
and inspiration
to generations of
students

America–Holy Land Studies

A Joint Project of the

American Jewish Historical Society
David R. Pokross, President
Dr. Maurice Jacobs, Chairman of the American
Jewish Historical Society–Institute of
Contemporary Jewry Liaison Committee
and the
Institute of Contemporary Jewry
The Hebrew University of Jerusalem
Dr. Daniel G. Ross, Chairman of the Institute's
International Planning Committee

Ongoing research for the America–Holy Land
Studies Project is made possible by grants
from the Memorial Foundation for Jewish
Culture and Irving and Bertha Neuman, New York.

Acknowledgments

Although the editor clearly assumes final responsibility for the scope and contents of this volume, it is hardly necessary to emphasize that both the colloquium and publication were a collaborative enterprise, and thanks are due chiefly to:

The authors, for contributing the fruits of their research;

The sponsoring organizations in the persons of:

Dr. Maurice Jacobs, then President of the American Jewish Historical Society and now Chairman of the American Jewish Historical Society–Institute of Contemporary Jewry Liaison Committee;

Dr. Daniel G. Ross, Chairman of the International Planning Committee of the Hebrew University's Institute of Contemporary Jewry;

Dr. James E. O'Neill, Deputy Archivist of the United States, and his associate, Ms. Elsie Freivogel;

Arleen Keylin, Editor, and Suri Fleischer, Assistant Editor, whose personal devotion was matched by their talents;

Arnold Zohn, publisher and friend, who took this project to his heart;

Above all, my colleagues Robert T. Handy, Nathan M. Kaganoff, Lucy K. Manoff, and Bernard Wax, whose programmatic and editorial acumen is an ever-present blessing.

Contents

Contributing Authors

W.D. BLANKS
Professor of Religion
Drake University, Des Moines, Iowa

WAYNE S. COLE
Professor of History
University of Maryland, College Park, Md.

JULES DAVIDS
Professor of American History and Diplomacy
Georgetown University, Washington, D.C.

MOSHE DAVIS
Stephen S. Wise Professor in American Jewish History and Institutions
Head, Institute of Contemporary Jewry
The Hebrew University of Jerusalem, Israel

RODERIC H. DAVISON
Professor of History
George Washington University, Washington, D.C.

YOHAI GOELL
Research Associate, America-Holy Land Studies Project
The Hebrew University of Jerusalem, Israel

MILTON O. GUSTAFSON
Chief, Diplomatic Branch
National Archives and Records Service, Washington D.C.

ROBERT T. HANDY
Dean of Graduate Studies and
Professor of Church History
Union Theological Seminary, New York, N.Y.

LAWRENCE N. JONES
Professor of Afro-American Church History
Dean, School of Religion
Howard University, Washington, D.C.

NATHAN M. KAGANOFF
Editorial Coordinator, America-Holy Land Project
Editor-Librarian
American Jewish Historical Society, Waltham, Mass.

MARTHA B. KATZ-HYMAN
Assistant Librarian
American Jewish Historical Society, Waltham, Mass.

MOSHE MA'OZ
Professor of History of the Muslim Countries
Director, Harry S. Truman Research Institute
The Hebrew University of Jerusalem, Israel

Colloquium Participants

HOWARD APPLEGATE
Director
Balch Institute, Society of American Archivists, Philadelphia, Pa.

HYMAN BERMAN
Professor of History
University of Minnesota, Minneapolis, Minn.

ANN BOWDEN
Associate Editor of the Papers of the
Bibliographical Society of America; Chairman,
Rare Books and Manuscript Section of the Association of College and Research Libraries, Austin, Tex.

MILES L. BRADBURY
Professor of History
University of Maryland, College Park, Md.

REVEREND WALTER BURGHARDT, S.J.
Professor of Patristics
Catholic University of America, Washington, D.C.

REVEREND PAUL A. BYRNES
Librarian, Missionary Research Library
Union Theological Seminary, New York, N.Y.

REVEREND PAUL CARLSON
Graduate Student
New York University, New York, N.Y.

JOHN B. CARMAN
Professor of Comparative Religion
and Director, Center for the Study of World Religions,
Harvard University, Cambridge, Mass.

W. D. DAVIES
George Washington Ivey Professor of Advanced
Studies and Research in Christian Origins
Duke University Divinity School, Durham, N.C.

WILLIAM R. EMERSON
Director
Franklin Delano Roosevelt Library, Hyde Park, N.Y.

MALCOLM FREIBERG
Editor of Publications
Massachusetts Historical Society, Boston, Mass.

C. C. GOEN
Professor of Church History
Wesley Theological Seminary; Preident-elect,
The American Baptist Historical Society, Rochester, N.Y.

LEONARD GOLD
Chief, Jewish Division
New York Public Library, New York, N.Y.

ROBERT M. HEALEY
Professor of Church History
University of Dubuque, Dubuque, Iowa

JOAN HOWARD
Supervisory Archivist, Office of Presidential
Libraries, representing
The Lyndon Baines Johnson Library, Austin, Tex.

MAURICE JACOBS
President
American Jewish Historical Society, Waltham, Mass.

I. L. KENEN
President
Near East Research, Washington, D.C.

PHILIP D. LAGERQUIST
Chief Archivist
Harry S. Truman Library, Independence, Mo.

STEVEN LOEWENSTEIN
Assistant Archivist and Research Associate
Yivo Institute for Jewish Research, New York, N.Y.

KENNETH LOHF
Librarian, Rare Books and Manuscripts
Butler Library, Columbia University, New York, N.Y.

LUCY MANOFF
Program Coordinator
Institute of Contemporary Jewry
The Hebrew University of Jerusalem, Israel

JAMES E. O'NEILL
Deputy Archivist of the United States
National Archives and Records Service, Washington, D.C.

DANIEL J. REED
Assistant Archivist for Presidential Libraries
National Archives and Records Service, Washington, D.C.

BARRY RAINISH
Graduate Student
The Hebrew University of Jerusalem, Israel

DANIEL G. ROSS
Chairman, International Planning Committee
Institute of Contemporary Jewry
The Hebrew University of Jerusalem, Israel

LOUIS RUCHAMES
Professor of History
University of Massachusetts, Boston
Chairman, Academic Council
American Jewish Historical Society, Waltham, Mass.

FREDERICK SCHALOW
Records Researcher
Presbyterian Historical Society, Philadelphia, Pa.

MENAHEM SCHMELZER
Librarian
Jewish Theological Seminary of America, New York, N.Y.

SHLOMO SLONIM
Head, Department of American Studies
The Hebrew University of Jerusalem, Israel

MARIE SYRKIN
Editor, *Jewish Frontier*
Professor Emeritus
Brandeis University, Waltham, Mass.

A. RONALD TONKS
Assistant Executive Secretary
The Historical Commission of the
Southern Baptist Convention, Nashville, Tenn.

SYLVIE TURNER
Research Archivist
John F. Kennedy Library, Waltham, Mass.

MELVIN I. UROFSKY
Chairman, Department of History
Virginia Commonwealth University, Richmond, Va.

BERNARD WAX
Colloquium Coordinator
Director
American Jewish Historical Society, Waltham, Mass.

JONATHAN WAXMAN
Graduate Student
Jewish Theological Seminary of America, New York, N.Y.

THOMAS WILKENS
Chairman
Department of Theology and Philosophy
Texas Lutheran College, Seguin, Tex.

RICHMOND D. WILLIAMS
Director
Eleutherian Mills Historical Library, Wilmington, Del.

DON W. WILSON
Assistant Director
Dwight D. Eisenhower Library, Abilene, Kans.

ROBERT WOOD
Assistant Director
Herbert Hoover Presidential Library, West Branch, Iowa

Introduction

This volume is an outgrowth of the Scholars' Colloquium on America–Holy Land Studies convened at the National Archives in Washington, D.C., in observance of the Bicentennial of the United States. The colloquium was jointly sponsored by the American Jewish Historical Society, the Institute of Contemporary Jewry of the Hebrew University of Jerusalem, and the National Archives and Records Service. Bringing together historians, archivists, and students, the sessions were devoted to a discussion of methods, norms, and sources for future research in the expanding field of America–Holy Land studies.

The colloquium itself had a prehistory. It began in a series of discussions, seminars, and papers in which my colleagues Prof. Selig Adler of the State University of New York at Buffalo and Prof. Robert T. Handy of the Union Theological Seminary and I attempted to map out the substantive and methodological dimensions of the relationships between the American nation and the Holy Land in regard to its nature and continuity.[1] Substantively, as both Professor Handy and I elaborate in our articles in the present volume, our working hypothesis is that the Holy Land, or Zion, theme is part of the continuing spiritual history of America, illuminating the interplay of ideas among its diverse religious and cultural elements.[2] Viewed methodologically, the subject reflects the cross-cultural and pluralistic experience in the United States.

When the American Jewish Historical Society and the Hebrew University's Institute of Contemporary Jewry joined together to sponsor this project, our editorial team gained the strength and talent of Dr. Nathan M. Kaganoff, Editor-Librarian of the Society, as editorial coordinator of the project and the assistance of Yohai Goell, research secretary in Israel. Recognizing the untilled condition of America–Holy Land studies, we decided to begin with the preparation of an annotated bibliographical guide. The papers and discussion that formed the basis for that decision were published in the *American Jewish Historical Quarterly*.[3]

To carry the research forward, two teams were formed, one in America and the other in Israel, working in accordance with a common plan, flexible to be sure, and modified as we moved along, but nevertheless in conformance with an overarching research design. That design follows from the project's substantive dimensions, which we organized into four major categories and subthemes:

Diplomatic Policy: backgrounds of American interest, consular protection, economic missions;
Christian Devotion: the Holy Land in the historic Christian tradition, Zion in American Christian churches;
Jewish Attachment: the Holy Land in the Jewish tradition, Eretz Yisrael in American Jewish life;
Cultural Aspects: Zion in American thought, American pilgrimage literature, the Holy Land in American culture.

The principal depositories of archival and other primary sources for this field, as this volume delineates, are to be found in the United States, Israel, and several other countries, including England and Turkey. A vast body of documentary materials—correspondence, manuscripts, periodicals, rare books and pamphlets, records, and so forth—needs to be ferreted out, sorted, and described before major interpretative research can be undertaken. Scholarly progress, it was quickly realized, could be achieved only through the organization of the research program on an inter-continental basis. At that point, the sponsoring organizations gave us the benefit of their administrative officers, namely, Bernard Wax and Menahem Kaufman, to serve as project coordinators respectively in the United States and Israel.

The next step was the preparation of specimen pages for the proposed guide, as the testing ground for our conceptual framework. The section chosen for this purpose was "American Individual and Institutional Presence in the Holy Land, 1620–1948."[4] "American presence" is, in effect, a microcosm of the entire historical venture and has the additional advantage of being a fresh subject which scholars have just begun to investigate. Broadly defined, "American presence" includes individual as well as corporate, institutional settlement. It differs from "pilgrimage and travel" insofar as these latter categories reflect occasional rather than permanent identification with the Holy Land.

In pursuing the sources of "American presence," our researchers faced a range of differing types of archives, from relatively well organized institutional depositories to private family collections; they have shaken the dust from many neglected, if not forgotten, files. In each case, the sources were carefully cited, listings were indicated, and items of special interest were featured. For most of the listings, the researchers were compelled to perform a double task—to locate the material and to catalogue it. That is to say, since most of the newly found sources are unorganized, description also became our responsibility. In many instances, almost as in a jigsaw puzzle, fragments of correspondence in one collection correlated with the material found in another. Thus, we know that sources dealing with the "presence" theme will undoubtedly turn up in files of many other subjects as we come to them. We have gathered and are gathering the material of which raw history is made.

The purpose of the specimen pages was not to submit a comprehensive list of findings. We sought to place before the critical scholarly community an example of our method in recording newly found materials for evaluation and informed guidance. And that helped bring us to the next stage—the colloquium in Washington. When the National Archives agreed to be a cosponsor of the colloquium, we cautiously decided on an additional preliminary step—to check our methodology with a representative national consultative committee. That meeting took place in September 1974 at the Union Theological Seminary in New York and opened new opportunities for analytical exchange. In addition to the sponsoring bodies, participants included representatives from the American Association for State and Local History; American Baptist Historical

Society; American Library Association; Cornell University Library; Eleutherian Mills—Hagley Foundation Library; Federal Records Management Division; Jewish Theological Seminary of America; Microfilming Corporation of America; National Archives and Records Service; New York Public Library, Jewish Division; Society of American Archivists; Southern Baptist Convention; Union Theological Seminary and Library; Yale University Library.

Following the consultative meeting in New York, research continued apace. To be specific, and also by way of expressing our gratitude to the agencies who cooperated so fully, I list alphabetically the libraries and repositories in the United States and Israel visited and studied by our research staff:

United States:
American Jewish Archives
American Jewish Historical Society
Boston University
Bostonian Society
Christian Science Center
Congregational Library
Franciscan Monastery, Washington, D.C.
Hadassah
Harvard University: Houghton Library; Semitic Museum; Widener Library
Jewish Theological Seminary of America Library
Massachusetts Archives Division, State House
Methodist Historical Society
National Archives and Records Service
New England Historic Genealogical Society
New York Public Library
Schlesinger Library, Radcliffe College
The Temple Library, Cleveland
Woodstock College Library
Yivo Institute for Jewish Research
Zionist Archives and Library

Israel:
Archives and Museum of the Jewish Labor Movement, Tel Aviv

Central Archives for the History of the Jewish People, Jerusalem
Central Zionist Archives, Jerusalem
Ein Hashofet (Kibbutz) Archives
Herzliya Municipal Archives
Institute of Contemporary Jewry, Oral History Division
Jabotinsky Institute in Israel
Jerusalem Municipal Archives
Jerusalem YMCA
Jewish National and University Library, Manuscript Division
Keren Hayesod Offices, Jerusalem
Southern Baptist Convention in Israel
Tel Aviv Municipal Archives
Yad Yitzhak Ben Zvi

Chief among all repositories are the vast historical storehouses of the National Archives in the United States and the Central Zionist Archives in Jerusalem.

Most important to the future direction of the America–Holy Land Project, this "prehistory" encouraged the prospect that we might overcome a major obstacle in our path, namely, the fragmentation of the source materials in literally scores of public and private collections on several continents. The vexing problem of fragmentation, as is now apparent, may be solved with the earnest assistance of archivists—indeed, in time, perhaps the development of a scholarly fraternity of the kind exemplified by the meeting in Washington—convening from time to time to review and assess the research output, to suggest new resources and approaches, and to delineate further areas for research and teaching. If this is accomplished as work in progress, the sensitive balance of thought and insight with facts and events may well be achieved. It is not too soon, then, to propose the creation of a specialized America–Holy Land documentary library of rare books, periodical literature, and unpublished manuscripts that could be photoduplicated in major centers for the benefit of scholars, graduate students, and general instruction.

The next phase of our project is to study the established libraries of American presidents, the Library of Congress, and church archives, as well as university and historical society libraries. In time, we hope to reap the rewards of fruitful analysis and critical apprais-al—and the vision that may rise from both.

Moshe Davis

Jerusalem
Washington's Birthday, 1977

Notes

1. See our respective contributions in the volume *Israel: Its Role in Civilization* (New York: Harper, 1956).
2. See also Robert T. Handy, "Studies in the Interrelationships between America and the Holy Land: A Fruitful Field for Interdisciplinary and Interfaith Cooperation," *Journal of Church and State*, 13, no. 2 (Spring 1971), pp. 283–301.
3. LXII, no. 1 (September 1972). Republished as a separate: *America and the Holy Land: A Colloquium* (Jerusalem: Institute of Contemporary Jewry, The Hebrew University of Jerusalem, 1972).
4. *Guide for America–Holy Land Studies* (Jerusalem: Institute of Contemporary Jewry, The Hebrew University of Jerusalem, 1973).

PART I

The Historical Perspective

The Holy Land Idea in American Spiritual History

Moshe Davis

THE OPPORTUNITY offered to all religious and ethnic groups to become an organic part of American society, despite some serious lapses, is an impressive phenomenon in history. Most significant has been the encouragement given such communities, in the spirit of American voluntarism, to develop their distinctive values and to contribute those values to the total complex of American civilization. This is a unique quality of the American experience. It is at the core of the spiritual history of America, as valuable for an understanding of American democracy as the political, economic, or cultural dimensions.

The concept *spiritual,* as I understand it, is not a synonym for *religious,* but encompasses the spectrum of religious, cultural, and ethnic history—the accumulated moral, ethical, and creative decisions made by individuals and groups. In this sense, the America–Holy Land theme is integral to America's spiritual history.

The broad concept of Holy Land, or Zion, or Eretz Yisrael (Land of Israel), has been a pervasive theme in American thought and action since the very beginnings of European settlement on the Western continent. This conception has appeared in many variations: from the earliest formulations in colonial times of the Puritan aspiration to a biblical commonwealth, where America itself was considered to be the embodiment of Zion; pilgrimages by Americans to the Holy Land; and in our own time, Restoration under Jewish sovereignty in which the United States played a strategic role.

Devotion to Zion has been shared by Americans of diverse backgrounds and cultural orientations. Attachment to the Holy Land extends into American homes, patterns of faith, and education, illuminating the interplay of ideas among different religions and cultures. Here many varied elements meet, sometimes antithetically, but most often cooperatively. To delineate the historical and contemporary impress of the Holy Land Idea on the American spirit, and more particularly on its Hebraic matrix, we select four elements: Biblical Heritage; Hebrew Language; The Holy Land as Zion, Land of Israel; and Jewish Restoration.

Biblical Heritage

In the American tradition, the Bible is the source of the common faith, a cohesive force in national aspirations. When the Congress, under the Articles of Confederation, voted in favor of appropriating funds to import twenty thousand copies of the Bible, its members voted, quite literally, to supply a household need. As the most widely read book in America during the colonial era and the nineteenth century, the Bible was the unimpeachable source for both supportive and conflicting opinions in the struggle for political independence and in the antebellum period. In trying as well as glorious times of American history, prophets and idolators, kings and commoners who lived centuries ago in ancient Israel rose to play contemporary roles.

The Fathers of the Republic, for example, did not cite Holy Scriptures in the past tense, but as living, contemporary reality. Their political condition was described as "Egyptian slavery": King George III was Pharaoh; the Atlantic Ocean nothing other than the Red Sea; and Washington and Adams—Moses and Joshua. What could have been a more appropriate seal for the underlying purpose of the Revolution, according to a committee composed of Franklin, Adams, and Jefferson, than the portrayal of the Israelites' exodus from Egypt? In the words of Thomas Jefferson: "Pharaoh sitting in an open chariot, a crown on his head and a sword in his hand passing thro' the divided waters of the Red Sea in pursuit of the Israelites: rays from a pillar of fire in the cloud, expressive of the divine presence, and command, reaching to Moses who stands on the shore and, extending his hand over the sea, causes it to overwhelm Pharaoh." The inscription—a motto by Benjamin Franklin—read: "Rebellion to Tyrants is Obedience to God."[1]

Puritan and Pilgrim identification with biblical thought permeated their political system and gave impetus to a distinctive principle of that system, namely, covenant theology. As Richard B. Morris points out, "This covenant theology (see Genesis 9:8–9, 17:2–4; Exodus 34:10, 28; Psalm 106; Jeremiah 31:31) . . . was the keystone to the democratic control of church government. . . . It is government based upon consent of the people, although the Puritan leaders maintained that it must be a government in accord with God's will."[2]

How this ancient civil polity was interpreted in the calls for revolutionary separatism is exemplified in one of the typical "election sermons"—a morality preachment delivered by Samuel Langdon, president of Harvard College, in the Massachusetts Bay Colony, on May 13, 1775:

> The Jewish Government, according to the original constitution which was divinely established, if considered merely in a civil view, was a perfect republic. . . . Every nation, when able and agreed, has a right to set up over themselves any form of government which to them may appear most conducive to their common welfare. The civil polity of Israel is doubtless an excellent general model; allowing for some peculiarities, at least some principal laws and orders of it may be copied to great advantage in more modern establishments.[3]

The Bible was more than a predominating influence on free American institutions. It influenced the individual lives of new Americans, immigrants who came to settle in their "Promised Land." Underlying the events which comprise the history of the United States are the individual sagas of men and women who, each in his or her own way, sought the purpose of their life, the meaning of human existence. To a great extent, this search was centered in the family circle, as its members drew together to study the Bible. Some of the most remarkable treasures may be found in the large family Bibles, in which the records of births, marriages, and deaths were inscribed and which were handed down from parent to child. In these family Bibles we discover the spiritual folklore of America.

Another manifestation of spiritual folklore is the map of America itself. If one's child was to be called by a biblical name, why not one's home, one's town and city?[4] Thus began to appear along America's expanding frontier hundreds of place-names of biblical origin.[5] Numerous places carry such names as Eden, Rehoboth, Sharon, Bethel, Canaan, Hebron, Mamre, Mt. Moriah, Mt. Tabor, Pisgah, Shiloh, Sinai, and Tekoa. Indeed, as one views the "biblical" map of America, one senses how a spiritual folklore was instituted by founders with an intimate knowledge of scriptural sources. Some locations are mentioned only once in the Bible: Elim, Nebraska (Exodus 15:27); Ai, Ohio (Joshua 8:18); Shushan, New York (Book of Esther); Elijah's Zarephath in New Jersey (I Kings 18:8). A Californian in search of gold named his settlement Havilah (Genesis 2:11).

Zion as a place-name reflected the organic relationship between the United States and the Land of Israel. At least fifteen locations are called Zion in almost as many states (Arkansas, Illinois, Iowa, Kentucky, Maryland, Minnesota, Nebraska, New Jersey, North Dakota, Pennsylvania, South Carolina, Utah, and Virginia). Uniquely, Zion City in Illinois was laid out with all its streets bearing biblical names. It was John A. Dowie who, at the end of the nineteenth century, established Zion City, intending it to be governed as a theocracy. For almost four decades the church controlled most of the town's industrial and commercial enterprises. In Shiloh Park, the city was constructed with the church site as its center; branching off it were streets with names taken from the Bible, such as Salem Boulevard, Ebenezer Avenue, Carmel Park, and Jerusalem Boulevard.

A much-favored biblical name dotting the map is Salem. There are no fewer than twenty-seven towns, cities and counties called Salem, and New Jersey has both a city and a county by that name. Thus the founders of these settlements symbolically extended their own "feast of peace" offerings (see Genesis 14:18) to neighboring inhabitants. As is well known, one of America's earliest settlements is Salem, Massachusetts. In 1626–1628, when the Pilgrims received corn from the Indians, they immediately associated the event with the patriarch Abraham and Melchizedek, king of Salem.

Of historical interest is the fact that this particular place-name symbolizes the movement termed progressive pioneering—the transmission of a familial belief from generation to generation. For example, Aaron Street the elder migrated from Salem, New Jersey, to Ohio, where he founded a town by the name of Salem. Together with his son, he moved to Indiana and there founded another town named Salem. The third lap of the journey was by the son to Iowa, where he plotted the Salem in Henry County.[6]

As biblical ideas and images pervaded early American consciousness, the Bible became *The Book* of common knowledge. From it children were taught reading; and as they grew and matured, the indelible pages of the Scriptures, their First Reader, served as their guide, and sometimes even as a determining factor in their vocational choice. One of the most remarkable testimonies of the direct connection between childhood biblical training and vocational purpose is that of the nineteenth-century archaeologist Edward Robinson, whose name today is so closely related to current excavations near the Western Wall. Robinson's Arch is one of the wonders of scholarly ingenuity evidenced for all who come to the reconstructed Temple Mount. In his three-volume *Biblical Researches in Palestine, Mount Sinai and Arabia Petraea,* Robinson writes that his scientific motivation issued from biblical fervor:

> As in the case of most of my countrymen, especially in New England, the scenes of the Bible had made a deep impression upon my mind from the earliest childhood; and afterwards in riper years this feeling had grown into a strong desire to visit in person the places so remarkable in the history of the human race. Indeed in no country of the world, perhaps, is such a feeling more widely diffused than in New England; in no country are the Scriptures better known, or more highly prized. From his earliest years the child is there accustomed not only to read the Bible for himself; but he also reads or listens to it in the morning and evening devotions of the family, in the daily village-school, in the Sunday-school and Bible-class, and in the weekly ministrations of the sanctuary. Hence, as he grows up, the names of Sinai, Jerusalem, Bethlehem, the Promised Land, become associated with his earliest recollections and holiest feelings. . . . With all this, in my own case, there had subsequently become connected a scientific motive. . . . [7]

Thus Americans expressed themselves in personal memory and around the family hearth.[8] In ordeal and triumph, whether in Abraham Lincoln's characterization of the Bible as "the best gift

God has given to man" or in Woodrow Wilson's insight that it is the "Magna Charta of the human soul," the biblical heritage became indissoluble from the American tradition.

Hebrew Language

From the very beginning of indigenous American culture, Hebrew was not just another "foreign" language documented in theological and literary writings—and molded into the seals of such major universities as Columbia, Dartmouth, and Yale. Hebrew was the Holy Tongue, *Leshon hakodesh,* bearer of eternal values, which brought Zion close to the basic elements of American civilization.

The story that Hebrew was proposed as the official language of the newly independent United States is an intriguing legend, which H. L. Mencken deflated in characteristic fashion. The legend originated in deep-seated anti-English feeling, which prompted a suggestion to adopt a language other than English as the official language of the United States. Actually, the suggestion was brought up by the traveler the Marquis de Chastellux. Greek, too, was considered, but rejected. As Charles Astor, grandson of John Jacob Astor, wrote in his essay "The English Language in America," ". . . it would be more convenient for us to keep the language as it is, and make the English speak Greek." Beyond these rationales and jesting, it is particularly interesting that the suggested substitute languages related to the two cultures underlying the Anglo-Saxon civilization—the Hellenic and the Hebraic.[9]

The continuing bond between Americanism and Hebraism, first established by the Puritans, who saw themselves as the renewers of the Bible in their generation, has undergone several transformations. From the colonial period until the beginning of the nineteenth century, the study of Hebrew was set in a strictly theological framework. Throughout the past century and until the turn of the twentieth, it was relegated to the realm of philology and was taught in the departments of Semitics existing in a few universities, far from the mainstream of contemporary thought. In our time, essentially because of its renaissance in Eretz Yisrael and the existence of a Jewish community there for whom Hebrew is the vernacular, the study of Hebrew has flourished, becoming a branch of general culture without in any way curtailing its role in the two previous areas.

This Bible-Hebrew-Holy Land nexus is quaintly expressed in Governor William Bradford's *History of Plimoth Plantation,* which includes portions of his Hebrew handwriting.

> Though I am growne aged, yet I have had a longing desire to see with my own eyes, something of that most ancient language, and holy tongue, in which the law and Oracles of God were write; and in which God and angels spake to the holy patriarchs of old time; and what names were given to things from creation. And though I cannot attaine to much herein, yet I am refreshed to have seen some glimpse hereof (as Moyses saw the land of Canan a farr of). My aime and desire is, to see how the words and phrases lye in the holy texte; and to discerne somewhat of the same for my owne contente.[10]

Puritan doctrine flowed easily into higher education. Samuel Johnson, the first president of King's College—now Columbia University—himself a Hebrew scholar, concluded that the Hebrew language "is essential to a gentleman's education"; hence all the teachers in his institution were to possess a knowledge of Hebrew.[11] The Reverend Ezra Stiles, who served as minister in Newport, Rhode Island, entertained a rewarding friendship with the messenger from "Hebron, near Jerusalem," Raphael Haim Isaac Carigal. After becoming president of Yale, Stiles made Hebrew a required part of the curriculum, claiming that he would be ashamed if any graduate should be entirely ignorant of the holy language when he ascended to heaven.[12]

Stiles's emphatic concern that his family and students should acquire a Hebraic education pervaded his thoughts even as revolutionary events raged about him. After giving a disturbing account of the Battle of Bunker Hill to Raphael Haim Isaac Carigal, who was in Barbados in July 1775, he adds:

> My son Ezra is gone to the University in Connecticutt to study Wisdom among the Sons of the prophets in the *bet midrash* [school]: May the Mantle of Elijah, the *ruach elohim* [God's spirit] defend & rest upon him. My son Isaac daily reads to me the grand Shema *shma yisrael* to *u-v'sh'arecha* ["Hear, O Israel": Deuteronomy 6:49]—Molly & the rest of the Children often inquire affectionately after Hocham R. Carigal. I shd take it as a favor if you will write to Ezra a short letter in Hebrew: for tho' he cannot answer it as yet in Hebrew, it may excite his Ambition & engage him more attentively to study that most excellent & devine Language. For the same purpose & to teach & p[er]fect

> me in the epistolary stile, I should be glad if you would write some of your Letters to me in Hebrew. May I hope for one in Answer to my long Hebrew Letter of 1773.[13]

Conceived as both language and bearer of a specific religious complex, the significance of Hebrew was enhanced in the consciousness of wider American circles. The account of Joseph Smith, founder of the Mormon Church, explains the reason and manner of his devotion to Hebrew, shedding light on a little-known aspect of American cultural and religious life.

The key to Smith's account is in a document which I found in the Mormon archives at Salt Lake City. Dated March 30, 1836, and signed by Joshua Seixas, it attests that Joseph Smith successfully completed a course of Hebrew under Seixas's guidance. Some years before, Smith had been in the process of recording his own version of the Bible because, according to the Book of Mormon, "many plain and precious things" had been removed from the Bible by the Gentiles. From time to time, according to Smith, several of these passages were revealed to him and written down by him. In 1830 he was instructed to stop his notation until he moved to Ohio. There Smith and his followers built a temple in the city of Kirtland.[14] They felt they needed to know Hebrew in order to fully understand the new revelations, especially to comprehend the differences between the Hebrew Scriptures and Smith's version. Special courses were organized and Joshua Seixas was engaged to teach them Hebrew.

Seixas, the son of Gershom Mendes Seixas of Shearith Israel in New York, was a Hebraist and teacher of Hebrew at several institutions of higher learning throughout the country, including Andover and Western Reserve. In 1833 he published *A Manual Hebrew Grammar for the Use of Beginners.* At the time he met Smith he was an instructor of Hebrew at Oberlin College.[15]

From selected entries in Joseph Smith's diary, we can follow some of the progress made by the founder of the church and his "school of prophets" in Seixas's Hebrew course.

> Tuesday, [January] 26. Mr. Seixas arrived from Hudson, to teach the Hebrew language, and I attended upon organizing of the class, for the purpose of receiving lectures upon Hebrew grammar. His hours of instruction are from ten to eleven, a.m.; and from two to three, p.m. His instruction pleased me much. I think he will be a help to the class in learning Hebrew.

> Thursday, [February] 4. Attended school, and assisted in forming a class of twenty-two members to read at three o'clock, p.m. The other twenty-three read at eleven o'clock. The first class recited at a quarter before two, p.m. We have a great want of books, but are determined to do the best we can. May the Lord help us to obtain this language, that we may read the Scriptures in the language in which they were given.
>
> Wednesday, 17. Attended the school and read and translated with my class as usual. My soul delights in reading the word of the Lord in the original, and I am determined to pursue the study of the languages [*sic*], until I shall become master of them, if I am permitted to live long enough. At any rate, so long as I do live, I am determined to make this my object; and with the blessing of God, I shall succeed to my satisfaction. . . .[16]

Smith's certificate was awarded to him by his teacher at the end of the month.[17] It read as follows:

> Mr. Joseph Smith Junr. has attended a full course of Hebrew lessons under my tuition; & has been indefatigable in acquiring the principles of the sacred Language of the Old Testament Scriptures in their original tongue. He has so far accomplished a knowledge of it, that he is able to translate to my entire satisfaction; & by prosecuting the study he will be able to become a [*sic*] proficient in Hebrew. I take this opportunity of thanking him for his industry, & his marked kindness towards me.
>
> J. Seixas
>
> Kirtland Ohio March 30th 1836

This document and its background help to explain much of the Mormon experience in Kirtland, Ohio, at a crucial moment in the evolution of its theology and program. Beyond that, some of the implications of the later relationship between Mormons and Jews become logical. Essentially, it was through this kind of experience that the inseparable bond of Mormon, Hebrew, Bible, and Holy Land was consecrated.

The trend away from the strictly theological study of the Hebrew language toward its philological conception began early in the nineteenth century; it was reflected in the beginnings of Hebrew grammar and didactic textbook writing.[18] Hebrew was taught as a classical language in several secular colleges established in the course of the century, as well as in those affiliated divinity schools where biblical subjects remained dominant. By 1917 the number of higher institutions which included Hebrew in their curriculum reached fifty-five, according to the *American Jewish Year Book.*[19]

While intellectual curiosity about the Hebrew language tapered off in the nineteenth century, its subsequent resurgence in this century is nothing less than phenomenal. Quite apart from its renaissance in Jewish culture, Hebrew today is taught in more than two hundred and fifty institutions of higher learning in the United States—colleges, universities, and Christian institutions and seminaries.[20] In 1940, only nine institutions taught modern Hebrew whereas sixty-eight had classical, or biblical, Hebrew in their curriculum. What is striking about this comparative statistic is that the trend shows continuing increase. Writing in a secular cultural vein, but yet reminiscent in spirit of Ezra Stiles's reflections, Edmund Wilson explained why he considered the study of Hebrew sources indispensable to any "ideal University."[21] In an autobiographical piece, Wilson tells us how he himself first came to study Hebrew.

> I discovered a few years ago, in going through the attic of my mother's house, an old Hebrew Bible that had belonged to my grandfather, a Presbyterian minister, as well as a Hebrew dictionary and a Hebrew grammar. I had always had a certain curiosity about Hebrew, and I was perhaps piqued a little at the thought that my grandfather could read something that I couldn't, so, finding myself one autumn in Princeton, with the prospect of spending the winter, I enrolled in a Hebrew course at the Theological Seminary, from which my grandfather had graduated in 1846. I have thus acquired a smattering that has enabled me to work through Genesis, with constant reference to the English translation and the notes of the Westminster commentaries, and this first acquaintance with the Hebrew text has, in several ways, been to me a revelation. In the first place, the study of a Semitic language gives one insights into a whole point of view, a system of mental habits, that differs radically from those of the West.[22]

What has given rise to this vital interest in Hebrew as language and culture? Certainly the rootedness of the American spirit in Hebraism is a pervasive influence. The indigenous quality of Jewish life in America, with its multifaceted communal and educational enterprise, is a correlative factor. However, the most salient force is the rapid emergence of the Yishuv in Eretz Yisrael as the contemporary embodiment of ancient Hebrew civilization—a phenomenon which has fired the imagination of the cultural and intellectual world. The fact that out of Zion have come forth literary figures, scholars, scientists, and artists has impelled an attitude of respect and appreciation for the language in which they live and create.

Holy Land

The personal attitude of Americans to the Holy Land may be examined mainly in two historical categories, both of which go back to the early days of the American nation: literary records, essentially pilgrimage literature; and actual settlement by individuals and groups.

The many sources of pilgrimage literature constitute a fruitful and largely untapped mine in the history of the American individual's involvement in the Holy Land.[23] Written by scholar or novelist, missionary or tourist, who were for the most part Christian pilgrims inspired by religious doctrine or by stories heard at their mother's knee about Zion and Jerusalem, this literature takes on a variety of forms. From it emerge not only the meditations and feelings of those who journeyed to the Holy Land and beheld it, but also its reflection of the yearnings and dreams of those who never so much as came near it.[24]

"Pilgrimage," wrote the Reverend Stephen Olin in 1844, then president of Wesleyan University, "is little less than to be naturalized in the Holy Land. Only then does the Bible become *real*."[25]

The real Holy Land seen by most nineteenth-century travelers largely dispelled the vision with which they had come. They were rudely shaken by the discrepancy between their expectation and the reality they encountered. "Renowned Jerusalem itself, the stateliest name in history, has lost all its ancient grandeur and is become a pauper village. . . ." "Palestine sits in sackcloth and ashes." These are not quotations from the book of Lamentations. These are the words of Mark Twain in *The Innocents Abroad,* a book recording his travels in Europe and the Holy Land in 1867 and subtitled *The New Pilgrim's Progress.* Mark Twain's humor vanished rather rapidly as he conveyed his shocked reactions to the scenes he witnessed.[26]

It took Herman Melville to draw the transcending conclusion. Melville went to the Holy Land in 1857 and set down his experiences in *Clarel,* a long philosophical poem.[27] For Melville, as Howard Mumford Jones pointed out, the Holy Land was, "in its ruined state, an outward and visible vision of the loss of religions among modern men and, to some degree, the ruin of the world."[28] Melville kept a special "Jerusalem" diary in which we read:

> Whitish Mildew pervading whole tracts of landscape—bleached—leprosy—encrustation of curses—old cheese—bones of rocks,—crunched, knawed & mumbled—mere refuse & rubbish of creation—like that lying outside of Jaffa Gate—all Judea seems to have been accumulations of this rubbish—You see the anatomy—compares with ordinary regions as skeleton with living & rosy man. So rubbishy, that no chiffonier could find any thing all over it. *No moss as in other ruins—no grace of decay—no ivy—the unleavened nakedness of desolation*—whitish [ashes]—lime kilns—black goats.[29]

Such was the land most travelers saw, wasted for centuries. But the dream persisted. Fortunately, many were able to see beyond the barren hillsides and dismal valleys. American Christian devotion to the Holy Land embraced a wide spectrum of religious trends in the United States. Individuals viewed the land not only through their own eyes but also through the prism of the religious tradition in which they were born and raised. In one acute passage, Mark Twain remarked:

> I am sure, from the tenor of books I have read, that many who have visited this land in years gone by, were Presbyterians, and came seeking evidences in support of their particular creed; they found a Presbyterian Palestine, and they had already made up their minds to find no other, though possibly they did not know it, being blinded by their zeal. Others were Baptists, seeking Baptist evidences and a Baptist Palestine. Others were Catholics, Methodists, Episcopalians, seeking evidences endorsing their several creeds, and a Catholic, a Methodist, an Episcopalian Palestine. Honest as these men's intentions may have been, they were full of partialities and prejudices, they entered the country with their verdicts already prepared, and they could no more write dispassionately and impartially about it than they could about their own wives and children. Our pilgrims have brought *their* verdicts with them.[30]

More than a century later we find a lyrical account of the influence of Christian upbringing, as expressed by Ralph McGill, then editor of the influential *Atlanta Constitution.* In his book *Israel Revisited,* he describes the strong impact of the Presbyterian tradition:

> As a boy, I came up in the country and in the Presbyterian faith, and if the hot breath of Calvin has not always been strong upon my neck, it is no fault of my family. I grew up knowing the old hymns in which Jordan's "Stormy banks," Galilee, and "Jerusalem the Golden" were

> sung mightily on the Sabbath and at Prayer Meetings. As a boy I used to dream of some day seeing the golden domes of Jerusalem and the blue reaches of the Sea of Galilee.
>
> My grandmother, who was a "Blue Stocking" Presbyterian, was responsible for this. She yearned all her years to see the Holy Land. In her last years, she would walk out on the front porch of our farm house in East Tennessee, which looked across a meadow and a bottom field where Indian corn grew every year, to the Tennessee River and say, reflectively, "Son, we've all got one more river to cross . . . the river of Jordan." I did not know, being then but a young boy immensely fond of his grandmother, that she was speaking symbolically. I used to ponder on it and wonder why all of us Presbyterians someday would have to cross over Jordan. At any rate, the pull of the ancient land there on the Mediterranean was planted in me as a child.[31]

This attachment to the Holy Land was confined for the most part to prayer and to home training. While some few American groups and individuals did attempt to settle in the Holy Land in the nineteenth century, most of those ventures were abortive. Yet as the incipient movements of scientific study, travel, and settlement coalesced, a new totality emerged, namely, the rediscovery of the Holy Land by the Western cultural world.

History and geography began to meet again. In his comprehensive study of the physical geography of the Holy Land, published in 1841, John Kitto succinctly established that relationship between land and people.

> But even considered in itself, Palestine is a country, small though it be, well worthy of attention, and in some respects as peculiar as the people whose history is inseparably connected with it. It does not, like most other small countries, constantly remind you that it is physically but part of a larger country, from which it is but conventionally separated; but it is a *complete country*—a compact, distinct, and well-proportioned territory. It offers, as it were, an epitome of all the physical features by which different countries are distinguished, and which very few possess in combination.[32]

Yehoshua Ben-Arieh develops this theme in his perceptive study "The Geographical Exploration of the Holy Land." He paraphrases Kitto's definition of the Holy Land as "a country of concentrated history" combining "two main factors which determine the landscape form of a settled country: natural conditions and man's activities."[33] Applying Kitto's conclusion to later nineteenth-century and early twentieth-century developments, Ben-Arieh puts his finger on the phenomenon which heightened "the process of rediscovery" of the Holy Land, thus differentiating it from other Oriental countries: "the renewed settlement of the Jewish people in its historic homeland." "It appears," he concludes, "that historical coincidence was primarily responsible for the particular circumstances which brought together the 'rediscovery' of the land and the 'rediscovery' of the people who wished to return to this land."[34]

Seen in such a light, while the specific efforts at personal settlement may largely have been failures, they assume a collective pioneer importance beyond the interest they contain in themselves. In 1852 the American "consul" at Jerusalem, Warder Cresson, who subsequently converted to Judaism and adopted the Hebrew name Michael Boaz Israel, tried to establish an agricultural colony in Emek Rephaim near Jerusalem. Another colony, "Mount Hope," was started by Clorinda Minor on land now situated in the Tel Aviv-Jaffa area; and in 1866 George Jones Adams, accompanied by 150 colonists from Maine, came to settle in Jaffa.[35] In the latter part of the nineteenth century and in the first decades of the twentieth, while the early Jewish colonies were taking root, some fresh attempts at American-Christian settlement were made. The history of the American Colony in Jerusalem was set down by Bertha Spafford Vester, who was brought to the land as a child of three, in her book called *Our Jerusalem.*[36]

Jewish colonization was also sporadic until the final decades of the century, when immigration to and settlement in the Holy Land gained impetus from the plight of the Jews in eastern Europe. Of course, American consuls, under the power of their capitulatory rights, played a crucial role in the Holy Land itself in granting protection to stateless Jews, who fled from persecution in the lands of their birth (particularly Russia) and had to face degradation on the part of the Muslim populace and Ottoman functionaries.[37]

A recently published document, the Articles of Incorporation of *Shelom Yerushalayim* (Peace of Jerusalem), aptly sums up this period. While it deals with an early attempt to establish an American *Kollel* (community) in Jerusalem in 1879, its content relates to that period in Holy Land history when not only American Jews but Jews from other lands who had never been granted citizenship and hence were totally disenfranchised, acquired legal status from American consuls. In this case it was to Consul J. G. Willson that the newly formed American community turned with a request "to protect it and to bring it under the shelter of his kindness."[38]

Programs for American Jewish settlement in the Holy Land were part of the *Hibbat Zion* (Love of Zion) movement in the last decades of the past century, and then of the Zionist movement. Jewish immigration to Eretz Yisrael from the United States in the course of that period involved a small segment of the American Jewish community, but its flow was constant. An early corporate American Jewish entity—which still exists in Jerusalem today—was established in 1896 and called "The American Congregation, The Pride of Jerusalem, or in Hebrew, 'Kollel America Tifereth Jerusalem.'"[39]

Other sporadic efforts resulted in a society called *Shavei Zion* (Returners to Zion), which counted Adam Rosenberg, Joseph Isaac Bluestone, and Alexander Harkavy among its founders.[40] Early in the twentieth century, a group of students from the Jewish Agricultural College at Woodbine, New Jersey, *Haikkar Hatzair* (the Young Farmer), started a settlement program which later developed through the initiative of Eliezer Jaffe, one of its founders, into the first cooperative small holder's settlement—Nahalal, in the Valley of Jezreel.[41] American Jewish settlement in Eretz Yisrael was also promoted by the creation of the *Achooza* land-purchasing company. Its main purpose was to prepare homesteads in Eretz Yisrael in anticipation of the members' future settlement.

Following the Balfour Declaration, there was a surge among American Jews to settle in Eretz Yisrael. Idealists such as Judah L. Magnes, Jessie Sampter, Henrietta Szold, and Alexander Dushkin looked forward to exemplifying in their life-style in deed those values they espoused in the United States and sought to realize them in the burgeoning young Yishuv. Judah Magnes, the first president of the Hebrew University, was widely respected as one of the most earnest spirits concerned with preserving Judaism in the United States. Arguing against the antinationalism which held sway in his circles, he maintained that contact with the living Jewish People—its Torah, language, custom, ceremony, and observances—was the certain way to bring American Jews out of their spiritual wasteland. For him, as he said on the eve of his departure for Eretz Yisrael in 1922, the Holy Land was "part and parcel of my whole Jewish makeup." In a trenchant essay, written in 1930, he stated:

> Three great things this poor little land has already given Israel in two

> generations. Hebrew has become a living possession and has thus restored to us and our children the sources of our history and our mind, and has thus given us the medium again for classic, permanent Jewish expression. The second great thing is the return of Jews to the soil, not only for the sake of a living from the soil but also for the sake of their love for this particular soil and its indissoluble connection with the body of the Jewish people. Third, the brave attempt on the part of the city-bred, school-bred young Jews—moderns of the modern—to work out in life, in the cities and on the land, a synthesis between the radicalism of their social outlook and their ancestral Judaism. It is problems of the same nature that a whole world in travail is laboring to solve; and among Jewry no more splendid attempt at a synthesis has been made than here, in everyday life and not in theory alone.[42]

In our own era, the old-new religious spirit was expressed by Walter Clay Lowdermilk, land conservationist par excellence. In his vision the Holy Land could indeed be again "a land of brooks of water, of fountains and depths springing forth in valleys and hills" (Deuteronomy 8:7). He thought that Palestine had become impoverished by political and social decay, by erosion and waste, and that "the contrast between Moses' description and the state of the country when Jewish colonists first began their work in 1882 afforded a graphic commentary on the misuse and neglect of resources in the Holy Land."

Speaking from Jerusalem in 1939, Lowdermilk formulated an "Eleventh Commandment," which he dedicated to the Jewish colonies whose "good stewardship in redeeming the damaged Holy Land was for me a source of great inspiration."

> Thou shalt inherit the Holy Earth as a faithful steward, conserving its resources and productivity from generation to generation. Thou shalt safeguard thy fields from soil erosion, thy living waters from drying up, thy forests from desolation, and protect thy hills from overgrazing by the herds, that thy descendants may have abundance forever.[43]

Jewish Restoration

"For I really wish the Jews again in Judea an independent nation." This key sentence in John Adams's letter of 1819 to Mordecai Manuel Noah is probably the first declaration by an American statesman in favor of a sovereign Jewish state in Eretz Yisrael. It is true that in the long line of declarations over the years, we come across many which reflect age-old attitudes of the Christian Church toward the Jews. In 1788, for example, a reader of the *Hartford Courant* vigorously protested against a resolution submitted to the Constitutional Convention (especially paragraph 24), which provided that the president of the United States was to be commander in chief of the armed forces. The reader was fearful that "should he [the president] hereafter be a Jew, our dear posterity may be ordered to rebuild Jerusalem."[44] Notwithstanding the eccentricity of this fear, we cannot ignore its implication, viz., the reader's conviction that Jerusalem might in effect be rebuilt and the Jewish People restored to its land. In fact, while Adams himself clearly expressed his favorable attitude to Jewish Restoration, the very last sentence of his letter shows just as clearly that this positive attitude is firmly rooted in Christian belief.

M. M. Noah Esq.

March 15th, 1819

Dear Sir

I have to thank you for another valuable publication your travels in "Europe & Africa" which though I cannot see well enough to read. I can hear as well ever & accordingly have heard read two thirds of it & shall in course hear all the rest. It is a magazine of ancient & modern learning of judicious observations & ingenious reflections. I have been so pleased with it that I wish you had continued your travels—into Syria, Judea & Jerusalem. I should attend more to your remarks upon those interesting countries than to those of any traveller I have yet read. If I were to let my imagination loose I should wish you had been a member of Napoleons [*sic*] Institute at Cairo nay farther I could find it in my heart to wish that you had been at the head of a hundred thousand Israelites indeed as well disciplined as a French Army—& marching with them into Judea & making a conquest of that country & restoring your nation to the dominion of it. For I really wish the Jews again in Judea an independent nation. For I believe the most enlightened men of it have participated in the ameliorations of the philosophy of the age, once restored to an independent government & no longer persecuted they would soon wear away some of the asperities & peculiarities of their character & possibly in time become liberal Unitarian christians for your Jehovah is our Jehovah & your God of Abraham Isaac & Jacob is our God. I am Sir with respect & esteem your obliged humble servant

John Adams[45]

These citations are adduced to demonstrate the highly complex nature of the American attitude to Jewish Restoration and the admixture of conflicting and often paradoxical positions taken not only by United States high officials and Christian sectarian spokesmen but also by Jewish groups and individuals.

In Protestantism, which of course is the main source for American Christian interest in the Holy Land before the present century, we must be particularly careful not to take for granted any consistency between church tenets and specific church action; or between an individual's avowed affiliation to a particular church group and the political and cultural activities in which he is engaged in a private capacity. Moreover, in any attempt to delineate the character of American Christian relations to the Holy Land, the Catholic position should also be taken into full account, particularly during those decades of its growth and influence, which brought about a major revision in the religious posture of the country.[46] Thus while the bulk of American Christians may have been denominationally neutral on any one issue concerning Holy Land Restoration, action on an individual basis has been often positive and constructive; and such action generally derived from the individual's Christian faith. In other words, while Christian denominations as such did not organize themselves on behalf of—or, for that matter, against—restoration of Eretz Yisrael to Jewish sovereignty (with a few exceptions on both sides of the issue), individual Christians did join with one another along transdenominational lines in favor of Jewish statehood.[47]

America's Jews were naturally not free from the impact of these prevailing norms and modes. They determined to design their Jewish Restoration goals in the American pattern. Like Americans in general, they did not evolve a unified response but, rather, differing approaches, some of which clashed or overlapped. Until the establishment of the State of Israel, most often disagreement centered on the political aspiration of Zionism. Agreement obtained in the areas of practical aid to the Yishuv in Eretz Yisrael, in effect adopting Restoration as a reality. In time, the preponderant elements of organized American Jewry agreed to a formulation which recognized the validity of Zionism in terms of the American Ideal and global concerns. On this basis it was possible for the American Jewish community to awaken public opinion in favor of Eretz Yisrael on many crucial issues.

The historian benefits from the gift of hindsight. He is mindful of the changing manifestations of Jewish Restoration within the multiple-organized American community. At the same time, he perceives contemporary American commitment as rooted in the beginnings of the American nation. It then becomes relatively simpler to trace the historical line of America's evolving polity on behalf of Jewish sovereignty in the Holy Land.

Whether by oration, prayer, or report by Catholic, Mormon, Jew, or Protestant, as we shall see in the following nineteenth-century illustrative sequence, the argument for Jewish Restoration was set forth as if with one mind: the decline of the Turkish Empire is imminent; the Jews, though now dispersed, will return to the Land; blessed will be that nation—hopefully America—which will induce Holy Land regeneration. Inevitably, the image of the biblical Cyrus rises as the symbol of inspired statesmanship.

A sincere introduction to this emergent formulation in the context of an American domestic issue came from Thomas Kennedy, a young Catholic who militated for equality for the Jews of Maryland. Kennedy had never seen a Jew. In his presentation in favor of the "Jew Bill" (1818), he declared:

> But if we are christians in deed and in truth, we must believe that the Jewish nation will again be restored to the favour and protection of God. The story of that wonderful people, from the days of Abraham unto the present time, is full of interest and instruction; their first emigration into Egypt; their leaving that country for the land of Canaan; their passage through the Red Sea; their journey in the wilderness; their settlement in Canaan; their captivity in Babylon; their restoration and final dispersion, afford a theme that never has been, never can be exhausted. They were once the peculiar people; though scattered and dispersed in every country and in every clime, their future state will no doubt be more glorious than ever. . . . And he who led their fathers through the deserts, has promised to lead them again to their native land. He who raised up and called Cyrus by name, can, by the same power and with the same ease, raise up a deliverer to his once favored nation; and it is probable that the time is not far distant when this great event shall take place. Who that has ever contemplated the rise and progress of the Russian empire, and noticed the decline and fall of that of Turkey, but will agree that wondrous changes will ere long take place in that part of the world; and when the crescent shall submit to the eagle, may we not hope that the banners of the children of Israel shall again be unfurled on the walls of Jerusalem on the Holy Hill of Zion?[48]

Thirteen years later, this time in the Holy Land itself, the Restoration theme was carried forward by Elder Orson Hyde, delegated to perform the first formal act of the Mormon Church: to travel to the Mount of Olives in Jerusalem to pray for the land's reclamation by the Jews. Hyde, who had been a fellow student of Joseph Smith in Joshua Seixas's Hebrew course, arrived in Jerusalem in October 1841 and offered the Church's prayer, which was incorporated into the Mormon prayer book, forming a cornerstone in the Church's faith:

> . . . Thou O Lord, did once move upon the heart of Cyrus to show favor unto Jerusalem and her children. Do thou also be pleased to inspire the hearts of kings and the powers of the earth to look with a friendly eye towards this place, and with a desire to see Thy righteous purposes executed in relation thereto. Let them know that it is Thy good pleasure to restore the kingdom unto Israel—raise up Jerusalem as its capital, and continue her people a distinct nation and government, with David Thy servant, even a descendant from the loins of ancient David to be their king.
>
> Let that nation or that people who shall take an active part in the behalf of Abraham's children; and in the raising up of Jerusalem, find favor in Thy sight. Let not their enemies prevail against them, neither let pestilence or famine overcome them, but let the glory of Israel overshadow them, and the power of the Highest protect them; while that nation or kingdom that will not serve Thee in this glorious work must perish according to Thy word—"Yea, those nations shall be utterly wasted". . . .[49]

One of the most imposing forerunners of Zionism in America was Mordecai Manuel Noah. Active on many fronts in American political life, Noah had suffered a stunning defeat in his attempt to found,in 1825, a city of refuge for the Jews on Grand Island near Buffalo, New York, naming it Ararat after the precedent of his biblical namesake. But this "Messiah: American Style," to borrow the title of Harry Sackler's drama, had learned an important lesson from the failure of his grandiose scheme.[50] He came to understand, as Herzl would almost half a century later, that no other place but Eretz Yisrael would do as the Jewish homeland. Only there could the Jews gather once again to fulfill the ancient prophecy of Return. This lesson was the most significant and enduring outcome of Noah's Ararat scheme. What interests us particularly is not only

Noah's "Zionist" outlook but the way he presented it before his American compatriots-as an American citizen who considered political restoration a means to rescue those Jews who were oppressed in other lands, he found it natural to direct his arguments to the conscience of the American nation. The approach of Noah and of those who were to follow him throughout the nineteenth century and well into the twentieth, presupposed that helping the Jews in Eretz Yisrael not only conformed to the spirit of America but enhanced it. America, Noah stated, was "the only country which has given civil and religious rights to the Jews equal with other sects. . . ." Consequently, an even greater responsibility devolved upon it.

> Where can we plead the cause of independence for the children of Israel with greater confidence than in the cradle of American liberty? . . . Let me therefore impress upon your minds the important fact, that the liberty and independence of the Jewish nation may grow out of a simple effort which this nation may make in their behalf. That effort is to procure for them a permission to purchase and hold land in security and peace; their titles and possessions confirmed, their fields and flocks undisturbed. They want only *Protection,* and the work is accomplished.[51]

The composite Jewish Restoration portrait assumes an unexpected gradation in the prescient and ofttimes poetic report of W. F. Lynch, naval commander of the United States expedition to the River Jordan. From the book written by Lieutenant Lynch, as well as from records preserved at the National Archives, we learn of America's interest that the Holy Land be settled by a stable population amicably disposed toward the United States. On Friday, March 31, 1848, when the American sailors pitched their tents outside the confines of Haifa, Lynch noted that

> For the first time, perhaps, without the consular precincts, the American flag has been raised in Palestine. May it be the harbinger of regeneration to a now hapless people! . . .
>
> It needs but the destruction of that power which, for so many centuries, has rested like an incubus upon the eastern world, to ensure the restoration of the Jews to Palestine. The increase of toleration; the assimilation of creeds; the unanimity with which all works of charity are undertaken, prove, to the observing mind, that, ere long, with every other vestige of bigotry, the prejudices against this unhappy race will be obliterated by a noble and a God-like sympathy. . . .

> . . . The fulfillment of the prophecy with regard to the Egyptians ensures the accomplishment of the numerous ones which predict the restoration of the tribes. . . .[52]

Within several decades, the vision of Restoration was darkened by the Russian pogroms of the 1880s. Yet it was the violence of the pogroms which gave rise in America, as elsewhere in the Jewish world, to the urgency of a Zionist solution to the Jewish plight. Without entering into the broad ramifications of the historical developments, suffice it to note Emma Lazarus's plea, which clarified the American Zionist position. Lazarus felt the pain and anguish of her fellow Jews in Russia and realized, much before others did in America and Europe, that Eretz Yisrael was the only possible destination for the Russian refugees. She who composed the inscription on the Statue of Liberty which called America the haven for the oppressed of the world also knew that Eretz Yisrael was the haven for the Jewish People.[53]

In 1882, the very year of the great pogroms and flight of the Jews, Samuel Sullivan Cox, member of the House of Representatives, wrote a "contemporary" editorial in his *Orient Sun Beams, or From the Porte to the Pyramids, By Way of Palestine.* Walking among the "Patriarchs in Israel" at the then "Wailing Wall," overlooking their old and worn volumes, Cox grasped the ultimate truth: Jerusalem and the Jew belong to one another.

> . . . in the full blaze of history, one cannot help but feel that this is especially the city of the Jews. Christians may fight for and hold its holy places; Moslems may guard from all other eyes the tombs of David and Solomon; the site of the temple on Mount Moriah may be decorated by the mosques of Omar and Aksa; but if ever there was a material object on earth closely allied with a people, it is this city of Jerusalem with the Jews. In all their desolation and wandering, was there ever a race so sensitive as to the city of its heart and devotion? All the resources, native and acquired, of this rare race, including its love of music and domestic devotion, have been called in to summarize and aggrandize the soreness of its weeping and the tearfulness of its anguish over the fate of Jerusalem and the restlessness of its exiles.[54]

It is of the essence of historical research to relate beginnings to ends, to discern permanent trends through the study of origins.

In this essay we have concentrated on one—albeit a singular—

dimension of the total continuing relationship between America and the Holy Land. Oral testimony which encases the thesis and written documentation was given by Harry S. Truman.[55]

In November 1953, the former President visited the Jewish Theological Seminary with his friend Eddie Jacobson. In the course of their conversation with Prof. Louis Finkelstein and Prof. Alexander Marx, Eddie Jacobson, pointing at HST, proclaimed, "This is the man who helped create the State of Israel." Truman called out: "What do you mean 'helped create'? I am Cyrus, I am Cyrus!"

Notes

1. *The Papers of Thomas Jefferson,* ed. Julian P. Boyd (Princeton: Princeton University Press, 1950), vol. 1, pp. 494–95, 677–79. For drawing of the seal by Benjamin J. Lossing, see Oscar S. Straus, *The Origin of Republican Form of Government in the United States of America,* 2nd rev. ed. (New York and London: G. P. Putnam's Sons, 1926), frontispiece. Compare Isidore S. Meyer, "The Book of Esther: American Midrash," *Hebrew Studies* XVII (1976), pp. 49–68. See especially the "sermon" (pp. 56–58), originally published on the first page of the *New York Journal or General Advertiser,* September 1, 1774, as moral support of the first Continental Congress, in which King George III is Ahasuerus and Lord North is Haman.
2. Richard B. Morris, "Civil Liberties and the Jewish Tradition in Early America," *Publications of the American Jewish Historical Society,* LXVI, no. 2 (September 1956), p. 22. Cf. I Maccabees 2:27.
3. *The Pulpit of the American Revolution,* ed. J. W. Thornton, pp. 239–40, quoted by Truman Nelson, "The Puritans of Massachusetts: From Egypt to the Promised Land," *Judaism,* 16, no. 2 (Spring 1967), p. 206.
4. Not all children were called by such patronymics as Abraham, Isaac, Jacob, and Israel. Even remote names, such as Nebuchadnezzar, were used. Family pets, too, were called by biblical appellations. Cf. Stanley D. Brunn and James O. Wheeler, "Notes on the Geography of Religious Town Names in the U.S.," *Names,* 14, no. 4 (December 1966), pp. 197–202. In this connection it is interesting to note the comment in the Talmud on the biblical text "Sidonians call Hermon Sirion, and the Amorites call it Senir" (Deuteronomy 3:9): "Senir and Sirion are mountains in the land of Israel; this verse, however, teaches us that every one of the nations of the world went and built for itself a large city, naming it after a mountain of the land of Israel, thus teaching you that even the mountains of the land of Israel are dear to the nations of the world." Babylonian Talmud, *Hullin* 60b (London: Soncino Press, 1948).
5. Lottie and Moshe Davis, *Guide to Map of Biblical Names in America: Land of Our Fathers* (New York: Associated American Artists, 1954).
6. Jerusalem as a name appears less frequently, perhaps out of awe of the Holy City. Yet there is a Jerusalem in four states. An illustrative anecdote of grass-roots immigrant amalgam in America was related about a mining town in Nevada. An Irishman and a Jew were two principal mine owners. As a delicate compliment to these leading citizens, the other miners left it to them to give the new camp a name. The Irishman stood out for a name taken from Gael, while the Jew wanted one that would be suggestive of Israel. After pressure from the impatient miners,

the pair came to a compromise: Tipperusalem. In 1875, New Jerusalem was founded in California. The selection of the title was made by Jewish settlers, according to one researcher, "surely because of the meaning Jerusalem had for these pioneers in their own tradition. . . ." See Lottie and Moshe Davis, op. cit.

7. Edward Robinson, *Biblical Researches in Palestine, Mount Sinai and Arabia Petraea* (Boston: Crocker & Brewster, 1841), vol. 1, p. 46. Henry W. Warren (1831–1912), a Methodist Episcopal clergyman, opened a chapter typically titled "Familiar Palestine" with the following lines:

> This is the first country where I have felt at home. Yet I have been in no country that is so unlike my own. Somehow this seems as if I had lived here long ago in my half-forgotten youth, or possibly in some ante-natal condition, dimly remembered. As I try to clear away the mists, bring forward the distant, and make present what seems prehistoric, I find myself at my mother's side and my early childhood renewed. Now I see why this strange country seems so natural. Its customs, sights, sounds, and localities were those I lived among in that early time, as shown to me by pictures, explained by word, and funded as a part of my undying property.

Henry White Warren, *Sights and Insights, or, Knowledge by Travel* (New York: Nelson and Phillips, 1874), p. 246.

8. Alexis de Tocqueville, *Democracy in America* (New York: Vintage Books, 1955), vol. 2, p. 152:

> On his return home he [the American] does not turn to the ledgers of his business, but he opens the book of Holy Scripture; there he meets with sublime and affecting descriptions of the greatness and goodness of the Creator, of the infinite magnificence of the handiwork of God, and of the lofty destinies of man, his duties, and his immortal privileges.

9. For the scholarly unraveling of this legend, see H. L. Mencken, *The American Language,* Supplement I (New York: Knopf, 1945), pp. 136–38; see also Marquis de Chastellux, *Travels in North America in the Years 1780, 1781 and 1782* (Chapel Hill: University of North Carolina Press, 1963), vol. 2, p. 498; *Quarterly Review,* January 1814, p. 528; A. W. Read, "The Philological Society of New York, 1788," *American Speech* IX, no. 2 (April 1934), p. 131.

10. In his introduction, Bradford stresses the value of knowing the Bible in the original. See Isidore S. Meyer, *The Hebrew Exercises of Governor William Bradford* (Plymouth, Mass.: Pilgrim Society, 1973). For a comprehensive study of Hebrew in colonial America, see Eisig Silberschlag, "Origin and Primacy of Hebrew Studies in America," (in Hebrew), *Hagut Ivrit Be'Amerika* (Tel Aviv: Brit-Ivrit Olamit, 1972), vol. 1, pp. 15–41. See also D. De Sola Pool, "Hebrew Learning among the Puritans of New England Prior to 1700," *Publications of the American Jewish Historical Society,* 20 (1911), pp. 31–83.

11. S. E. Morison, *The Puritan Pronaos* (New York: New York University Press, 1936), pp. 41–42; Isidore S. Meyer, "Doctor Samuel Johnson's Grammar and Hebrew Psalter," *Essays on Jewish Life and Thought; Presented in Honor of Salo Wittmayer Baron* (New York: Columbia University Press, 1959), pp. 359–74.
12. One of Stiles's students recorded this. See *Memoirs, Auto-biography and Correspondence of Jeremiah Mason* (1873; reprint ed., Kansas City, Mo.: Lawyers International Pub. Co., 1917), p. 11:

    During our Senior year the President took the whole charge of our instruction. Ethics constituted our chief class study, and Locke's treatise our only text-book. Some attention was paid to a general review of our previous college studies and the President insisted that the whole class should undertake the study of Hebrew. We learned the alphabet, and worried through two or three Psalms, after a fashion; with most of us it was mere pretense. The President had the reputation of being very learned in Hebrew, as well as several other Eastern dialects. For the Hebrew he professed a high veneration. He said one of the Psalms he tried to teach us would be the first we should hear sung in heaven, and that he should be ashamed that any one of his pupils should be entirely ignorant of that holy language.

    For Stiles's own version of the teaching of Hebrew at Yale, see *The Literary Diary*, ed. F. B. Dexter (New York: Scribner's, 1901), vol. 3, p. 397:

    From my first accession to the Presidency 1777–1790 I have obliged all the Freshmen to study Hebrew. This has proved very disagreeable to a number of students. This year I have determined to instruct only those who offer themselves voluntarily, and that at subsecivis horis only without omitting any of the three daily classical Recitations to their Tutor. Accordingly of 39 Fresh 22 have asked for Instruction in Heb. and these Accordingly I teach at iv. P.M. Mondays, Wednesdays, Fridays. I have besides several of the other classes at other times.

    See also George Alexander Kohut, *Ezra Stiles and the Jews; Selected Passages from his Literary Diary Concerning Jews and Judaism* (New York: Philip Cowen, 1902).
13. *The Event Is with the Lord,* edited with an introduction by Stanley F. Chyet (Cincinnati: American Jewish Archives, 1976). The story of their friendship is told by Lee M. Friedman, *Rabbi Haim Isaac Carigal: His Newport Sermon and His Yale Portrait* (Boston, privately printed, 1940).
14. From details furnished in a letter dated May 17, 1965, from Lauritz G. Petersen of the office of the Church Historian, The Church of Jesus Christ of Latter-Day Saints, Salt Lake City. For an enlightening study

of Mormon Jewish relations, see Rudolf Glanz, *Jew and Mormon: Historic Group Relations and Religious Outlook* (New York, privately printed, 1963).

15. Seixas's biography is somewhat obscure. For his relations with the Mormons see Leroi C. Snow, "Who was Professor Joshua Seixas?" *The Improvement Era,* February 1936, pp. 67–71.
16. *History of the Church of Jesus Christ of Latter-Day Saints* (Salt Lake City, 1950), vol. 2, p. 385ff.
17. Published by courtesy of the Archives of the Church of Jesus Christ of Latter-Day Saints, Salt Lake City, Utah.
18. William Chomsky, "Hebrew Grammar and Textbook Writing in Early Nineteenth-Century America," *Essays in American Jewish History* (Cincinnati: American Jewish Archives, 1958), pp. 123–45. See also William J. Leonard, "The Study of Hebrew in American Protestant Institutions of Higher Learning," *Hebrew Studies* XVII (1976), pp. 138–43. An early example of Jewish encouragement to spread the knowledge of the Hebrew language in American universities is recorded by Bertram Wallace Korn, *The Early Jews of New Orleans* (Waltham, Mass.: American Jewish Historical Society, 1969), p. 249.
19. "American Colleges in which Hebrew Is Taught," *American Jewish Year Book 1917–1918,* p. 406. See also Abraham I. Katsh, *Hebrew Language, Literature and Culture in American Institutions of Higher Learning* (New York: Payne Educational Sociology Foundation, 1950); David Mirsky, "Hebrew in the United States: 1900–1920," *Herzl Year Book* 5 (1963), pp. 83–111. Note Mirsky's citation (p. 85) of Henry Hyvernat, "Hebrew in Our Seminaries," *Catholic University Bulletin* 14 (1898), p. 384.
20. David Rudavsky, "Hebraic and Judaic Studies in American Higher Education," *Bulletin of the Council of the Study of Religion,* 6, no. 2 (April 1975), p. 4, and letter to writer, March 12, 1976. The figures are based on the Modern Language Association biennial study for the fall semester 1972–1973. For earlier studies, see Abraham I. Katsh, op. cit.; *Hebrew in Colleges and Universities,* ed. Judah Lapson (New York: Hebrew Culture Service Committee for American High Schools and Colleges, 1958); Arnold J. Band, "Jewish Studies in American Liberal-Arts Colleges and Universities," *American Jewish Year Book,* 67 (1966), pp. 3–30.
21. Edmund Wilson, "The Need for Judaic Studies," *A Piece of My Mind: Reflections at Sixty* (Garden City, N.Y.: Doubleday & Co., 1958), pp. 146–53.
22. Edmund Wilson, "On First Reading Genesis," *Red, Black, Blond and Olive* (New York: Oxford University Press, 1956), p. 387.
23. For a bibliography of representative writings by Americans who visited or worked in the Middle East prior to 1850, see David H. Finnie,

Pioneers East: The Early American Experience in the Middle East (Cambridge, Mass.: Harvard University Press, 1967), pp. 287–94. For the second half of the nineteenth century, see Yohai Goell and Martha B. Katz-Hyman, "Americans in the Holy Land, 1850–1900: A Select Bibliography," in this volume.

24. Jesse Lyman Hurlbut, *Traveling in the Holy Land through the Stereoscope* (New York: Underwood and Underwood, 1900), pp. 12–13.
25. Stephen Olin, *Travels in Egypt, Arabia Petraea, and the Holy Land* (New York: Harper and Brothers, 1844), vol. 1, p. x. See also David Millard, *A Journal of Travels in Egypt, Arabia Petraea, and the Holy Land* (New York: Lamport, Blakeman and Law, 1853), pp. v–vi; Henry C. Potter, *The Gates of the East: A Winter in Egypt and Syria* (New York: E. P. Dutton & Co., 1877), pp. 247–53.
26. Mark Twain, *The Innocents Abroad* (Hartford: American Pub. Co., 1869), 2 vols. The voyage to the Holy Land is described in vol. 2, beginning with chap. 14.
27. Herman Melville, *Clarel: A Poem and Pilgrimage in the Holy Land,* ed. Walter E. Bezanson (New York: Hendricks House, 1960).
28. Howard Mumford Jones, "The Land of Israel in the Anglo-Saxon Tradition," *Israel: Its Role in Civilization,* ed. Moshe Davis (New York: Harper & Brothers, 1956), p. 248. For a penetrating analysis of Melville's understanding of the Jewish relationship to the Holy Land, see Miriam Baker and Ruth Miller, "'New Canaan's Promised Shores': The Idea of Jerusalem in American Literature, 1630–1894," (in Hebrew), *Keshet,* 18, no. 4 (Summer 1976), especially pp. 128–32.
29. Herman Melville, *Journal of a Visit to Europe and the Levant, October 11, 1856—May 5, 1857,* ed. Howard C. Hornsford (Princeton: Princeton University Press, 1955), pp. 137–38.
30. Mark Twain, op. cit., vol. 2, p. 243.
31. Ralph McGill, *Israel Revisited* (Atlanta: Tupper & Love, 1950), pp. 1–2.
32. John Kitto, *Palestine: The Physical Geography and Natural History of the Holy Land* (London: Charles Knight and Co., 1841), p. xxix. On this, compare Allan Nevins: "Any Gentile visitor to Israel is struck by the fact, never clearly realized by the mere reading of books, that Biblical history is local history writ large; for Palestine is smaller than many an American county, and the immortal place names, from Beersheba up to Nazareth, Tiberias, and Safed, are the names of villages sprinkled over that tiny map as villages besprinkle Putnam County and Dutchess County." "The Essence of Biography: Character Study," *The Writing of American Jewish History,* ed. Moshe Davis and Isidore S. Meyer (New York: American Jewish Historical Society, 1957), p. 439.
33. Yehoshua Ben-Arieh, "The Geographical Exploration of the Holy Land," *Palestine Exploration Quarterly,* 104 (1972), pp. 81–92. A thorough summary of American scientific exploration of the Holy Land is found in Philip J. King, "The American Archaeological Heritage in the

Near East," *Bulletin of the American Schools of Oriental Research,* 217 (February 1975), pp. 55–65.

34. Yehoshua Ben-Arieh, op. cit., pp. 91–92.
35. On Cresson see Abraham J. Karp, "The Zionism of Warder Cresson," *Early History of Zionism in America,* ed. Isidore S. Meyer (New York: American Jewish Historical Society and Herzl Press, 1958), pp. 1–20; Frank Fox, "Quaker, Shaker, Rabbi—Warder Cresson: The Story of a Philadelphia Mystic," *The Pennsylvania Magazine of History and Biography,* 95 (1971), pp. 147–94. Clorinda Minor's work is recorded in her diary and letters, in accounts by travelers, and in several studies. See J. E. Hanauer, "Notes on the History of Modern Colonisation in Palestine," *Quarterly Statement of the Palestine Exploration Fund* (1900), pp. 128–32; N. M. Gelber, "A Pre-Zionist Plan for Colonizing Palestine: The Proposal of a Non-Jewish German-American in 1852," *Historia Judaica,* I (1939), pp. 82–85; Edward Robinson, *Later Biblical Researches in Palestine, and in the Adjacent Regions: A Journal of Travels in the Year 1852* (Boston: Crocker and Brewster, 1857), p. 274. Mrs. Minor was in contact with Isaac Leeser, who published one of her letters in *The Occident,* XII (1854), pp. 200–206. See Leeser's announcement of her death, ibid., XIII (1856), p. 603. On the Adams Colony: Peter Amann, "Prophet in Zion: The Saga of George J. Adams," *The New England Quarterly,* 7 (1964), pp. 477–500; Shlomo Eidelberg, "The Adams Colony in Jaffa 1866–1868," *Midstream,* 3 (Summer 1957), pp. 52–61, based upon the Hebrew press of the period. For contemporary accounts by two American travelers, see Robert Morris, *Freemasonry in the Holy Land* (New York: Masonic Pub. Co., 1872), pp. 265–69; John Franklin Swift, *Going to Jericho: Or Sketches of Travel in Spain and the East* (New York: A. Roman & Co., 1868), pp. 190–204. The Manuscript Department of the Jewish National and University Library in Jerusalem holds archival material relating to the Adams Colony (Ms. Var. 849), consisting of correspondence with senators from Maine and the Department of State, who investigated the colonists' plight.
36. Bertha Spafford Vester, *Our Jerusalem: An American Family in the Holy City, 1881–1949* (Garden City, N.Y.: Doubleday & Co., 1950).
37. See David Landes, "Palestine before the Zionists," *Commentary,* 61, no. 2 (February 1976), pp. 47–56, and the discussion in letters to the editor, ibid., May 1976, pp. 18–22; Frank E. Manuel, *The Realities of American-Palestine Relations* (Washington, D.C.: Public Affairs Press, 1949), pp. 35–44.
38. The original document, dated 22 Adar 5639 (17 March, 1879), is in the National Archives of the United States, Records of Foreign Service Posts of the Department of State-R.G. 84 Jerusalem, and was published in facsimile in *Guide for America–Holy Land Studies: Section on American Individual and Institutional Presence, 1620–1948: Specimen Pages* (Jerusalem: Institute of Contemporary Jewry, The Hebrew University

of Jerusalem, 1973). A free translation from the Hebrew, by Nathan M. Kaganoff, has now been deposited at the Archives. For the background and the outcome of this attempt, see Frank E. Manuel, op. cit., pp. 34–35.

39. For the constitution of the American "community," see J. D. Eisenstein, *Constitution of the American Organization* (New York, 1898). A full description of its early days, including a list of members, is found in Simcha Fishbane, "The Founding of Kollel America Tifereth Yerushalayim," *American Jewish Historical Quarterly*, LXIV (1974–1975), pp. 120–36.
40. Israel Klausner, "Adam Rosenberg: One of the Earliest American Zionists," *Herzl Year Book*, I (1958), pp. 232–87; Hyman B. Grinstein, "The Memoirs and Scrapbooks of the Late Dr. Isaac Bluestone of New York City," *Publications of the American Jewish Historical Society*, 35 (1939), pp. 53–64.
41. The full story of *Haikkar Hatzair*, whose members sought to contribute to the regeneration of the Holy Land through introduction of American agricultural methods, remains to be told. For brief treatments, see Joseph Brandes, *Immigrants to Freedom: Jewish Communities in Rural New Jersey since 1882* (Philadelphia: University of Pennsylvania Press, 1971), pp. 245, 337–38; Alex Bein, *The Return to the Soil: A History of Jewish Settlement in Israel* (Jerusalem: Youth and Hechalutz Dept. of the Zionist Organization, 1952), pp. 88–91, 223–27.
42. Judah L. Magnes, *Like All the Nations?* (Jerusalem: 1930), p. 26.
43. Walter Clay Lowdermilk, *Palestine, Land of Promise* (New York and London: Harper and Brothers, 1944), frontispiece. Cf. James Parton, "Our Israelitish Brethren," *Atlantic Monthly*, XXVI (October 1870), pp. 387–88.
44. *Hartford Courant*, January 28, 1788, p. 3.
45. The original letter is in the Adams Papers, Massachusetts Historical Society, and is reprinted by permission of the Adams Memorial Trust. Noah quotes part of the letter in the preface to his *Discourse on the Restoration of the Jews* (New York: Harper, 1845), p. 5. The book referred to by Adams is Noah's *Travels in England, France, Spain and the Barbary States in the Years 1813–14 and 15* (New York: Kirk, 1819). For an analysis of Adams's interest in Judaism and the Jews, see Isidore S. Meyer, "John Adams Writes a Letter," *Publications of the American Jewish Historical Society*, 37 (1947), pp. 185–201.
46. See Esther Feldblum, "On the Eve of a Jewish State: American Catholic Responses," *American Jewish Historical Quarterly*, LXIV (1974–1975), pp. 99–119.
47. See Robert T. Handy, "Studies in the Interrelationships between America and the Holy Land: A Fruitful Field for Interdisciplinary and Interfaith Cooperation," *Journal of Church and State*, 13 (1971), pp. 290–93, 298–300.

48. *Votes and Proceedings of the House of Delegates of Maryland, 1818 Session* (Annapolis: John Green, 1819), p. 26; E. Milton Altfeld, *The Jew's Struggle for Religious and Civil Liberty in Maryland* (Baltimore: M. Curlander, 1924), p. 22. For background on the "Jew Bill," see Edward Eitches, "Maryland's 'Jew Bill,'" *American Jewish Historical Quarterly*, LX (1970–1971), pp. 258–79; *The Jews of the United States 1790–1840: A Documentary History*, ed. Joseph L. Blau and Salo W. Baron (New York and London: Columbia University Press, 1963), vol. 1, pp. 33–49.
49. *History of the Church of Jesus Christ of Latter-Day Saints*, vol. 4, pp. 456–59. See also Marvin Sidney Hill, "An Historical Study of the Life of Orson Hyde, Early Mormon Missionary and Apostle, from 1805–1852" (Typescript, 1955), pp. 43–65, 113–18.
50. Louis Ruchames, "Mordecai Manuel Noah and Early American Zionism," *American Jewish Historical Quarterly*, LXIV (1974–1975), pp. 195–223; Bernard D. Weinryb, "Noah's Ararat Jewish State in Its Historical Setting," *Publications of the American Jewish Historical Society*, XLIII (1953–1954), pp. 170–91; Selig Adler and Thomas E. Connolly, *From Ararat to Suburbia* (Philadelphia: Jewish Publication Society of America, 1960), pp. 5–9.
51. M. M. Noah, *op. cit.* pp. 10, 51.
52. William Francis Lynch, *Narrative of the United States' Expedition to the River Jordan and the Dead Sea* (Philadelphia: Lea and Blanchard, 1849). For a discussion of the Lynch expedition, see D. H. Finnie, op. cit., pp. 262–70; and for a characterization of Lynch, see especially pp. 269–70.
53. Emma Lazarus, *An Epistle to the Hebrews* (New York: Cowen, 1900), especially pp. 73–74, 77.
54. Samuel S. Cox, *Orient Sun Beams, or From the Porte to the Pyramids, By Way of Palestine* (New York: G. P. Putnam's Sons, 1882), pp. 295–96.
55. Confirmed in a letter to author, April 30, 1969.

Sources for Understanding American Christian Attitudes toward the Holy Land, 1800-1950

Robert T. Handy

AMERICAN Christian interest in the Holy Land increased markedly early in the nineteenth century when citizens of the United States began to visit there in greater numbers. As Frank S. De Hass, former United States consul in Palestine, put it in the early 1880s, "No other land is so fruitful a theme for meditation or so hallowed in its associations; and what is remarkable, it never loses its interest. . . . The more we know about Palestine the more interest it awakens."[1] The focus of this paper is on the major white Protestant denominations and the Holy Land in the nineteenth and the first half of the twentieth centuries, with some brief mention of other Christian traditions.

Both American Protestantism and the Holy Land were changing realities during this period. American Protestantism was steadily growing in size, from an estimated membership of less than half a million to more than fifty million in the 150-year period.[2] It was becoming increasingly diversified into many branches, large and small, through immigration, schisms, and the founding of indigenous bodies.[3] Protestants had accepted the practice of religious liberty and the separation of Church and State, but nevertheless were finding ways of working together in voluntary societies with the intention of making the United States a fully Christian nation by persuasive means. All through the nineteenth century and into the twentieth, they believed that they were moving toward that goal and vowed they would not cease their efforts until, in Horace Bushnell's words, "the bands of a complete Christian commonwealth are seen to span the continent."[4] They not only anticipated a Christian America but also a Christian world, and sent a swelling stream of missionaries to many lands across the seas to that end. Toward the turn of the century, their expectations were so high that they now sound very naive; as one missionary put it, "Christianity is the religion of the dominant nations of the earth. Nor is it rash to prophesy that in due time it will be the only religion in the world."[5]

If American Protestantism was dynamically changing and growing in the period under review, the Holy Land by contrast—one that many Americans drew—seemed unchanging, static, decaying. The changes came at last, with a rush, especially during and after World War I. An American longtime resident in the Holy Land recalled the excitement when Gen. Edmund H. H. Allenby entered Jerusalem late in 1917. "We thought then we were witnessing the triumph of the last crusade," she wrote. "A Christian nation had conquered Palestine!"[6] Col. John H. Finley, head of the American Red Cross in Palestine, later editor of the *New York Times,* devoutly read Isaiah 35, noting it as "the chapter of the prophecy of the Great Restoration, which was also seemingly coming to pass."[7] Although there were those who would have been pleased with an American mandate over the now rapidly changing Holy Land, it went to Great Britain in 1920. This fact can serve to remind us that, though this paper focuses on American Christianity and the Holy Land, the religious forces—Jewish, Muslim, and Christian—of many other countries also had their own important concerns in this land that is holy to all of them in varying ways. As the Reverend Adolf A. Berle put it, "Palestine is a land dear to the heart of the whole world."[8] In our effort to assess American Christian attitudes toward the Holy Land, we must not forget the influence of other nations on America, especially that of Great Britain, with respect to this and other matters.

The interest and curiosity of American Protestants in the Holy Land increased in the nineteenth century because of their strong religious commitments to Jesus Christ, the Holy Bible, and foreign missions. For most Christians, the land is holy because Jesus lived, labored, suffered, died, and rose again there. In his magisterial book

The Gospel and the Land, W. D. Davies shows how this has been a concern of Christianity since the days of the early church.

> The need to remember the Jesus of History entailed the need to remember the Jesus of a particular land. Jesus belonged not only to time, but to space; and the space and spaces which he occupied took on significance, so that the *realia* of Judaism continued as *realia* in Christianity. History in the tradition demanded geography.[9]

Even a quick glance at the vast but scattered materials that record the attitudes of American Protestants to the Holy Land confirms this again and again. Former American Consul Frank De Hass wrote:

> Though we may not be able to determine the precise spot where the events occurred which render sacred these places, such is the influence of the name of Jesus, and the glory of his personal presence, the whole land seems fragrant with his memory. What hallowed recollections the walls and towers of Zion awaken![10]

And, typical of many a pastor who visited Jerusalem, Maltbie D. Babcock wrote back to his parishioners at New York's Brick Presbyterian Church:

> What if the old buildings are gone! what if the gorges are filled up with the wreck of centuries!—here He walked; the outline of these changeless hills He saw; on this holy hill He lifted his eyes to heaven. Nearer still to Him we felt ourselves when we walked through the Via Dolorosa, and under the church of the Sisters of Zion saw the old pavement deep below the present road; saw the foundation of the Pretorium that ran to the rock level of the Tower of Antonia.[11]

John R. Mott, that Methodist layman who was so central a figure in the missionary and ecumenical movements for over half a century, was typical of many Christians whose piety was especially stirred as they gazed on the Sea of Galilee. In 1895, while on a three-week pilgrimage, he wrote, "My heart was deeply moved as I thought of what Christ did and taught around this little lake. . . . A majority of [His] miracles were performed on the lake, or on its shore, or in sight of its waters."[12] The unpublished letters of Mott, now being utilized by C. Howard Hopkins in a forthcoming biography, show how important in Mott's spiritual life his Holy Land experiences were. There are probably thousands of letters like the ones Mott wrote, some resting in various collections of documents and records, others still dispersed in personal or family papers. Many of these undoubtedly emphasize the point that is being made here, so neatly summarized in the motto of the Jerusalem YMCA, "Where the feet of Jesus have trod is the Holy Land."

The devotion to the Bible that has been so strong in Protestant history meant that millions of believers had developed a familiarity with the Holy Land, and those who were able to travel there often felt much at home. Edward Robinson of New York's Union Theological Seminary, whose great three-volume archaeological work of 1841 laid solid foundations for much of the investigation that followed, "the first American scholar whose main work was published simultaneously in English and German,"[13] explained how he first became interested in the Holy Land in these words:

> As in the case of most of my countrymen, especially in New England, the scenes of the Bible had made a deep impression upon my mind from the earliest childhood; and afterwards in riper years this feeling had grown into a strong desire to visit in person the places so remarkable in the history of the human race. Indeed in no country in the world, perhaps, is such a feeling more widely diffused than in New England; in no country are the Scriptures better known, or more highly prized. From his earliest years the child is there accustomed not only to read the Bible for himself; but he also reads or listens to it in the morning and evening devotions of the family, in the daily village-school, in the Sunday-school and Bible-class, and in the weekly ministrations of the sanctuary. Hence, as he grows up, the names of Sinai, Jerusalem, Bethlehem, the Promised Land, become associated with his earliest recollections and holiest feelings.[14]

Though in the latter part of our period critical and naturalistic approaches to sacred literatures eroded this spirit in many quarters, the tradition long persisted. So Ralph McGill, writing in 1950, could say:

> I grew up knowing the old hymns in which Jordan's "Stormy banks," Galilee, and "Jerusalem the Golden" were sung mightily on the Sabbath and at Prayer Meetings. As a boy I used to dream of some day seeing the golden domes of Jerusalem and the blue reaches of the Sea of Galilee.[15]

At last he did, and so did many like him. But even those who were not raised in deeply religious homes were likely to hear much about the Holy Land. For in the nineteenth century the King James version of the Bible occupied an important and familiar place in American literature and education. In his article "The place of the Bible in American Fiction," Carlos Baker reported that "this intimacy, this warm sense of association with Adam and Eve, Job and Jonah, David and Jonathan, Esau and Jacob, Ruth and Boaz, Isaiah and Ezekiel, and even Sodom and Gomorrah, appears constantly in the so-called 'local color' movement in nineteenth-century American fiction."[16]

Enthusiasm for foreign missions swept across Protestant churches in the early years of the past century, and for a hundred years and more the supporters of this expanding movement were determined, aggressive, and confident. R. Pierce Beaver has explained that in the earlier part of the century "the salvation of the perishing was popularly the most important motive in vocations and support. Few doubted that the unbelieving heathen perished in everlasting torment." By the middle of the century, however, the stress was more on

> the providential new opportunities for preaching the gospel to all people. Each decade thereafter some prominent voice or pen read the signs of the times to show the providential working of the Almighty in favoring the mission and to demonstrate a new readiness of the heathen to accept the gospel. One of the last instances occurs as late as 1931 when John R. Mott interpreted the favorable omens of the day in his book *Present Day Summons to the World Mission of Christianity.*[17]

In view of the Christocentrism and Bibliocentrism of Protestantism, the Holy Land could hardly be omitted from missionary strategies.

These three commitments of evangelical Protestantism in various combinations lay behind the desire of many Americans to visit or work in the Holy Land in the period under study. Early prominent among them were the missionaries. The first of the major American missionary societies, the American Board of Commissions for Foreign Missions, which originally was supported by Congregationalists, Presbyterians, and Reformed, appointed in 1818 Pliny Fisk and Levi Parsons, and later Jonas King, to go as missionaries to Muhammadan lands of the Near East. As the board saw it, the whole population of those lands, Islamic, Jewish, and Christian, was in a state of "deplorable ignorance and degradation." The missionaries were to go primarily to the Oriental churches, for as Rufus Anderson put it,

> We may not hope for the conversion of the Mohammedans, unless true Christianity be exemplified before them by the Oriental Churches. To them the native Christians represent the Christian religion, and they see that these are no better than themselves. They think them worse; and therefore the Moslem believes the Koran to be more excellent than the Bible.[18]

With characteristic enthusiasm and self-confidence, the missionaries hoped to succeed with both Oriental Christians and Muslims. On the eve of departure, Pliny Fisk delivered a sermon, "The Holy Land as an Interesting Field of Missionary Enterprise," in which he asserted that, "firmly as Mohammedans are shielded against Christianity, there are some favorable appearances, even among them."[19]

The missionaries found a troubled Palestine, however, and converts were very few indeed. Nor did they make much headway with the Oriental churches; certainly their attitudes were hardly helpful to the opening of doors. After a visit to the Church of the Holy Sepulchre, King uttered this not untypical comment in an account published in the *Missionary Herald:* "The Greeks and Armenians profane the temple of the Lord, and seem to know very little about the true nature of Christianity."[20] The mission at Jerusalem was not successful; the workers did what they could in distributing Scriptures and tracts and in helping the sick when plagues swept the land. The mission in Syria and Lebanon went better, and in 1844 it was decided to close the Jerusalem station. American Protestants thereafter tended to leave Palestine to others, especially the British, while their own work was carried on in other lands of the Middle East. Yet they did not give up their interest in and travels to the Holy Land. One member of the Syrian mission, William M. Thomson, wrote a massive two-volume work, *The Land and the Book,* which has been called "the most popular book ever written by an American missionary, and one of the best."[21] He viewed the Holy Land as "one vast tablet whereupon God's messages to men have been drawn, and graven deep in living characters by the Great Publisher of glad tidings, to be seen and read of all to the end of time."[22] The American missionary presence was never wholly withdrawn from the Holy

Land, for other American bodies entered the field. A report from the middle 1930s found four denominations from the United States at work, along with some "independent forces."[23] A number of books tell part of the story of these missions, but the full story lies in the archives of the missionary societies and in the voluminous back files of the periodicals that kept the American public in touch with the work of their servants abroad. My own research on this topic so far has been done in the Missionary Research Library of Union Theological Seminary, a rich mine of information.

Undoubtedly the largest number of Christian Americans to come to the Holy Land can be classed as travelers, pilgrims, and tourists—the lines between these categories get blurred, especially as one approaches the present century. There have been thousands of such persons; the founder of the American Colony of Jerusalem, Horatio Spafford, once noted that "at one time or another the world and his wife come to Jerusalem."[24] Many of those who came were prominent ministers or lay leaders, not a few of whom wrote books and articles about what they saw and experienced. The trips from Jaffa to Jerusalem and from Jerusalem to Bethlehem and Hebron, to Jericho and the Dead Sea, and to Nazareth and the Sea of Galilee were described hundreds of times. The list of church leaders who visited the Holy Land would be a long one indeed, and it would include many of the names that stud the books on American church history. Such persons as Philip Schaff, Henry Van Dyke, Phillips Brooks, William E. Blackstone, Maltbie D. Babcock, T. DeWitt Talmage, Dwight L. Moody, John R. Mott, John Haynes Holmes, and Harry Emerson Fosdick are but a few of those who were giants in their day whose pilgrimage to the Holy Land influenced what they did and said. Hundreds came who were less well known; many hastily followed routinized paths, but others stayed longer and probed more carefully. To pick an example from the latter part of our period, Frank McCoy Field spent a summer in travel and study and then shared his findings with several congregations over a period of seven months, finally putting his reflections in book form. He said, "In these journeys it was my endeavor to leave the beaten paths and not to see only the accustomed places visited by tourists, but to learn more thoroughly the Bible backgrounds and to capture the atmosphere of Bible times to a degree that an ordinary tour would not make possible."[25]

Not all the visitors to the Holy Land would rate high on the scale of mental stability; how can we state this in a charitable way? Perhaps the lines of Mrs. Vester of the American Colony will serve.

> Jerusalem attracts all kinds of people. Religious fanatics and cranks of different degrees of mental derangement seemed drawn as by a magnet to the Holy City. Some of those who particularly camė into our lives were men and women who thought themselves the reincarnation of saints, prophets, priests, messiahs, and kings.[26]

Not all of those were Americans, but Herman Melville somehow brushed up against many unusual Americans in his short stay. As Lewis Mumford summarized Melville's experience in this regard, "in Jerusalem he had encountered all sorts of queer people: an old commercial man giving tracts to people whose language he did not understand; . . . a fanatical American missionary going about Jerusalem with an open Bible, looking forward to the opening asunder of Mount Olivet and in the meanwhile preparing the highway for the procession of the dead; a crazy American woman who had opened an agricultural academy for the Jews without converting a single Jew to either agriculture or Christianity."[27] Did some of these have followers back home, who played a role in the shaping of American attitudes to the land that is holy to three world religions?

Probably the most important single group in guiding American Christian thought about the Holy Land were the dedicated and disciplined band of biblical scholars, beginning with Edward Robinson and Eli Smith. By the twentieth century they were coming in significant numbers, many under the leadership of the American School of Oriental Research in Jerusalem, which began its work in 1900. A forceful figure in the field of biblical archaeology was William Foxwell Albright of Johns Hopkins, an indefatigable excavator and an enthusiastic interpreter of the results. As a boy he had worried that by the time he got to Palestine all the tells would have been excavated, but when he finally got there in 1919, he found plenty to do. He served for many years as director of the American School and for thirty-seven years edited its influential *Bulletin.*[28]

Here we must digress for a moment to refer to an important development in Protestant life and thought in the late nineteenth and early twentieth centuries. The emergence of evolutionary, naturalistic, historical, and critical thinking posed problems for those reared in the certainties of older views of traditional biblical and doctrinal authority. Congregations and denominations experienced internal tension, sometimes quite sharp and painful, between those who favored the older views and those who swung to the newer, liberal attitudes. There were many who clung to a mediating position, who saw values on both sides and were concerned about maintaining the fellowship and witness of the churches. The biblical archaeologists of the present century inclined to the liberal side, for their approach by definition was historical. Yet most of them remained rooted in the faith, and their deep concern with clarifying the Bible was a modernized version of the traditional Protestant devotion to the Scriptures. As he did so many times, Albright expressed views widely accepted among scholars in 1932 when he said:

> Archaeological research in Palestine and neighbouring lands during the past century has completely transformed our knowledge of the historical and literary background of the Bible. It no longer appears as an absolutely isolated monument of the past, as a phenomenon without relation to its environment. It now takes its place in a context which is becoming better known every year. . . . However, the uniqueness of the Bible, both as a masterpiece of literature and as a religious document, has not been lessened, and nothing tending to disturb the religious faith of Jew or Christian has been discovered.

He went on to say that archaeological research made a contribution to theology in two ways.

> On the one hand, the excessive skepticism shown toward the Bible by important historical schools of the eighteenth and nineteenth centuries, certain phases of which still appear periodically, has been progressively discredited. Discovery after discovery has established the accuracy of innumerable details, and has brought increased recognition of the value of the Bible as a source of history.

But on the other hand, Albright insisted that the theory of verbal inspiration had been proved to be erroneous.[29] Overall, the teaching of the Bible was deeply influenced by the impressive archaeological work done in the Holy Land in the twentieth century; the education of church leaders in both conservative and liberal seminaries was deeply affected. The general attitude of American Christians to the Holy Land was also influenced by the views of those scholars who had lived and worked there, and who were clarifying the Book that continued to be central in the life of the churches. Hence, a person attempting to understand fully American attitudes to the Holy Land needs to inquire not only into the technical results of biblical scholarship, but also into the broader attitudes to the Holy Land of those who taught and those who learned in the American School of Oriental Research and similar institutions. A study of the American careers of those who served a season or two on a dig and then taught in a college or seminary would help us to see the larger picture more clearly.

A much smaller, but very interesting, group of Americans in the Holy Land were those who went there to plant Christian colonies. There were a number of efforts, many of them short-lived. In the *Guide for America–Holy Land Studies, Section on American Individual and Institutional Presence, 1620–1948, Specimen Pages,* attention is given to the resources in Israel for studying the Mount Hope Colony, established in Jaffa in 1853 by Clorinda Minor and a group of American Millerites, and a later (1866) group, largely from Maine, which came to the same place under the leadership of George Jones Adams.[30] At least a nucleus of the latter group survived until 1917. Better known is the American Colony of Jerusalem, which has already been mentioned several times. It was founded in 1881 by Horatio and Anna Spafford, following the loss of four daughters in an accident at sea. These devout laypersons had so emphasized a theology of all-embracing divine love that they had been asked to leave the Presbyterian congregation in Chicago in which they had been active. Mr. Spafford explained his determination to found the colony by saying, "Jerusalem is where my Lord lived, suffered, and conquered, and I wish to learn how to live, suffer, and especially to conquer."[31] The colony grew to include about 150 persons and carried out ministries of welfare, teaching, and nursing—similar to settlement houses in England and America. The older missionaries did not trust or like this group of autonomous laypersons, and neither did the Reverend Selah Merrill, American consul in Jerusalem, who opposed them bitterly for some eighteen years. Yet the colony prospered; during World War I it was feeding up to 6,000 persons daily. In the 1920s, a New York committee for the colony was formed, with Harry Emerson Fosdick as president. Located near Mount Scopus, the colony was caught during the 1948 war in the cross fire between the contending parties. The collection of primary and secondary materials concerning these colonies and what their influence on segments of the American public was, could be an important part of the America–Holy Land Project.

Reference to Selah Merrill calls attention to another set of Americans who were in a position to influence American attitudes—the United States consuls in Palestine. Some of them were ministers or former ministers, and the devotional tone of some of their writings marks them as coming out of the "Christian America" period of our national history. Frank S. De Hass, D.D., has also already been mentioned; he began his big book, *Buried Cities Recovered,* by saying frankly, "The author's object in accepting an appointment under the United States Government was not the honor or emoluments of office, but a desire to visit the lands of the Bible, that he might see for himself how far the manners, customs, and traditions of the people and topography of those countries agreed with the inspired word." He made little effort to hide his prejudices; for example, he wrote: "The Christian population is made up of Greeks, Latins, Armenians, Syrians, Copts, and a few Protestants. With the exception of those earnest workers connected with the Protestant missions there is very little vital piety among any of them, everything formal, ceremonial, mechanical."[32] Another consul whose Protestant piety shows in his writing was the Reverend Edwin Sherman Wallace, for five years a resident of Jerusalem in the late nineteenth century. With a directness that would now be quite unseemly for such an official, he criticized Oriental Christianity sharply as "little else than lifeless form" as he surveyed Christian work then extant in Jerusalem.[33] Research in the National Archives and in personal papers on the lives of United States consuls in Palestine may add important dimensions to our overall understanding of America–Holy Land relationships.

Even a cursory survey of these five groups of Protestant Americans in the Holy Land can allow us to draw some preliminary conclusions about the general picture that they reflected back to the American Christian public. Certainly, they conveyed in their letters and writings a sense of fascination and consuming interest. De Hass spoke of the land as

> the theatre of the most stirring and momentous events in the history of our world. Learned divines, historians, and antiquarians for ages have been visiting this land, giving us glowing descriptions of their

> travels, with the results of their investigations, until our libraries teem with volumes on these subjects; and yet the desire to know more about this country was never greater than at present.[34]

Yet, with few exceptions, the knowledge that the faithful Protestants sought primarily was about the Holy Land of the Bible, not of the nineteenth and twentieth centuries. E. S. Wallace noted that visitors to Jerusalem had a strong sentiment about this matter, preferring "to see a city untouched by the hand of modern improvement."[35] After World War I, those who came often congratulated themselves when they could find something that must have been just that way in Bible times. Colonel Finley rejoiced to give this report in 1919, following a walk across the plains south of Jerusalem:

> Nowhere else in lower Palestine was the far past so close. There was no near association for the most of the way across the plain to disturb the consciousness of the past, and I was free to spend most of the time in the company of Abraham and his boy Isaac, Elijah, David, and others of those ancient days.[36]

Frank McCoy Field, writing at the very end of our period, declared, "We can be thankful that, until about the time of the Second World War, Palestine has been a land of few changes."[37] The biblical scholars were professionally dedicated to recovering the Palestine of the past.

The impression I have gathered on the basis of evidence seen so far is that American Protestants' interest in the Holy Land was primarily a function of their religious sensibilities, and was directed to the land of the Book much more than to the land of the living. There are some exceptions, of course, but this impression comes across very strongly. It needs to be tested against a wider range of evidence awaiting investigation in our libraries and archives.

A confirmation of the judgment that has been offered comes in a somewhat negative way by observing the distaste that many American Protestants seemed to have not only for the Palestine they actually found but also for the kind of Christianity they found there. For example, the first missionaries were critical of what Levi Parsons described as "the disgraceful exhibition" of the Holy Fire at the Church of the Holy Sepulchre on the anniversary of the crucifixion, "the supposed miraculous descent of the Holy Spirit under the similitude of *fire*."[38] They also sharply criticized the bitter quarrels between the warring Christian sects at the Holy Places—but never referred to their own divided houses back home. When the decision was made to close the first American Protestant mission to Jerusalem, Dr. Joel Hawes of the American Board of Commissioners spoke words that seem impersonal and callous. Speaking of the population of the city, he said:

> It is composed of well-nigh all nations and of all religions, who are distinguished for nothing so much as for jealousy and hatred of each other. As to the crowds of pilgrims who annually visit the Holy City,—a gross misnomer, by the way, as it now is,—they are certainly no very hopeful subjects of missionary effort; drawn thither, as they are, chiefly by the spirit of superstition; and during the brief time they remain here, kept continually under the excitement of lying vanities, which without number are addressed to their eyes, and poured in at their ears.[39]

This negative note toward the land and the people as they were persists throughout our period. De Hass exclaimed, "You see nothing but ruin and desolation everywhere. The people are poor and ignorant, the land neglected and barren, and the towns filthy and cheerless."[40] And John Haynes Holmes wrote, after his trip to Bethlehem in 1929, "I was disgusted by the Church of the Nativity, with its preposterous shams of the stable and the manger, and its equally preposterous divisions of area between Latin, Greek, Coptic and other warring Christian sects."[41] Of course, there are some statements of quite a different tone; one thinks of the ability of the members of the American Colony to appreciate many variant styles of life and piety. And one must remember that it was only toward the end of the period treated here that what I have elsewhere called the "second disestablishment" of Protestant Christianity in America took place and the actual highly pluralized religious situation was seriously recognized.[42] Only toward the end of the period did the ecumenical and paraecumenical movements help to bring about a more open attitude to the rich variety of Christian bodies and to other world religions. Only after the middle of the twentieth century did the dramatic change in Protestant-Catholic relations take place, with the pontificate of Pope John XXIII and Vatican II. Indeed, a major reason why considerable archival work in depth is now needed is to test and improve such generalizations as are being suggested here and as have been proposed by others, and to put them in the historical contexts of these earlier decades.

Our topic is "Sources for Understanding American Christian Attitudes toward the Holy Land, 1800–1950," and after having given attention to five groups of Americans who traveled or lived there, we must ask, But how much of this played a role in shaping the attitudes of Christians in the United States? I'm convinced that the answer is: A great deal; indeed, that it was of the essence of American opinion. The missionaries had large followings back home; their journals and letters were regularly published in the periodicals. Levi Parsons died in Alexandria a year after he had arrived in Jerusalem. A historian of the mission he served wrote of him, "Though scarcely thirty years of age, such was the impression he made on the Christian community at home, that his death was widely lamented; the more, doubtless, because of the intimate association of his name with Jerusalem, Zion, Gethsemane, and the scenes of the crucifixion."[43] Those who lived went home to report to the home constituency; a revealing note about Jonas King, Parsons's successor, stated that "he returned home at the close of the summer of 1827, and soon after the annual meeting of the Board made a tour as agent through the Southern and Middle States, which occupied him till April of the following year."[44] So most missionaries have spent considerable time on speaking tours, helping to shape the attitudes of those who heard them. The articles and books they wrote also made their impact, especially W. M. Thomson's *The Land and the Book,* which sold nearly 200,000 copies. One authority reported "seeing his volumes in the libraries of universities, colleges and theological schools, in the homes of pastors and teachers, in Sunday-schools and public schools: quoted by scholars, preachers and teachers, in commentaries, books of travel, and encyclopedias."[45]

The work of the biblical scholars was also highly influential. The foundational contributions of Edward Robinson have already been mentioned. Popular interest was focused on the Holy Land in the latter part of the century by such figures as William Rainey Harper and John Heyl Vincent; the latter, a founder of the famous Chautauqua Assembly, virtually turned it into "a gigantic Palestine class."[46] The work of the biblical archaeologists was made available in a noncontroversial way to church leaders and Sunday school teachers in a twentieth-century book with an incredibly long life, George A. Barton's *Archaeology and the Bible.* Published by the American Sunday School Union, it appeared first in 1916 and then went through edition after edition, the most recent of which I have seen was the fourth printing of the seventh edition, printed in 1946. Probably more Protestant attitudes were formed in the Sunday school than in any other place; an interesting research project might be to study the major curricular materials published by the churches in order to see precisely what views of the Holy Land were being transmitted.[47]

Of course, not all the reports from Palestine were by the convinced Protestants of whom I have been speaking, for statements were also made by such persons as Herman Melville and Mark Twain. And sometimes the enthusiasm of the convinced backfired. Willie Morris, editor of *Harper's Magazine,* in talking about growing up Methodist in Mississippi in the 1940s, says:

> By the time I was thirteen I had reached my quota on preachers who had gone to the Holy Land, subsidized by the congregation, and had returned with innumerable notes, trinkets, Kodak slides, sand from the desert, bones, second-hand garments, rocks, dirt, jars full of water from the Sea of Galilee, and more inside knowledge of the place after a two-week vacation than Moses got in a lifetime—all this stretched out over three or four Sundays in a row. They would give minute-by-minute descriptions of meals they had eaten, conversations they had exchanged with fellow preachers from Alabama or Arkansas, prayers they had prayed on seeing some natural wonder, remarks their wives had made, exact hours of arrival and departure and retiring and awakening. No, I never want to hear another lecture about the Holy Land again, and at the age of thirteen I had already promised myself I would never go there, no matter what the inducements or how exceptional the circumstances.[48]

This may be an indication of a generation gap, or a sign of a massive change of perception and feelings among young persons brought up in conventional Protestantism. For our period this was exceptional; far more common were the sentiments expressed in a song I have heard many times in the churches, "I Walked Today Where Jesus Walked." Characteristic lines are "Those little lanes, they have not changed" and "I saw the mighty Jordan roll / As in the days of yore."[49] One is reminded of John R. Mott's finding the Jordan to be a narrow, crooked, dirty stream—but characteristically he added that it was probably "the most famous river in all the world."[50] Not only the hymns that refer to the Holy Land, but also the pictures and maps that one so often sees in parish halls and church educational centers have played their part in shaping attitudes.

The backgrounds that have been traced are important in understanding American Protestant reactions to the tension between Arab and Jew in the Holy Land, and to the emergence of the Jewish State. In part it was the sense of familiarity with the Holy Land of Bible times which prepared presidents like Wilson and Truman to take some of the measures important to the emergence of modern Israel that they did; in part it was their religious sensibilities which encouraged certain senators and representatives to vote for important joint resolutions in 1922 and 1945.[51] It was in part an awareness of the long and troubled history of the Jews that led Christians like William E. Blackstone in 1891 to urge the return of Palestine to the Jews, and encouraged Adolf A. Berle to say in 1918, "Looked upon by many as a silly or idle dream for years, there is now something resembling a probability that there will arise in Palestine a Jewish state under the protectorate of the great powers, or some of them, which will have a significance to the world far beyond, probably, what even its most ardent advocates dream."[52] Hence, coupled with the reaction to the Holocaust, important support for Israel in the 1940s came from Christian sources. In his *Political World of American Zionism,* Samuel Halperin offered as a salient finding of his study "the fact of widespread and influential Christian support for the Zionist cause," and concluded "that opinions of Christian Zionist sentiment were both genuine and indigenous to American culture."[53] The sentiment was also expressed by some prominent churchmen, notably Reinhold Niebuhr, and by some articulate groups, especially the American Christian Palestine Committee, active with some 15,000 supporters in the late 1940s.

American Protestant attitudes to the Holy Land, however, had long been influenced by the missionaries, of whom those serving the Middle East were oriented primarily to the other lands. Joseph L. Grabill has noted that by 1914, "about 75 per cent of all the Western Protestant enterprises in Asia Minor and European Turkey were under American Board control," and that the Presbyterian Board had done extensive work in Syria.[54] Years ago, Frank E. Manuel had observed that missionaries "had built American universities and had become a dominant civilizing agent in the Near East. Apprehensive that the penetration of Palestine by a Jewish state would introduce into the Near East an element to compete with their own cultural concepts, they were vigorous antagonists to Zionism."[55]

The biblical scholars, to name another influential group, were not of one mind on issues relating to the emergence of Israel. But many had first made their contacts in Palestine when the Arabs were the dominant group, and then found the period of the mandate to their liking. In describing some of the great archaeological achievements, Ernest Wright observed that "it all took place at the best of all possible periods from the archaeologist's point of view—the time of mandates, when the countries in question welcomed western work and control was maintained by western directed departments of antiquities. Today that period is past and will not again return, at least in our time."[56]

Such were some of the streams of thought that influenced American Protestant opinion toward some of the political developments in the Holy Land in 1948 and after, described in such books as Hertzel Fishman's *American Protestantism and a Jewish State.*[57] Though Protestantism has been changing with some rapidity in the latter half of the twentieth century, the attitudes, feelings, and commitments of the previous century and a half persist, and the effort to understand them and their effects is a contribution to freedom.

My own research thus far has focused primarily on the leading white denominations; for me an as yet unexplored aspect of the topic is the attitudes of the black churches to the Holy Land. Certainly, along with other Christians they appropriated the imagery of Zion and the Promised Land in their search for religious truth and social justice. As Lawrence N. Jones has summed it up,

> they looked forward to the New Jerusalem—the city of God. . . . At different periods in the history of the last two centuries, the intensity of the dream of the New Jerusalem has been in direct proportion to the prospects for achieving the beloved community, though the struggle for the latter has never been entirely abandoned.[58]

At crucial moments in black church history, the "Promised Land" across Jordan became very vivid, but it was rehistoricized to mean the North. James H. Cone quotes Frederick Douglass, who insisted that "the *North* was our Canaan," and goes on to say that,

> as with Douglass, [Harriet] Tubman's concept of "de promised land on de oder side of Jordan" was not just a transcendent reality. It was the North and later Canada.[59]

The missions of the black churches have been primarily to Africa and the West Indies. But I suspect that there is a chapter about the attitudes of blacks to the Holy Land yet to be written; attention needs to be given to the reports of the visit of black Christians and the attitudes of leaders like Ralph Bunche, who played a major role in the peace settlement of 1948–1949.

The attitude of American Roman Catholics to the Holy Land is a topic that needs extensive research. Certainly there are many parallels with Protestant attitudes; a typical book, *The Catholic Shrines of the Holy Land,* declares that "the Holy Land is ever essentially the same—sacred because of God's frequent visitations and because it is the Son of God's birthplace."[60] Characterized by a strong sacramental concern, Catholics have traditionally emphasized the Holy Places, a number of which they have maintained for centuries. The late Esther Feldblum indicated some of the archival collections that invite study before we can arrive at sound scholarly judgments concerning this important part of the whole topic. She called attention to the records of the Catholic Near East Welfare Association, the Pontifical Mission to Palestine, the Franciscan Commissariat of the Holy Land, and the Notre Dame de Sion, and also to the archives of certain dioceses and the papers of Myron Taylor, Franklin Roosevelt's personal representative at the Vatican.[61] Papers relating to the building of the Church of all Nations by the Franciscans at the Garden of Gethsemane, which "was undertaken by American Catholics who subscribed almost the entire cost of construction,"[62] might also be instructive.

There is another group of Catholic Christians who have played some role, as far as I know not yet studied in detail, in shaping American attitudes to the Holy Land. Among the many streams of immigrants to the United States in our period from Palestine and other Arab lands were Melchites (Greek Catholics) and Maronites, both groups in communion with Rome. Some returned years later to their original settings, while others remained. They need to be studied, too, for the fullest understanding of American Christian attitudes toward the Holy Land.[63]

This paper has dealt primarily with the familiar evangelical Protestant denominations; I suspect that certain of the attitudes to the Holy Land that have been considered were reflected to a degree in some of the indigenous religious bodies that arose on American soil—groups as diverse as Latter-day Saints, Seventh-Day Adventists, Jehovah's Witnesses, and Christian Scientists. The late Yona Malachy devoted scholarly attention to the attitude of several of these movements to Zionism;[64] we would now profit from careful study of the nuances of their views of the Holy Land. In time I hope we shall see fruitful comparative studies across the spectrum of Christian churches, but first there is much basic work of research and interpretation to be done in our libraries and archives.

Notes

1. Frank S. De Hass, *Buried Cities Recovered, or, Explorations in Bible Lands,* 10th ed. (Philadelphia: Bradley & Co., 1885), p. 10.
2. Edwin Scott Gaustad, *Historical Atlas of Religion in America* (New York: Harper & Row, 1962), p. 111.
3. For extensive treatment of religion in the United States, see Sydney E. Ahlstrom, *A Religious History of the American People* (New Haven: Yale University Press, 1972); a more compact account is by Winthrop S. Hudson, *Religion in America,* 2d ed. (New York: Charles Scribner's Sons, 1973).
4. See the author's *A Christian America: Protestant Hopes and Historical Realities* (New York: Oxford University Press, 1971); the quotation from Horace Bushnell's *Barbarism the First Danger* is on pp. 27 and 64. See also Martin E. Marty, *Righteous Empire: The Protestant Experience in America* (New York: Dial Press, 1970).
5. Sidney L. Gulick, *The Growth of the Kingdom of God* (New York: Fleming H. Revell Co., c. 1897), p. 307.
6. Bertha Spafford Vester, *Our Jerusalem: An American Family in the Holy City, 1881–1949* (Garden City, N. Y.: Doubleday & Co., 1950), p. 262.
7. John H. Finley, *A Pilgrim in Palestine: Being an Account of Journeys on Foot by the First American Pilgrim after General Allenby's Recovery of the Holy Land* (New York: Charles Scribner's Sons, 1919), p. 15.
8. Adolf A. Berle, *The World Significance of a Jewish State* (New York: Mitchell Kennerley, 1918), p. 31. I am grateful to Dr. Glenn T. Miller for calling Dr. Berle's work to my attention.
9. W. D. Davies, *The Gospel and the Land: Early Christianity and Jewish Territorial Doctrine* (Berkeley: University of California Press, 1974), p. 366.
10. De Hass, op. cit., p. 123.
11. Maltbie D. Babcock, *Letters from Egypt and Palestine* (New York: Charles Scribner's Sons, 1902), p. 80.
12. "Palestine letter #2," October 28, 1895. I am indebted to Dr. C. Howard Hopkins for sharing with me the typescript of his account of Mott's tour of the Holy Land, based on the unpublished letters.
13. G. Ernest Wright, "The Phenomenon of American Archaeology in the Near East," in James A. Sanders, ed., *Near Eastern Archaeology in the Twentieth Century: Essays in Honor of Nelson Glueck* (Garden City, N.Y.: Doubleday & Co., 1970), p. 3.
14. Edward Robinson, *Biblical Researches in Palestine, Mount Sinai and Arabia Petraea: A Journal of Travels in the Year 1838. . .* (Boston: Crocker & Brewster, 1841), vol. 1, p. 46.

15. Ralph McGill, *Israel Revisited* (Atlanta: Tupper & Love, 1950), p. 2.
16. In James Ward Smith and A. Leland Jamison, eds., *Religious Perspectives in American Culture* (Princeton: Princeton University Press, 1961), p. 248.
17. R. Pierce Beaver, "Missionary Motivation through Three Centuries," in Jerald C. Brauer, ed., *Reinterpretation in American Church History* (Chicago: University of Chicago Press, 1968), pp. 127–29.
18. Rufus Anderson, *History of the Missions of the American Board of Commissioners for Foreign Missions to the Oriental Churches,* rev. ed. (Boston: Congregational Publishing House, 1884), vol. 1, pp. ix, 1. See also Paul Rowden, "A Century of American Protestantism in the Arab Middle East, 1820–1920" (Ph.D. dissertation, Dropsie College, 1959).
19. Pliny Fisk, *The Holy Land an Interesting Field of Missionary Enterprise. A Sermon, preached in the Old South Church, Boston, Sabbath Evening, Oct. 31, 1819, just before the Departure of the Palestine Mission* (Boston: Samuel T. Armstrong, 1819), p. 32.
20. *The Missionary Herald,* XX (March 1824), p. 68.
21. David H. Finnie, *Pioneers East: The Early American Experience in the Middle East* (Cambridge: Harvard University Press, 1967), p. 187.
22. William M. Thomson, *The Land and the Book: or, Biblical Illustrations Drawn from the Manners and Customs, the Scenes and Scenery of the Holy Land* (New York: Harper & Bros., 1859), vol. 2, p. xv.
23. John A. De Novo, *American Interests and Policies in the Middle East, 1900–1939* (Minneapolis: University of Minnesota Press, 1963), p. 346.
24. Quoted by Vester, op. cit., p. 74.
25. Frank McCoy Field, *Where Jesus Walked: Through the Holy Land with the Master* (New York: Exposition Press, 1951), p. 7.
26. Vester, op. cit., p. 119.
27. Lewis Mumford, *Herman Melville* (New York: Harcourt, Brace & Co., 1929), p. 308.
28. Albright's work is discussed by Wright, in Sanders, op. cit., pp. 22–28.
29. William Foxwell Albright, *The Archaeology of Palestine and the Bible* (New York: Fleming H. Revell Co., 1932), pp. 127–28.
30. Moshe Davis, ed. *Guide for America–Holy Land Studies* (Jerusalem: Institute of Contemporary Jewry, 1973), pp. 37, 45–46.
31. Quoted by Vester, op. cit., p. 56.
32. De Hass, op. cit., pp. 9, 116.
33. Edwin S. Wallace, *Jerusalem the Holy: A Brief History of Ancient Jerusalem: with an Account of the Modern City and Its Conditions Political, Religious and Social* (New York: Fleming H. Revell Co., 1898), p. 321.
34. De Hass, op. cit., p. 10.
35. Wallace, op. cit., p. 85.
36. Finley, op. cit., p. 106.
37. Field, op. cit., p. 16.

38. Isaac Bird, *Bible Work in Bible Lands; or, Events in the History of the Syria Mission* (Philadelphia: Presbyterian Board of Publication, 1872), p. 40.
39. Anderson, op. cit., vol. 1, pp. 38–39.
40. De Hass, op. cit., p. 130.
41. John Haynes Holmes, *Palestine Today and To-morrow: A Gentile's Survey of Zionism* (New York: Macmillan Co., 1929), p. 57.
42. Handy, *op. cit.*, pp. 184–225.
43. Anderson, op. cit., p. 14.
44. Ibid., p. 28.
45. Henry Harris Jessup, *Fifty-three Years in Syria* (New York: Fleming H. Revell Co., 1910), vol. 1, p. 62.
46. Leon Vincent, *John Heyl Vincent: A Biographical Sketch* (New York: Macmillan Co., 1925), p. 91. An example of the way knowledge about the Bible and its setting was transmitted to the Christian public is John H. Vincent's *Little Footprints in Bible Lands; or, Simple Lessons in Sacred History and Geography, for the Use of Palestine Classes and Sabbath Schools* (New York: Carlton & Lanahan, 1861).
47. On the importance of the Sunday school in American Protestant history, see Robert W. Lynn and Elliott Wright, *The Big Little School: Sunday Child of American Protestantism* (New York: Harper & Row, 1971).
48. Willie Morris, *North toward Home* (New York: Dell Publishing Co., 1967), p. 43. I wish to thank Art Jester for mentioning this passage to me.
49. Words by Daniel S. Twohig, music by Geoffrey O'Hara, published by G. Schirmer, Inc., New York, 1937.
50. See note 12.
51. On the attitudes of the presidents, see the following articles by Selig Adler: "The Palestine Question in the Wilson Era," *Jewish Social Studies,* X (1948), 303–34; "Backgrounds of American Policy toward Zion" in Moshe Davis, ed., *Israel: Its Role in Civilization* (New York: Harper & Bros., 1956), pp. 251–83; and "United States Policy on Palestine in the FDR Era," *America and the Holy Land: A Colloquium* (Jerusalem: Institute of Contemporary Jewry, 1972), pp. 11–18. (The report of the colloquium was first published in the *American Jewish Historical Quarterly,* LXII [1972], p. 362.) On the 1922 joint resolution, see Reuben Fink, ed., *America and Palestine* (New York: American Zionist Emergency Council, 1944), p. 37; on the one in 1945, see Samuel Halperin, *The Political World of American Zionism* (Detroit: Wayne State University Press, 1961), p. 294.
52. Berle, op. cit., p. 12. I touched on some of the reasons why certain Christians anticipated a restoration of the Jews to the Holy Land in a previous article, "Studies in the Interrelationships between America and the Holy Land: A Fruitful field for Interdisciplinary and Interfaith Cooperation," *Journal of Church and State,* 13 (1971), pp. 283–301, re-

printed in James E. Wood, Jr., *Jewish-Christian Relations in Today's World* (Waco, Texas: The Markham Press Fund of Baylor University Press, 1971), pp. 105–23.

53. Halperin, op. cit., p. 187.
54. Joseph L. Grabill, *Protestant Diplomacy and the Near East: Missionary Influence on American Policy, 1810–1927* (Minneapolis: University of Minnesota Press, 1971), p. 33.
55. Frank E. Manuel, *The Realities of American–Palestine Relations* (Washington, D.C.: Public Affairs Press, 1949), p. 3.
56. In Sanders, op. cit., p. 18.
57. Hertzel Fishman, *American Protestantism and a Jewish State* (Detroit: Wayne State University Press, 1973), esp. pp. 64–107.
58. Lawrence N. Jones, "They Sought a City: The Black Church and Churchmen in the Nineteenth Century," *Union Seminary Quarterly Review,* XXVI (1971), p. 257.
59. James H. Cone, *The Spirituals and the Blues: An Interpretation* (New York: Seabury Press, 1972), pp. 88–89. See also Davies, op. cit., pp. 116–17, n. 108.
60. Paschal Kinsel and Leonard Henry, *The Catholic Shrines of the Holy Land* (New York: Farrar, Straus & Young, 1951), p. 8.
61. *America and the Holy Land, A Colloquium,* pp. 33–35; see also her study "The American Catholic Press and the Jewish State, 1917–1957" (Ph.D. dissertation, Columbia University, 1973). For a bibliographical note on the papers of the Franciscan Commissariat of the Holy Land, see *Guide for America-Holy Land Studies . . . Specimen Pages,* pp. 27–28.
62. Kinsel and Henry, op. cit. p. 157.
63. See the remarks by Professor Zvi Ankori in *America and the Holy Land: A Colloquium,* pp. 31–32.
64. Yona Malachy "Jehovah's Witnesses and Their Attitudes toward Zionism and the Idea of the Return to Zion," *Herzl Year Book,* V (1963–64), pp. 175–208; "Seventh-Day Adventists and Zionism," Ibid., VI (1964–65), pp. 265–301.

Afro-Americans and the Holy Land

Lawrence N. Jones

UNTIL recent decades, a distinguishing characteristic of the life of many blacks in America is that they did not bifurcate experience into sacred and secular dimensions. There are historical reasons for this unitary view of experience. Some writers trace it to the African past and point out that the radical separation of the religious from the secular is a Euro-American phenomenon. While there is merit in this line of reasoning, there are reasons which are more readily validated in the immediate past of Afro-Americans.

The blacks who came to America as slaves did not come as empty pitchers waiting to be filled with whatever cultural content might be poured into them by their enslavers. They were persons with world views, with opinions that we would call religious, with convictions about deity, or the "supreme being," as they typically referred to God, and with beliefs about the meaning of life and death. What they lacked when they came to America, having come from so many diverse tribes and geographical areas, was a common language. For most of the slaves, the verbal communication to which they were immediately exposed was the specialized vocabulary of agriculture, trade, and the conventional conversation of the larger social grouping into which they were introduced. Since only a few slaves were taught to read or managed to learn to read through their own ingenuity (approximately five percent of the slaves could read at the time of the Emancipation Proclamation), they had only limited access to philosophical concepts or systems of religious belief other than those that they had brought with them. The workaday world provided few formal resources for dealing with the meaning of their lives beyond those of African origin. From the earliest times, a few slaves, whose masters professed either Christianity or Judaism, were introduced to these belief systems, and some appropriated their teachings. The number of converts was never great. As a matter of fact, even after the vigorous efforts of the major Protestant denominations to subject blacks to religious instruction, only twelve to fifteen percent were listed on church rosters at the end of the Civil War. It is axiomatic, however, that the impact of religion upon blacks cannot be captured fully in a statistical net. Despite the limited numbers who formally accepted membership in religious bodies, the folk literature and the limited historical data available from the period indicate that the Christian religion provided both the concepts and the language by means of which blacks began to reflect upon, to talk about, and to philosophize and theologize about their existence in America. It was via the Bible and the church that blacks first encountered the "Holy Land."

Blacks did not begin to make pilgrimages to the Holy Land until very late in the nineteenth century. Prior to that time, it was known through preaching, Bible study, and song as the place in history where God revealed himself through mighty acts on behalf of the "Children of Israel" and then on behalf of all humankind through Jesus of Nazareth. Through the pictures in religious literature, blacks were enabled to visualize in imagination the cities and towns, the rivers and lakes, the gardens and buildings, the mountains and deserts, the hills and the valleys where God revealed himself with unalloyed clarity in the lives of an historic people. The land, with its configurations and buildings, provided a backdrop for the faith. One of the functions the Holy Land served, as a place, was to lend credibility to the religious beliefs with which the black converts had been indoctrinated.

But if the Holy Land was important to black believers as the stage upon which "holy history" was enacted, it was the particular actions of God in the Exodus and in other situations where persons were dramatically liberated that fostered and sustained faith. Names, personages, and ideas were assigned contemporary meaning in the slaves' day-to-day activity. The language of religion was not objectionable to the slaves' masters; indeed, religiousness was an attribute that some masters fostered in the belief that it made slaves more tractable. It was fortuitous, then, that the slave community began to adopt religious language in their efforts to mitigate and to subvert the conditions of their bondage. Although a slave would not have dared to address his master as Pharaoh, he could sing about pharaoh with impunity. The other slaves would know that he was speaking about "old marse," but the object of his criticism would not. Similarly, "Canaan Land" referred not to heaven but to the North. The advantage of utilizing religious language to make nonreligious statements was clear: it was approved by the master community, but it was also a vehicle for criticizing the system and for publishing notices. The susceptibility of religious language to double meaning admirably suited it as the bearer of apparently innocent conversation that was actually potentially quite subversive. Gabriel Prosser and Nat Turner are excellent examples of black slave leaders who used religious language to advance revolutionary activity. Under cover of holding religious meetings, Prosser and Turner gathered their followers together to work out the strategies of their uprisings. The image of liberation that these men found in the Old Testament encouraged them in the belief that their revolutionary initiations had divine warrant.

Not only was everyday language replete with religious symbolism derived from the Holy Land via the Bible, but the spirituals, the earliest religious songs created by blacks, are heavily laden with it.[1] Drawing upon the images from the Old Testament, these folk songs are filled with references to persons, places, and events which became for the slaves luminous paradigms for understanding and interpreting their life situations. They identified with the stories that dealt with slavery, oppression, deliverance from danger, liberation from "pharaoh," and similar examples of God's continuing concern for the poor and the dispossessed. This identification with the oppressed people of the Bible was a ground of hope for their own liberation. One spiritual queries, "Didn't my Lord deliver Daniel? Then why not every man?" In another vein, to raise the song "Steal Away to Jesus" around the slave quarters might very well have been the announcement that a clandestine meeting would be held at a commonly understood time and place. The spirituals reveal the amazing versatility of the language of faith as a bearer of both sacred and secular meanings.[2]

Blacks did not become frequent travelers to the "sights and scenes" of the Holy Land until well into the twentieth century. The earliest account that I find of a black making the pilgrimage is that of Dr. C. T. Walker, who made the journey in 1891, when he was pastor of the Tabernacle Baptist Church in Atlanta, Georgia. The Tabernacle congregation proudly asserted that it was "the first colored church in this country to send its pastor on a trip to Europe and to the Holy Land."[3] In the nineteenth century, it was more common for Afro-Americans to visit Africa than the Holy Land. But what was an exceptional occurrence in the nineteenth and early twentieth centuries is now a commonplace event. Tours leave from most major urban centers with persons going to "walk where Jesus walked." It is a fair conjecture that early Afro-American visitors to the Holy Land were clergypersons sponsored by their congregations. It is also probably true that black and white pastors utilized their experiences in similar ways—to give credibility to the faith, to enliven their preaching, and to expose their parishioners to the larger world of Europe and the Middle East. It is reported that when Walker returned from the Holy Land, he described how he had stood in the place where Joshua commanded the sun and the moon to stand still (Josh. 10:12). On other occasions this popular clergyman made graphic reference to his journey over routes traveled by Roman emperors and Christian crusaders on their way to the land of the Bible. His sermons and lectures contained dramatic word pictures of his bathing in the Jordan River and of his visit to the site where the Children of Israel crossed over into the Promised Land. Although the uses to which the experience of going to Palestine were put by churchpersons were probably the same for blacks and whites, the meaning of the experiences is different. The Holy Land, for blacks, is supremely the place where God through his action communicated his concern for the poor and the oppressed and where he demonstrated his sovereign power over his creation. It is a theological meaning supported by everyday religious experience which echoes the events in the Old and New Testament that constitutes the present significance of the Holy Land for blacks. This holy space, in the biblical sense, engenders confidence in the prophetic tradition and in the ethics of the Bible. In a religious sense, it is Jesus the Son of God, rather than Jesus the son of Mary and prophet, that is important for Afro-American Christians. In their view, Jesus transcended his Jewishness and becomes, in fact, the embodiment of the love of God.

As I suggested earlier, the contact of blacks with the Holy Land is not exhausted in the Christian community, for there are so-called Black Jews for whom Palestine is the motherland. Some of these persons trace their affiliations with Judaism back to slave plantations presided over by Jewish masters. Others are more recent converts, while still others belong to one of the several black religious groups that have gathered around persons like the late Rabbi Samuel Matthew, who trace their origins to Ethiopia. Still others belong to groups that have gathered around charismatic persons whose religious practice varies from strict adherence to the rituals and belief of Orthodox Judaism to a superficial mimicking of Jewish rituals and worship.

Still other blacks who profess the Islamic faith also look to the Holy Land as sacred space. But regardless of their religious affiliation, the Holy Land has been for Afro-Americans more than a place. It is the context in which a sustained interpenetration of divine activity with creation and history occurred over time, the meaning of which has been appropriated by an oppressed people as a clue to the meaning of their own experience and as a basis of their struggle and hope for liberation.

Notes

1. Frederick Douglass was one of the first persons to report on the double entendre of the spirituals. See Frederick Douglass, *Narrative of the Life of Frederick Douglass, an American Slave* (Cambridge, Mass.: The Belknap Press of Harvard University Press, 1967), pp. 36–38. This dimension of meaning in the spirituals is fully explored in Miles Mark Fisher, *Negro Slave Songs in the United States* (New York: The Citadel Press, 1953), 54ff.
2. See James Weldon and J. Rosamond Johnson, eds., *The Book of American Negro Spirituals* (New York: The Viking Press, 1969). This is one of the most complete compilations of the religious music of the slaves. The best and most recent study of the spirituals is that of John Lovell, *Black Song: The Forge and the Flame* (New York: Macmillan, 1972).
3. Silas X. Floyd, *Life of Charles T. Walker, D.D.* (New York: Negro Universities Press, 1969), pp. 56–69. Dr. Walker was one of the most famous black preachers of his time. His trip to the Holy Land was similar to that being made by other pastors of the time. He traveled via Europe to Palestine. Upon his return he developed a very popular lecture entitled "The Holy Land; What I Saw and Heard." For a number of years he delivered this lecture throughout the country. His sermons reveal that his trip was a rich source of "scenes from the Holy Land."

PART II

The Ottoman-Muslim Era

America and the Holy Land During the Ottoman Period

Moshe Ma'oz

IT IS well known that America's interest in the Ottoman Empire and its Palestinian districts was limited in both duration and scope, particularly when compared with the involvement of France, Russia, and England. The relatively late participation of the United States in the international community and the vast geographical distance that separated America from the Middle East were not the only factors. The government of the United States had neither strategic aims nor political ambitions concerning the Ottoman Empire prior to the present century. Even its economic interests in the Middle East were minor in comparison with those of the other powers. We should note, however, that the absence of American political interests in the Ottoman Empire served for a long time to establish cordial relations between the two countries, based on mutual respect and understanding and an absence of suspicion. From the Ottoman point of view, the United States had become involved in the area with a "clean record," unlike other Christian powers, all of which had a long history of political and economic intervention or military encroachment.

Some examples will provide the necessary perspective. When the thirteen colonies declared their independence in 1776 and sought to establish relations with powers overseas, czarist Russia was already engaged in driving the Ottomans out of territories north of the Black Sea, obtaining special naval and commercial privileges in Turkish waterways and provinces, and establishing *de facto* protection over the Greek Orthodox subjects in the empire. In 1772, as part of the Russian military offensive, a naval squadron advanced to the eastern Mediterranean, engaging in two battles against Ottoman troops in an area just north of Palestine. A similar difference in American and French relations with the Ottomans is seen some thirty years later. In 1799, President John Adams appointed an American mission to Turkey to seek a treaty of amity and commerce; a year earlier, a French military expedition landed in Alexandria and occupied Ottoman Egypt, from where it advanced toward Palestine, capturing key towns along the way.

In Palestine itself, the contrast between the influence of the United States and that of the European powers was equally apparent during most of the nineteenth century. In the early 1840s, before an American consulate was established in Palestine, British Consul Wood noted with some arrogance in one of his dispatches that "British influence . . . was not only paramount but the country may be said to have been administered by us."[1] In the late 1840s, another British consul complained, not without bias and envy, that "the French have succeeded in establishing a system of terror all over Syria by means of which they have become the virtual rulers of the country."[2] As for the Russians, a historian of modern Palestine has noted that "Russian expansion was the most striking among all the European nations. They had established [in Jerusalem] a consulate on a grand scale; lands had been purchased, residences constructed for the bishop and the consul and a hospice built for pilgrims."[3] By contrast, a local Arab historian informs us that when the American consulate was first opened in Jerusalem, the Turkish governor refused to salute the hoisted American flag or fire the citadel guns.[4]

Apparently the American consuls in Jerusalem were not very enthusiastic about their post. In the 1860s and 1870s, the consuls, complaining about the climate and their personal ailments, followed one another in rapid succession.[5] They certainly could not complain about being overly busy, since their regular duties of managing the affairs of local American citizens were not extensive. In the late 1850s, the number of American citizens in Jerusalem did not exceed "the number of a hand's fingers," according to an Arab source.[6] In 1870, twelve American citizens were registered in the consulate;[7] this number increased to 184 in 1882 and 317 in 1891.[8]

The commercial transactions handled by the American consulate were also not especially burdensome throughout the nineteenth century. This was true for the Ottoman Empire in general, where "for decades commerce was sluggish."[9] The goods that the United States exported to and imported from the immediate area were typical of its trade relations with the empire at large. According to American Consul Merrill, "most vessels which bear the U.S. flag arriving here [in Beirut] come with cargoes of petroleum,"[10] while American vessels departing from Mediterranean ports carried back mainly wool, oil, figs, and opium. But even with the gradual growth of trade in eastern Mediterranean ports, the United States was last in the foreign trade return in the port of Jaffa for the years 1904 to 1910.[11]

Indeed, American relations with the Ottoman Empire and Palestine should not be measured by tons of cargo; or by the number of local American citizens or the size of the American consulates; and certainly not by political status or influence with the Ottoman authorities. American activity in Ottoman dominions, notably Palestine, should rather be examined within the wider context of human interest in which consuls and officials played the role of participants, assistants, or protectors. The personal involvement of many Americans came primarily from humanitarian motives and religious feelings or beliefs, as well as from a scientific thirst for knowledge or a dilettantish curiosity. The major concerns of these Americans who were involved with Ottoman Palestine were the Holy Land and the places holy to Judaism and Christianity, the relevant biblical and archaeological sites, and—not less important—the people of the Holy Land, notably, "the Children of Israel."

American travelers, like their European counterparts, came to Palestine to visit the shrines and tour the sites. Among them were several prominent scholars and researchers who made important contributions to biblical and archaeological research as well as to our geographical knowledge of Palestine. The outstanding individual in this group was Edward Robinson, who conducted his research in 1838 and 1852, and who has been described as a "meticulous researcher" by an Arab chronicler of Nazareth,[12] and as the "progenitor of Eretz Yisrael research" by an Israeli geographer.[13] Among

Robinson's discoveries was "Robinson's Arch" in the Western Wall, which was named after him. A similar impact was made on Palestine by the famous traveler and researcher Lieutenant Lynch of the U.S. Navy, who, in 1848, explored the Jordan River and laid the foundations for the bathometric mapping of the Dead Sea. A strait was named after him. Many contemporary writers refer to Lynch's expedition, and he is mentioned in some Arabic sources because of his connection with Aqil Agha, the legendary bedouin chief who escorted him and his men.[14] But apart from travelers and researchers, American Protestant missionaries were interested in Palestine too.

Several attempts to establish a permanent status in Jerusalem were made sporadically from the early 1820s to the mid-1840s by the American Board of Commissioners for Foreign Missions. Although a number of schools were founded in Palestine, American missionary efforts were met by vigorous opposition from Eastern churches, an evasive attitude on the part of the Druze, and stubborn resistance by the Jews. The American missionaries were also hampered in their efforts by the influential Anglican mission in Palestine, and eventually had to submit to the superiority of their British colleagues.

Yet American missionary work continued without interruption in other parts of the Ottoman Empire and, in fact, expanded throughout the nineteenth century. But faced with the strict Ottoman ruling which forbade the conversion of Muslims, the missionaries operated almost exclusively among the "nominal," or Eastern, Christians, notably, the Armenians in Anatolia and the Christian Arabs in Syria. Through their educational network and printing presses, American missions contributed during the last decades of the nineteenth century towards the development of a cultural renaissance and national awakening among Protestant Armenians in Turkey and Christian Arabs in Lebanon. Especially effective in this was the Protestant College in Beirut, which became an important center of Arab revival for young Christian and Muslim Arabs. At the same time, however, American missionary activity promoted sectarian schism among the Christian communities, inspiring many Christians to emigrate to America. It also helped tarnish the reputation of the Muslim Turks in the eyes of the American public and drew the government of the United States into increased political involvement in Turkey, which resulted in a deterioration of relations between the two countries.

At the same time, a somewhat similar situation developed in American-Ottoman relations vis-à-vis the position of the Jewish community in Palestine. American consuls, motivated both by their Protestant convictions and by the persuasive efforts of American Jews, helped Jewish immigrants, American and non-American alike, to settle in Palestine and realize their national aspirations. The consuls worked to abolish Turkish restrictions on Jewish immigration and Jewish residence in Palestine; they also assisted Jews to engage in productive labor and acquire land. On the other hand, American consular involvement helped create dissension between American and European Jews and fostered antagonism between the "old Yishuv" and the more recent Zionist settlers.[15] Jews were also encouraged to seek American consular protection, and in a sense this contributed indirectly to the emigration of Russian Jews from Palestine to the United States.[16]

Furthermore, American intervention on behalf of Jews in Palestine strained relations between some American officials and Turkish government officials in Jerusalem and Constantinople; consequently, U.S. political activity met with the disapproval and criticism of certain American consuls in Palestine as well as senior officials within the State Department in Washington.[17] Thus, while American economic interests increased in the first decade of the twentieth century, American official sympathy towards the Jews in Palestine was on the decline.

A revival of nineteenth-century humanitarian and favorable attitudes towards the Jews in Palestine occurred during the presidency of Woodrow Wilson. The Wilson administration helped prevent the deportation of some 100,000 Jews from Ottoman Palestine and provided relief for the Jewish community there. Wilson also supported the Balfour Declaration of 1917, thereby opening a new era in America–Holy Land relations.

Resources for Research

The study of America's presence in the Holy Land during the Ottoman era is still in its early stages. Works published in the last few decades deal either with specific aspects of the subject or with the much broader scope of American interest and policy in the Middle East. Only Frank Manuel, in his *Realities of American–Palestine Relations,* has come close to dealing with the entire problem during the nineteenth century. He utilized resources which fall mainly into three categories: (a) American consular dispatches, official reports, and memoranda and papers of American diplomats and statesmen; (b) memoirs and accounts of American (and some European) diplomats, missionaries, observers, and travelers; and (c) memoirs and personal accounts of Jewish personalities in Palestine, as well as reports printed in Hebrew periodicals of the late nineteenth century.

Such resources are of great value for the study of the American presence in nineteenth-century Ottoman Palestine, particularly since these materials, both official and nonofficial, evolved primarily in connection with the Jews of the Holy Land. The consular reports and other official accounts provide an overall picture of the policies and attitudes of the United States towards the Ottoman authorities and the Jewish population. The accounts and memoirs of Jewish contemporaries show how the diverse Jewish communities in Palestine viewed the United States and how they hoped it would act.

Nevertheless, it must be stressed that many of these sources present a rather narrow, frequently one-sided, and occasionally biased approach to the realities of Ottoman Palestine. On the one hand, both American and Jewish authors were likely to describe various issues and problems as a reflection of their official assignments, personal attitudes, or religious convictions. On the other hand, frequently they did not justly evaluate the position and aspirations of the Turkish government, the Muslim majority population, or the Christians of the East. Many of the American consuls, Protestant missionaries, Jewish leaders, and Western travelers knew neither Arabic nor Turkish; moreover, they were not familiar with Islamic tradition, the Oriental way of life, or the historical background of Ottoman Palestine. Thus, for example, a Protestant scholar writing in 1832 in *Palestine, or the Holy Land* could state:

> As the civil history of Palestine for three centuries is nothing more than a relation of the broils, the insurrections, the massacres, and changes of dynasty which have periodically shaken the Turkish Empire in Europe as well as in Asia, we willingly pass over it, as we thereby only refrain from a tedious recapitulation of names and dates which could not have the slightest interest for any class of readers.[18]

Many American missionaries, travelers, and diplomats expressed similar generalizations concerning the Muslim faith and the Ottoman Empire. Some wrote about the "immoral character" of the founder of Islam, and "its polygamy, permission of slavery and fatalism."[19] They also maintained that "Islam tends to depopulation . . . to the destruction of wealth,"[20] and pointed out "Mohammedan hostility to Christianity."[21]

Even Lieutenant Lynch, the keen observer who displayed a sympathetic attitude toward local Muslim leaders and the Ottoman judicial system ("Justice was administered with all the promptitude and simplicity of the East"[22]), was imbued with the Western concept of the "white man's burden." When he first reached the shores of Palestine, he wrote: "For the first time, perhaps . . . the American flag has been raised in Palestine. May it be the harbinger of regeneration to a now hapless people." Upon his departure he referred to "the fanaticism of the Turks" and concluded:

> The Muhammedan rule, that political sirocco which withers all before it, is fast losing the fierce energy which was its peculiar characteristic, and the world is being gradually prepared for the final dismemberment of the Ottoman Empire.
>
> It needs but the destruction of that power which, for so many centuries, has rested like an incubus upon the eastern world, to ensure the restoration of the Jews to Palestine.[23]

Similar views can be detected in various contemporary Jewish sources concerning the Ottoman authorities, the Muslim population, and the Christian minorities.

By citing these references, it is not intended to imply that the observations of the authors were unfounded or that their generalizations lacked any substantial elements of truth. The annals of Ottoman rule in Palestine and in other areas are indeed replete with upheavals and disturbances and with long periods of government repression alternated with anti-Christian fanaticism and violence initiated by Muslim notables and Ottoman rulers. The anti-Christian massacres of 1860 in Damascus and the Armenian massacres of 1894–1895 and 1915 come readily to mind.

Yet, upon examining the other side of the coin—the Muslim and Ottoman position—one should not overlook certain forces at work. Side by side with the Islamic tradition of religious and political superiority over Christians and Jews, one must note the major Ottoman efforts at reform and modernization during the nineteenth century aimed at creating a new political community in which both

Muslims and non-Muslims could become equal members. Similarly, as a background to Muslim intolerance and violence, one should not overlook the process of Ottoman disintegration in the face of the impact of European powers: this resulted in frustration and the need for self-defense against European military pressure and Western cultural and economic encroachment.

To grasp these factors fully, the student and researcher of America–Holy Land relations should consult Ottoman and Arabic sources, European consular reports, the records of the Eastern churches, and minutes of local organizations, as well as private papers.

Here again, it is likely that the documents will manifest parochial, tendentious, or biased approaches. Indeed, the tendency to glorify oneself and criticize others is a common phenomenon in a great number of source materials. Just as family papers tend to magnify the role of family members in local history and cast aspersions on their rivals, so the records of the Eastern Christian churches are filled with antagonism toward missionary societies and their protectors, the Western consuls. The dispatches sent by European consuls show them to be often critical of their colleagues in other consulates, at times unaware of the nuances of prevailing local conditions, and occasionally patronizing towards the Turkish authorities. The Turkish pashas in *their* reports tend to be self-complacent in their efforts to please their superiors.

Nevertheless, most of these source materials are invaluable not only to check and balance other sources, but also to furnish a fuller spectrum of attitudes and trends, fill important lacunae in historical records, and provide a more complete chronology of events. Much of this can be supplied primarily by the Ottoman and Arabic sources.

Generally speaking, Ottoman source materials are located in most former Ottoman dominions in the Middle East and in southeastern Europe. The main bulk of documentation is stored at the National Archives of Turkey, which is one of the richest historical repositories in the world. Its more than forty million documents, which start with the founding of the Ottoman Empire in the fourteenth century, are classified in a number of categories. The documents relevant to our subject are to be found within the *Mühimme Defterleri,* i.e., directives and orders of the grand viziers (from 1559 to 1906); and the *Irade Defterleri* (from 1832 on), containing various documents on internal and foreign affairs, as well as orders (*irades*) issued by special legislative bodies. Among these, the *Hariciye* (foreign and minority affairs), the *Imtiyaz ve Mukavelat* (capitulatory privileges and foreign contracts) and *Mesail Mühimme* ("important problems" such as those concerning the Protestant community) are the most pertinent to our concern. Other important records are the *Kilise Defterleri* (church registers) for the years 1869–1921 and *Gayri Müslim Cemaalara ait Defterleri* (registers concerning non-Muslim communities), covering the period from 1830 to 1918.

It should be noted that these collections probably contain but a small number of documents pertaining to the American presence in the Holy Land or in the Ottoman Empire. Indeed, the United States is not even listed under the various classified subheadings of countries or special problems. The reasons for this omission have been indicated above. In our own research on Syria and Palestine in the mid-nineteenth century, we did not come across any major documents regarding American activities. The only references indicating American presence pertain to the negative influence of the missionaries in Syria.

For the later period, we assume that the number of documents concerning the United States will be larger, for they deal with problems of consular jurisdiction over American Jewish citizens and protégés in Palestine. It might be particularly illuminating to trace the Ottoman exposition of Article IV of the American–Turkish Treaty of commerce and navigation (1830), particularly in its application to Palestine in the 1880s. (This article deals with litigations and disputes between Ottoman and American subjects, as well as with offenses committed by American citizens in Ottoman dominions.) The reports of Turkish governors in Palestine about U.S. consular matters pertaining to American citizens, Jewish immigration, and land purchases by American protégés might prove equally interesting.

Important Ottoman data is also available in Israel. The Israel State Archives contains census registers (Nüfus) for the years 1884–1917, which also listed foreign subjects; and registers of the governor (*Mutasarrif*) of Jerusalem for 1906–1908, which contain documents on Jewish immigration and settlement, and reports on foreign visitors, including Americans. Other possibly useful source materials are the registers of the Provincial Council (*mejlis–i idare*) in Jerusalem for 1910-1915, which deal with administrative affairs; and records of the notary public in Jaffa from 1896 onwards, which cast some light on economic and business life in the area.

Source materials even more valuable for the study of economic, social, and political developments in Ottoman Palestine are located in the Muslim court (*shari'a*) records (*sijill*) in Jerusalem and Jaffa. Some of these materials are available in Xerox at the Institute of Asian and African Studies of the Hebrew University of Jerusalem. The Jerusalem records cover the entire period of Ottoman rule in Palestine, while the Jaffa *sijill* are restricted to documents from the early nineteenth century.

The Muslim records, written by hand in both Ottoman Turkish and Arabic, represent a sort of Public Records Office: they contain government orders and regulations as well as notarial and juridic proceedings brought before the *qadi*. These include title deeds and certificates for property transactions and other legal actions such as civil claims concerning the sale and loss of property and matters of personal status. Matters of personal status for members of various Protestant churches, which did not enjoy official recognition, were occasionally settled in the *Shari'a* court of Jaffa.

Printed Arabic documents of nineteenth-century Ottoman Palestine are less numerous and contain but few references to the American presence in the area. One of these, for example, concerns Mr. Chasseaud, the American vice-consul in Beirut who was appointed U.S. consul for all Syria, including Palestine, in 1836, during the period of Egyptian rule. An order to this effect was issued by Ibrahim Pasha to the local governor in the country, directing him to treat the consul well. This document appears in a collection, *Arabic Sources for the History of Syria during the Period of Muhammad Ali*, edited by the great Lebanese scholar Asad Rustum.[24] This author also compiled a summary of documents for the same period, which are located in the Egyptian Archives.

Both collections, like other corpora of documents, local chronicles, town histories, biographies of Muslim notables, and contemporary journals, provide important data on the social, political, and cultural conditions in the area, and are thus indispensable for the researcher in this field. Insofar as American activities are concerned, sources refer for the most part to the missionary work conducted in Lebanon and Syria. References to the American presence in Palestine are sporadic, dealing with the work of Robinson and Lynch and with the establishment of the American consulate in Jerusalem and the American colonies in Jaffa and Jerusalem. The references to Robinson and Lynch place them in a favorable light, whereas the ones pertaining to the consulate and the Jaffa Colony reflect the strong opposition of the Muslim population to both.[25] These few references should not be interpreted as revealing a hostile attitude on the part of the Muslim population in Palestine to Americans as such. The Muslim common people of that period hardly distinguished Americans from Russians, Britons, or Frenchmen. All were regarded as infidels by the intolerant masses and as *ifranj* ("Franks," Europeans) by the indifferent Muslims. We may safely assume that the great majority of the Muslim population in Palestine was not even aware that there was any kind of American presence in the Holy Land until World War I. At that time, the Muslim-Arab nationalists, particularly in Syria, began to show an interest in the United States as a factor in the region's politics as well as in Wilson's doctrine of self-determination for national minorities.

Undoubtedly the local Christians had closer contact than the Muslims with the American presence in Palestine, but their religious leaders were just as hostile toward the Protestant missionaries, whether British or American. Valuable source materials on American activities in the Holy Land may very likely be found in the archives of the various patriarchates—Greek Orthodox, Greek Catholic, Armenian, and Latin—as well as in the archives of the Catholic missionary organizations. For example, the Franciscan archives at Terra Sancta contain several collections of manuscripts and documents, among them many firmans and legal documents in Turkish and Arabic. From personal knowledge we can point also to the rich collection of Ottoman firmans located in the Armenian Patriarchate of Jerusalem, in the Greek Orthodox Patriarchate of Jerusalem, and in Saint Catherine's Monastery at the foot of Mount Sinai. Most of the documents in these archives deal with the status of the various Christian communities and the holy sites in Jerusalem and Bethlehem, internal organization, tax collection, etc. The references to American presence are presumably few and hostile.

More detailed and balanced data about the American establishments in Palestine in the nineteenth century can be found in the

German Templars Archives in Stuttgart, West Germany, and in the State Archives in Jerusalem, which contains the records of the German Colony in Haifa. Members of this group came from Württemberg and settled in Jaffa, Haifa, and Jerusalem in the late 1860s. In Jaffa, the Templars first established themselves on the remains of the American colony, which they had purchased from Adams. They helped finance the return journey of the Americans, who, according to a letter from Adams to the Templar leader Hoffmann, were on the verge of extinction. In Haifa, the link between the German Templars and the Americans was more fortuitous. Mr. Schumacher, the leader of the local German colony, also served as American vice-consul in the city.[26]

Other German sources that might provide valuable data about American activity in the Holy Land are the Archives of the German Foreign Office in Bonn (from 1867 on), which contain, *inter alia,* files on the "protection of the Christians in Palestine" and on "the Protestants in Turkey;" and the Archives of the Prussian-German consulate in Jerusalem (1842–1917), stored in the Israel State Archives. The latter contain a great deal of information on various political, social, economic, and religious matters as recorded by German consuls and consular agents in several Palestinian towns.

The consular dispatches of other European consuls in Palestine—British, French, Russian, Austrian, and Italian—are equally invaluable for research on Ottoman Palestine. But the quantity and quality of their materials pertaining to the American presence depend to a certain extent on the political and personal attitudes of the individual consuls. Obviously, the dispatches of the British consuls on matters relating to the United States are usually informative and often sympathetic. These dispatches also give us the most reliable and objective information on internal developments in nineteenth-century Palestine, for there was a large network of British consular posts throughout the land and the British were actively involved in the affairs of Ottoman Palestine. Original and unique records of the British consulate in Jerusalem are available in the Israel State Archives, and a complete collection of the London Foreign Office consular dispatches on Palestine exists on microfilm at the Hebrew University's Institute of Asian and African Studies (which also contains French, Italian, and Austrian consular documents).

Important deposits of source materials on Ottoman Palestine, including aspects of American interest in the Holy Land, are located in various other institutes and libraries in Israel, notably, at the Institute of Contemporary Jewry of the Hebrew University, the Central Zionist Archives, the Ben-Zvi Institute, and the Aaronsohn Archives. Many of these materials reflect the complex relationship between the Jews of Palestine and American official and unofficial representatives—a relationship that constituted a central factor in the role of America in the Holy Land.

Notes

1. Great Britain, Public Records Office, FO 78/499. Wood to Ponsonby, Beirut, 17 February 1841.
2. Ibid., FO 78/1385. Moore to Clarendon, Beirut, 19 February 1858.
3. F. E. Manuel, *The Realities of American–Palestine Relations* (Washington, 1949), p. 13.
4. 'Arif al-'Arif, *Ta'rikh al-Quds* (Egypt, 1951), p. 262.
5. Manuel, op. cit., p. 13.
6. 'Al-'Arif, op. cit., p. 262.
7. Manuel, op. cit., p. 38.
8. Ibid., p. 69.
9. J. L. Grabill, *Protestant Diplomacy and the Near East* (Minneapolis, 1971), p. 37.
10. Selah Merrill, *East of the Jordan* (London, 1881), p. 5.
11. D. Trietsch, *Palästina Handbuch* (Berlin, 1921), pp. 209-10.
12. As'ad Manṣur, *Ta'rikh al-Naṣira* (Egypt, 1924), p. 81.
13. Y. Ben Arieh, *The Rediscovery of the Holy Land in the Nineteenth Century* (in Hebrew) (Jerusalem, 1970), p. 69.
14. Manṣur, op. cit., p. 74.
15. Manuel, op. cit., p. 45.
16. According to the American consul in Jerusalem, some 3,000 people, mostly young, emigrated in 1913 from the *mutasarriflik* of Jerusalem to the United States. Of these, 35 percent were Jews, 35 percent Muslims, and the remainder Christians. See Charles Issawai, *The Economic History of the Middle East, 1800–1914* (Chicago, 1966), p. 272.
17. Consul Merrill, for example, claimed that the Jews "are becoming a burden and a menace for our Government." Manuel, op. cit., p. 94.
18. Michael Russell (Edinburgh, 1832), p. 325.
19. Grabill, op. cit., p. 116.
20. A. L. Tibawi, *American Interests in Syria, 1800–1901* (Oxford, 1966), p. 270.
21. Ibid., p. 264.
22. W. F. Lynch, *Narrative of the United States Expedition to the River Jordan and the Dead Sea* (Philadelphia, 1849), p. 156.
23. Ibid., p. 119.
24. Asad Rustum, *al-uṣul al-arabiyya li-ta'rikh Surriyya fi 'ahd Muhammad Ali* (Beirut, 1930–34), p. 97.
25. As'ad Manṣur, op. cit., pp. 74, 81, 144; 'Arif al-'Arif, op. cit., p. 262.
26. A. Carmel, *The German Colonies in Palestine at the End of the Ottoman Period* (in Hebrew) (Jerusalem, 1973), p. 12.

Observations on America-Holy Land Relations in the Period before World War I

Nathan M. Kaganoff

THERE are not many books dealing with the relationship between the United States and the Holy Land, and although some are excellent, they all confine their discussions to merely a few aspects of the subject. A comprehensive study of the America–Holy Land relationship has not been published. However, the present state of research clearly indicates that contacts between the two geographical areas, even before the twentieth century, ran the entire gamut of relationships normally prevailing among countries in modern times.

The first official contact between the United States and the Middle East was made in 1799, when President John Adams appointed an American mission to arrange a treaty of friendship and commerce with the Sublime Porte of Turkey, but the actual treaty was not concluded until 1830. In 1829 an unusual incident occurred, which is especially noteworthy when compared with the negotiations and discussions conducted in the Middle East today. A document in Hebrew, bearing the date November 1829, has recently been found among the Phillips Family Papers at the American Jewish Historical Society. It is a letter of introduction for Charles Rhind to the Jewish communities in Russia and Turkey.[1] By itself it would seem to have no relation to the other materials in the collection, but further research, especially at the National Archives, reveals an intriguing story behind this document. Charles Rhind, a successful merchant in New York City and a very active Republican, applied to serve as consul at Odessa, Russia. In a communication to Martin Van Buren, a copy of which was sent to President Jackson, Rhind noted that the post in Odessa was not his prime interest. He was more concerned with negotiating a commercial treaty with Turkey, for he had been heavily engaged in trade in the Mediterranean. Rhind indicated that the British and French would undoubtedly try to prevent the conclusion of such a treaty, because they feared American economic penetration in the area. Hence the only way a treaty could be successfully negotiated would be to appoint him, Rhind, a government agent.

> Let government give plenary powers to the Commodore commanding in that station to conclude a treaty—a merchant of intelligence (and if possible, one known in that quarter) then to be selected who would proceed in his private capacity to Constantinople and through one of the first Jewish bankers, commence a negotiation with the Reis Effendi, more as a business matter than a diplomatic one. . . . The Jewish bankers are men of the highest standing in that country and at the present moment . . . they could operate with more effect than at any other time. It would be easy for me to obtain such introduction to those gentlemen as would secure their cordial cooperation.[2]

President Jackson replied that he did not feel he could issue such an order because of security reasons, but it is interesting to note the suggestion made at the time, that the only means by which the American presence could be secured in the Middle East was by Jewish intervention.

The first salaried American consul in Palestine was appointed in 1856. One of the major duties of the different American consuls throughout the latter half of the century was to protect Jewish residents in the Holy Land, who were apparently covered by American capitulatory rights. This was especially true during the Russo-Turkish War of 1877, when a large number of Russian Jews were registered at the American consulate. To the best of my knowledge, no adequate explanation as to why American officials were so involved in the protection of non-American citizens has ever been advanced.

Much has been made in many published works of the visit to Palestine of the U.S.S. *Delaware* in 1835, but research in the Archives reveals that other American ships, namely, the U.S. sloop

John Adams, the U.S.S. *Shark,* and the U.S.S. *Constitution,* also arrived there at this time. The culmination, of course, was the very famous expedition of William F. Lynch along the Jordan River in 1848–1849.[3]

There are numerous accounts of the work of Edward Robinson and his famous scholarly travels between 1838 and 1841, but there is as yet no comprehensive or systematic study of the various archaeological endeavors of Americans and American institutions in the Holy Land.

What led the American School for Oriental Research, Harvard University, the University of Chicago, the University of Pennsylvania, and many other institutions to undertake extensive archaeological digs in Palestine? Dr. William G. Dever, director of the Albright Archaeological Institute in Jerusalem, in an unpublished address delivered several years ago, attempts to explain this phenomenon as part of the late nineteenth-century American controversy between fundamentalism and modernism in Protestant theological circles. Basically, the archaeological explorations were an attempt by the fundamentalist group to prove the literal accuracy of the Bible by scientific means. Whether we accept this thesis or not, it is a fact that the major American archaeologists working in the Holy Land did not necessarily have scientific, but rather theological, backgrounds.[4] Two outstanding examples are William Foxwell Albright, son of a Methodist missionary who combined "a devotion to Evangelical Christianity with a scientific approach to the problem of archaeology and the Bible,"[5] and Nelson Glueck, Albright's student, who was rabbinically trained at the Hebrew Union College in Cincinnati and eventually became its president.[6]

Generally, the accounts describing the relationship between America and the Holy Land note that these contacts were primarily philanthropic and humanitarian. This is true, but only in part. American Christian missionaries established schools in Jerusalem as early as 1829, and a Quaker school functioned in Ramallah in the early part of the twentieth century.[7] Jewish philanthropic contacts date back over two centuries. We discovered a letter requesting financial aid which was written to Michael Gratz in Philadelphia from Hebron in 1763.[8] During the nineteenth century, at least three Jewish organizations were officially established to raise funds among American Jews to alleviate conditions of the Jewish communities in

Palestine: these were the North American Relief Society for the Indigent Jews in Jerusalem, Palestine; *Hebra Tarumot Hakodesh*; and the Palestine Relief Fund in Cincinnati. Other organizations, such as the Board of Delegates of American Israelites, included Palestine relief among their activities.

Research on the formal organized attempts of Americans to settle in the Holy Land during the Ottoman period has been generally neglected. Oddly enough, the three attempts at organized settlement in the nineteenth century were made by American Christians, while the approximately twenty organizations that appeared in the early part of the twentieth century in the United States were all established by Jews. These attempts were unlike all the earlier European migrations to the United States, which had been motivated by the desire for religious and political freedom or economic opportunity. In the American migrations to Palestine, the endeavors of individuals to find spiritual or ideological fulfillment were the impelling motives of both the Christians and the Jews.

The three Christian settlement ventures were those of Clorinda Minor, a Millerite who established the Mount Hope Colony near Jaffa; George J. Adams of the Church of Messiah Immigration Association, who set up a colony also near Jaffa; and the Spafford family, who established the American Colony in Jerusalem. A contemporary report has the following to say concerning the Adams Colony: "Religiously they believed that Christ's government will be established in Palestine and that the whole land will enjoy a prosperity and glory unparalleled in history."[9] Clorinda Minor reports in a letter to Isaac Leeser that "through the devout study of the Hebrew scriptures, we became convinced that the appointed time of the Gentiles treading down the sanctuary and the host of Israel was accomplished."[10] An official account of the establishment of the American Colony states that it originated from a group of American Christians from Chicago, who strove to create a more meaningful spiritual fellowship.[11]

Most Jewish efforts of the twentieth century were, of course, connected with the newly born political Zionist movement, but here too the desire to relocate in the Holy Land was primarily spiritual or ideological. The following excerpts are typical of the numerous letters written by American Jews interested in joining the Achooza Societies prior to the outbreak of World War I:

> . . . behold I saw the earth and it was corrupt and we didn't like it because Judaism and the Torah fell to the most lowest degree, for most of the population are sabbath desecrators openly and my soul was depressed greatly. . . .
>
> We want our children educated and married in Palestine in an atmosphere where the Jew and the human being can develop into one integrated personality.
>
> . . . there are very few Jews that are born in the American atmosphere who will sacrifice their success in business for a good education for their children.[12]

Further research is necessary to determine whether these efforts to settle in the Holy Land reflect a certain condition of late nineteenth-century American society with a strong spiritual undertone as was evidenced in the explanation for the archaeological efforts noted above.

What characterized the meeting of Eastern and Western civilizations in nineteenth-century Palestine? Can conclusions be drawn from the experiences of American settlers? Two examples are offered for consideration.

The first involves the Jewish community. Toward the end of the nineteenth century, there were a sufficient number of Americans residing in Jerusalem who were dissatisfied with the financial arrangements then in vogue in the city, whereby funds collected from Jews abroad were distributed to various individuals. An autocratic organization called the *Vaad Hakelali* was responsible for the distribution of these funds, and while many groups were affected by the undemocratic procedures, a practice quite common in the Ottoman Empire and among Jewish communities throughout the world, the Americans challenged the authority of the *Vaad* and formally organized a *Kollel America* (American community). In the conflict that ensued, the *Kollel America* was a prime factor in eliminating the *Vaad* and bringing about the downfall of the entire system.[13]

The new arrangements provided for a direct and fairer distribution of funds from the overseas Jewish communities to the beneficiaries in the Holy Land. Although many of the American immigrants had lived in the United States for only a few years prior to their settling in Palestine, this residency had imbued them with sufficient zeal and confidence in American democratic values to challenge the autocratic authority and secure benefits they believed were their due. Members of the communities of European origin had not attempted such an action.

The second example involves American Christians. The Adams Colony was a dismal failure. The causes for this failure, including the question of whether the founder was or was not actually a charlatan, have been discussed in the literature. In many cases, the more than 150 individuals who settled the colony came from fairly comfortable American backgrounds. Although their prime motivation for emigration was spiritual, one of the reasons for the failure was the fact that the money originally collected was used to purchase lumber in Maine, which was then shipped to Palestine to build comfortable housing for the new immigrants. Consequently, bankruptcy followed very shortly. A contemporary account relates that, although the financial conditions of the colony were very bad, the buildings were comfortable, being made of wood and plastered and finished in a very tasteful manner. There were a hotel, a schoolhouse, and a store, but no travelers to patronize the hotel and no local population to purchase supplies from the store.[14]

Does this phenomenon reflect in a sense the American peculiarity of seeking out American comforts no matter where they travel? The causal relationships of historic events are of course difficult to prove. This is especially true of the impact of one culture upon another.

Notes

1. Document dated Nov. 13, 1829, in Phillips Family Papers, American Jewish Historical Society, Waltham, Mass.
2. Microcopy no. 639, Letters of Application and Recommendation during the Administration of Andrew Jackson, 1829–37, Roll 20, Rh-Ry, National Archives, Washington, D.C.
3. W. F. Lynch, *Narrative of the United States Expedition to the River Jordan and the Dead Sea* (London, 1849).
4. Stellof Lecture at the Hebrew University of Jerusalem, available on tape at Albright Institute, Jerusalem.
5. *Encylcopedia Judaica* article on Albright.
6. G. E. Wright, "The Achievement of Nelson Glueck," *Biblical Archaeologist,* XXII (1959), p. 99.
7. American Board of Commissioners of Foreign Missions Papers, Houghton Library, Harvard University, Cambridge, Mass.
8. Gratz Family Papers, American Jewish Historical Society, Waltham, Mass.
9. *New York Times,* April 15, 1867. For a comprehensive study of the colony, see Peter Amann, "Prophet in Zion: The Saga of George J. Adams," *New England Quarterly,* vol. XXXVII (1964), pp. 477–500.
10. *The Occident,* vol. 12, p. 202.
11. Report of researcher Deborah Goldman on America–Holy Land Project. Copies of reports are deposited at the Institute of Contemporary Jewry, Jerusalem and the American Jewish Historical Society, Waltham.
12. Bernard I. Sandler, "Hoachoozo—Zionism in America and the Colonization of Palestine," *American Jewish Historical Quarterly,* LXIV, 2 (December 1974), pp. 138–39.
13. Simcha Fishbane, "The Founding of Kollel America Tifereth Yerushalayim," Ibid., p. 121.

Appendix

Sources for the Study of America–Holy Land Relations Found at the American Jewish Historical Society at Waltham, Mass.

Although the major quantity of archival material located at the library of the Society pertains to America–Holy Land contacts in the post–World War I period, several collections do contain significant data and information on relations between the two areas for the Ottoman period. The following should be noted as being particularly useful for further research and for providing us with a much broader appreciation of the range of relationships that existed.

1. The Gratz Family Papers (P–8) contain two Hebrew letters written from Hebron, Palestine, in 1763 to Michael Gratz in Philadelphia, requesting financial assistance.
2. The Hebra Tarumot Hakodesh Papers (I–33), covering the years 1824–1851, contain information on the establishment of this society and include a large group of letters in Hebrew and English from Palestine acknowledging the receipt of funds sent from America. These letters note the names of several American contributors as well as the various Jewish communities that provided the money.
3. The Papers of the North American Relief Society for the Indigent Jews in Jerusalem, Palestine (I–14), which cover the years 1853–1887, provide both data on the organization and information on the various funds sent to Palestine.
4. The Papers of Congregation Shearith Israel in San Francisco (I–97) contain correspondence about the funds sent to Palestine from 1868 to 1872, which were personally delivered by Moses Montefiore.
5. The Board of Delegates of American Israelites Papers (I–2) contain material on various aspects of American Jewish involvement in the Holy Land. The board was established in 1859 as the first successful national organization of Jewish congregations in the United States. Within the surviving archives are a large number of letters dated 1877 concerning United States consular protection of American and Russian Jews in Palestine during the Russo-Turkish War. Over one hundred items contain information on various phi-

lanthropic ventures that the board engaged in. These included support for the agricultural school in Jaffa (1873–74), the Bikur Holim Hospital (1872–73), and the pilgrim dwellings near Jerusalem (1870–72); charitable work conducted with Moses Montefiore; and economic assistance for indigent American citizens through contacts with the American consulate.

6. The Myer Samuel Isaacs Papers (P–22) contain several letters in French relating to American assistance of the work of the Alliance Israelite Universelle on behalf of the Jews in Palestine.

7. The Stephen S. Wise Papers (P–134) are one of the major resources of American Jewish communal history for the twentieth century. Although a major part of the material reflects American contacts with Palestine in the post-Ottoman era, a substantial number of items contain data relevant for the earlier period as well. Several letters contain information on the American involvement in the language controversy over the use of German or Hebrew in Palestine in 1913. There are also several letters to Wise from Jacob E. Spafford of the American Colony in Jerusalem describing conditions in the Holy Land in the years 1913 and 1914.

The Search for Sources

Roderic H. Davison

WHEN Sultan Selim I led a great army from the north to conquer Syria in 1516, wresting it from the Mamluks of Egypt, Palestine came under Ottoman Turkish control. It remained under Turkish rule until 1917–1918, when British forces aided by Arabs, French, and Anzacs pushed in from the south. The government of the last sultan in Istanbul recognized the loss in the Treaty of Sèvres of 1920; the Turkish government of Ankara confirmed it in the treaty of Lausanne of 1923, when Palestine was already in fact under British mandatory administration.

Throughout its four hundred years as a part of the Ottoman Empire, Palestine was important in a number of ways. It was a border area where the desert and the sown met, and thus was intended to provide protection for the settled populations against Bedouin raids. It flanked the pilgrim route from Damascus to Mecca, which had to be made safe for the annual *hajj*. It was also a vital link in the land route by which officials, soldiers, and messengers traveled from Istanbul to Cairo. These aspects of Palestine's geographic location were important principally in relation to the Ottoman Empire's own peoples and domestic concerns, although the *hajj* caravans were joined by many pilgrims from abroad. Other aspects were important to foreign countries as well as to the empire. One was Palestine's location not far from the Suez Canal, which was opened to navigation in 1869. Another was its suspected potential, about the time of the

Great War of 1914–1918, as a source of petroleum. But the major importance of Palestine was religious; it was the site of shrines and places holy to Christianity, Judaism, and Islam. Muslim Turks, as well as Jews and Christians, often called it the Holy Land (*arazi-i mukaddese*).[1]

The administration of Ottoman Palestine, as of other Ottoman territories, generated quantities of written records. Many of them have been preserved in various archives. The most important are those in Istanbul, primarily the Başbakanlik Arşivi, the Prime Ministry Archive, which is the major depository for documents from the early days of the Ottoman Empire to its end, from many offices of the sultan's government. The significance of this archive for the history of Palestine has already been demonstrated by various scholars, such as Uriel Heyd, Moshe Ma'oz, and Bernard Lewis. They have used documents preserved there to explore questions relating to population, administration, defense, property, taxation, commerce, and religious groups in Palestine in the sixteenth and nineteenth centuries.[2] Many more records on Palestine in the Prime Ministry Archive undoubtedly await scholarly use. For the archive is extraordinarily rich. While there are, in fact, many archives from the Ottoman period, including collections of court records in various provincial centers both inside and outside of present-day Turkey, and other central archives in Istanbul and Ankara, the Prime Ministry Archive is the largest.[3] Its holdings in the 1940s were estimated at roughly 30,000,000 documents, in addition to thousands of bound registers.[4] A decade later, the director of the archive made an estimate of 50,000,000 documents.[5] I have seen informal estimates run as high as 90,000,000.[6] Whatever the total, which cannot be precisely known, the number of documents is enormous.

It is logical to assume that these vast holdings may contain records relating not only to the religious importance of Palestine for Muslims, Jews, and Christians in the empire, but also to the interest of other countries and peoples in Palestine as a religious center and place of pilgrimage. The Prime Ministry Archive would, therefore, be a likely place in which to seek information on American interest in the Holy Land.

A number of limitations must be borne in mind, however. During much of the period of Ottoman rule in Palestine, there was no United States, which is a relatively young country. Selim I's conquest of

Syria occurred barely three years after Balboa became the first European to sight the Pacific Ocean on its American side, about ninety years before the first permanent settlement of English-speaking colonists at Jamestown, and over two and a half centuries before American independence. On the other hand, the French, Austrians, English, Dutch, and Italians of various city-states did develop fairly close relations with the Ottoman Empire. They engaged in commerce and acquired extraterritorial rights and religious privileges along with diplomatic representation in Istanbul. In 1774 Russia joined the group. During all this time, no specifically American connection with the Ottoman Empire existed. Before 1776, then, and in fact before 1880, one would not expect to find Ottoman records concerning the United States, excepting perhaps a few on a trickle of commerce and a few on the Barbary pirates who operated out of Ottoman provinces in North Africa. Likewise, there would probably be no records concerning the interest of individual Americans in Palestine.

A second limitation has been mentioned by Professor Ma'oz. Among the countries that maintained diplomatic and consular representation in the Ottoman Empire, and interests in Palestine, the United States was relatively insignificant. This was true even after this country signed a treaty of navigation and commerce with the empire in 1830 and opened a legation in Istanbul a year later. Unlike the European powers, the United States did not participate in the international politics of the Near East.[7] The Eastern Question—the question of the ultimate fate of the Ottoman Empire's territories—was of very peripheral interest to the United States. But Russia, France, Britain, and Austria were constantly involved with it; by the late nineteenth century, Germany and Italy had joined in. As for Ottoman Palestine, the Catholic states—France, Austria, and Italy—devoted much attention to its shrines, monks, religious hierarchies, and pilgrims, France taking the lead as self-proclaimed protector of Roman monks and missionaries. Russia set herself up as protector of the Greek Orthodox shrines and clergy in Palestine. Almost all the foreign pilgrims who swarmed into Jerusalem and Bethlehem at Easter or Christmas time were Roman Catholic or Greek Orthodox, and probably few among them came from predominantly Protestant America. Protestant England expressed greater religious interest in Palestine, through establishments of the Anglican Church, than did the United States. By the late nineteenth century, Protestant Germany, too, made her presence felt. Furthermore, all these European powers held political interests, whether direct or indirect, in Palestine. Sometimes these interests came dramatically to the fore, as in the dispute over the Holy Places in 1852–1853 between Russia and France, which culminated in the Crimean War, or the visit of Kaiser Wilhelm II to Jerusalem in 1898, when a new path yet untrod by human foot was blasted for the emperor through the wall of the city. These are the kinds of interest on the part of the European powers that the documents in the Ottoman archives will primarily reflect. American interests in the Holy Land will undoubtedly find only modest reference in the documents.

A third limitation should also be considered: the extent to which records in the Prime Ministry Archive are as yet uncatalogued. Progress is made constantly, documents are being sorted, new lists and catalogues are being prepared. Yet the archive is run by a limited staff and its needs are much larger than its budget can meet. Furthermore, in the last days of the empire and during the transition to the republic, considerable shifting of documents took place, causing disorder and some loss. As a result, millions of documents must yet be sorted, classified, and described. No one can estimate how long the process will take. The problem is compounded for the nineteenth and twentieth centuries because, just at the period when the United States appears on the Near Eastern scene, the archival records tend to be documents on single sheets, which are easier to scatter and harder to put in order than the bound registers, containing many documents in a series, so common in earlier periods.

Despite these limitations, there is probability that documents will be found here concerning American interest in Palestine. Certain classifications of documents in the Prime Ministry Archive are more likely than others to contain material relevant to this subject. Moshe Ma‘oz mentions some of the most pertinent ones in his paper, although I think he is overoptimistic about one classification. This is the *Mühimme Defterleri* (registers of important matters), an excellent source through the eighteenth century but far less complete and useful for the nineteenth; the series practically ceased to be kept up after mid-century.

Three classifications of documents from the nineteenth century seem, from my own experience, perhaps more likely to contain material on the America-Holy Land theme. One is the *Cevdet tasnifi* (Cevdet classification), so called after a scholar who headed a committee which classified documents in the 1930s. Catalogues for the subcategory *Hariciye* (foreign) of this classification contain many mentions of "Amerikan" or of "Protestan" activities, often in connection with schools or missions; perhaps some of these activities related to Palestine. Another classification, *Iradeler* (orders, or decrees), particularly in its "foreign" subcategory, also contains documents concerning Protestant activities and presumably concerning Americans. An *irade* was an order on the basis of a memorandum describing a situation and requesting the sultan's approval of a course of action; the memoranda are often quite informative and are preserved with the reply, which was usually written on the lower margin of each memorandum.[8]

One further classification of documents in the Prime Ministry Archive is of particular interest because it originates in the era of Sultan Abdulhamid II (1876–1909), known for his autocratic rule and his fear of subversive influences, religious influences included. This is the *Yildiz* classification, a rather large group of documents which the sultan collected in his Yildiz palace and which, after the Young Turks deposed him, were transferred in large part (some were lost, purloined, or destroyed, and some deposited elsewhere) to the archive.[9] All kinds of records are included, among them personal papers of prominent statesmen, reports on various provinces of the empire, and reports on foreign influences and on groups suspected of subversive activity. The catalogue for the Yildiz classification makes occasional references to Americans, Palestine, Protestants, Jews, and other religious groups.

It should be pointed out that research in this classification is not a simple matter (not that it is so in other classifications). The principles of organization in the different classifications vary. Some classifications are based on provenance—on the government office from which, or to which, the document came. Some are based on a geographical area in the empire, some on the nature of the document (like the *irade*). Some classifications are arranged chronologically and some are not. Some are based on no recognizable scientific or modern archival principle. The *Yildiz* classification obviously belongs to the latter category; its contents are heterogeneous partly owing to the sultan's interests and whims, and partly owing to chance. The subcategories within it, furthermore, are often illogical and uninformative. For example, one subcategory is labeled "Cartons and registers connected to private and official documents concerning various subjects." Under this subcategory rubric in the catalogue, there is at least one entry referring in one context to American missionaries and in a separate context to Palestine. Finally, the descriptive entries for each document in any of the archive's catalogues may be sufficient to give a good idea of what the document contains, but may also be insufficient. Moreover, one catalogue entry may indicate a whole bundle of documents or a single sheet only; fortunately, this is usually specified. The archivists are aware of all these difficulties, which stem from years past when registers were made in various offices of the sultanate, or when documents were grouped by chance, or when the arranging was done by nonhistorians and nonarchivists. Archivists can sometimes offer considerable help. The researcher must forever be grateful not only that so many documents have survived, but that there are catalogues of any kind. He must be prepared, however, to go at his task slowly, to spend weeks if not months with catalogues, and then to examine hundreds or thousands of documents with the near certainty that only a small proportion will contain what he seeks. The sources are rich, but the labor is long. Sometimes the feeling is like that of looking for a needle in a haystack.

There is another archive in Istanbul which may also contain documents that would shed light on American interest in Palestine. This is the Archive of the (Ottoman) Foreign Ministry, the Diş-Işleri Bakanliği Hazine-i Evrak, maintained in Istanbul by the Foreign Ministry of the Republic. The Foreign Ministry Archive is far smaller than that of the Prime Ministry, since its records come from a single government department, which was established in its modern form as late as 1836. Some documents that date back to the late eighteenth century have been added, but these are exceptional. The Foreign Ministry records become detailed only after the 1850s. The bulk of the documents concern Ottoman relations with the major European powers, as seen in communications from Ottoman diplomatic and consular representatives abroad to the Sublime Porte in Istanbul, and vice versa. But there are also documents concerning relations with the United States and many other countries. Since many of the international questions related to provinces in the empire, this archive also contains materials on Syria and Palestine. The documents in this archive that are available to research (some are said to be stored and unsorted) are fairly well ordered. Still, there are occasional difficulties: some of the catalogue entries, made over a half-century ago, no longer correspond to existing cartons or files in the depository, while some cartons or files that are correctly catalogued turn out, on examination, to have been emptied of documents years ago, usually when these were sent to another ministry.

The archives of the great European powers, in their respective capitals, undoubtedly contain materials relating to interests and activities of Americans in the Holy Land. The best sources would probably be British diplomatic and consular reports from the area, as Moshe Ma'oz indicates; and then, in descending order, French, German, Russian, Austrian, and Italian reports. Archives of the Vatican might also prove quite useful.[10] To some of these countries the Americans were friends; to others they were rivals, especially if they were Protestant missionaries. Here again, however, references to American activities in Palestine are likely to be few and scattered.

My own experience in research on the Ottoman Empire of the nineteenth and twentieth centuries, limited though it is in regard to Palestine, suggests that the major sources for information on the America–Holy Land relationship lie in the United States rather than abroad. A mine of information is the archive of the American Board of Commissioners for Foreign Missions (ABCFM), now on deposit in the Houghton Library at Harvard University. Despite their usually strong evangelical bias, their parochial missionary concerns, and their opposition to the Eastern Christian churches as well as to Islam, some of the missionaries had broad interests and many were good observers. They reported not only on the work of the mission but on events and conditions around them. My impression is that most of them were fluent in the language of the country where they were stationed; those in Syria knew Arabic, and when traveling in the Holy Land, they could talk with the inhabitants. It is unfortunate, from the viewpoint of records, that the Jerusalem mission was closed in 1844, leaving only centers just north of Palestine. Another possible source of information about Americans in Palestine would be personal papers of missionaries, and even of the staff members of the Syrian Protestant College, established in Beirut in 1866. Many of them certainly traveled to Palestine, with the Bible and Thomson and Robinson in their saddlebags.

The records of the State Department, now in the National Archives, containing diplomatic and consular reports from various posts in the Ottoman Empire, are well known as a major resource and are described in Milton Gustafson's paper. The researcher soon discovers that information in these records on Palestine does not come only from posts like Jaffa and Jerusalem located within Palestine. For instance, information about the ill-starred Adams Colony of 1866 at Jaffa turns up in consular reports from Alexandria and from Beirut, and in dispatches of the American minister in Constantinople. (It may be worth mentioning also that the ABCFM records refer to the Adams venture.)

Another productive source in the United States, one might surmise, would be the records of oil companies, at least of the Standard Oil Company of New York (Socony). Thinking that Palestine might be flowing not only with milk and honey but with petroleum, Socony began explorations there in 1913, just before World War I. At the end of the war, Socony ran into stiff opposition from the British occupation forces. Much of the story comes across in the State Department records, but there is undoubtedly more in Socony archives.[11] Again, one can expect that the records of steamship and travel companies might reveal a good deal about American travel to, and therefore interest in, the Holy Land. It may well be, however, that in the Ottoman period travelers would more frequently resort to British rather than to American companies. Certainly Thomas Cook and Sons were preeminent in the travel field: they were the ones who organized the Kaiser's visit to Jerusalem, and Cook's tourists became so well known to natives that they were called "Kukiyya." Americans had a hand in the tours, as well; two survivors of the Adams Colony in Jaffa became Cook's representatives and guides.[12]

Another fruitful American source may well be records of Freemasonic lodges or jurisdictions. Freemasons clearly felt a tie to the land where their order was said to have originated, the land of King Solomon and of Hiram of Tyre. The connection may have been more one of romantic interest, of bridging the seas and the centuries with a leap of imagination, than of actual contact with Palestine. Masonic lodges in the nineteenth-century Ottoman Empire were few and of recent European parentage, and none appear to have existed in Palestine itself at the time. Records of American Freemasonry may shed more light on the actual connection. Yet there was at least some direct contact with Palestine. Robert Morris, a dedicated and enthusiastic Mason, prolific author of Masonic books and poems, published a long account of his "Masonic Holy Land Mission" to Syria and Palestine in 1868. As he went about visiting biblical sites, he "dedicated" them to groups of American Masons, and on a number of monuments he chiseled the square and compass, the symbols of the order. He reports that on the winding steps of the Damascus Gate of Jerusalem he "cut the *Square and Compass* so deeply that the city may be captured another seventeen times before it fades out."[13] Morris also visited the Adams Colony at Jaffa. Adams and three other colonists were also Masons. While Morris approved of some of the others, he found Adams a deplorable character, "vain, conceited, intemperate"; "of all men living he was one of the last to undertake to manage a colony upon the Syrian coast."[14]

Obviously most of the American interest in the Holy Land in the Ottoman period was personal and unofficial, rather than public and official. In the total context of American interests in the Near East, the interest in Palestine was comparatively small. Books such as David Finnie's *Pioneers East: The Early American Experience in the Middle East*[15] and Leland Gordon's *American Relations with Turkey, 1830–1930: An Economic Interpretation,*[16] when added to the works by Grabill, Manuel, and Tibawi cited by Moshe Ma'oz, help to put America's Palestine interest in perspective. Particularly useful in this regard are James Field's *America and the Mediterranean World, 1776–1882*[17] and John De Novo's *American Interest and Policies in the Middle East, 1900–1939.*[18] One should not expect, then, to find official American records exhibiting major concern with the Holy Land in the Ottoman period. Compared to the interests of Europeans, with their passionate involvement with the holy sites, their concern for the possible breakup of the Ottoman Empire, and their jockeying for strategic, political, economic, and religious position, the American interest was indeed minor.

Yet the American interest existed as a constant thread, sometimes only in vague terms, and mostly in the realm of thought and attitudes. Undoubtedly the sort of influence that Robert Handy describes—Bible study, Sunday school lessons, hymns, devotional poems—was the major link at least between Protestant Americans and the Holy Land. There may be one other link, subtle but perhaps just as pervasive—the given names of individuals. Perhaps the United States census records may be a source for demonstrating American interest in the Holy Land. For here one might discover what percentage of Americans bore Christian names like Samuel, Ruth, Ezra, Obadiah, Sarah, Ebenezer, Esther, Eli, Zechariah, and so on for a long, long list. Perhaps each American who bore a Hebrew name from Palestine felt subconsciously some personal connection, however tenuous, with the Holy Land, the land of the Bible.

Notes

1. Uriel Heyd, *Ottoman Documents on Palestine, 1552–1615* (Oxford: Clarendon Press, 1960), p. 39.
2. Ibid., passim, especially pp. xv–xviii and 3–6, on the Mühimme Defterleri; Moshe Ma'oz, *Ottoman Reform in Syria and Palestine, 1840–1861* (Oxford: Clarendon Press, 1968); Bernard Lewis, *Notes and Documents from the Turkish Archives: A Contribution to the History of the Jews in the Ottoman Empire* (Jerusalem: Israel Oriental Society, 1952); idem, "Studies in the Ottoman Archives—I" *Bulletin of the School of Oriental and African Studies* (London), 16:3 (1954), pp. 469–501.
3. Some idea of the archival resources, both in the Prime Ministry Archive and elsewhere, may be obtained from Midhat Sertoğlu, *Muhteva bakimindan Başvekalet Arşivi* (The Prime Ministry Achive from the Viewpoint of its Contents) (Ankara: Türk Tarih Kurumu, 1955), pp. 84–86; Stanford J. Shaw, "Archival Sources for Ottoman History: The Archives of Turkey," *Journal of the American Oriental Society,* 80:1 (January–March 1960), pp. 1–12; Roderic H. Davison, "Archives in the Near East, with Special Reference to Ottoman History," *News from the Center* (Center for the Coordination of Foreign Manuscript Copying, Library of Congress), IV (Fall 1968), pp. 2–11. See also the informative review of Sertoğlu's book by Andreas Tietze in *Oriens,* 10:2 (31 December 1957), pp. 302–3.
4. I. H. Uzunçarşili, *Osmanli Devletinin Saray Teskilati* (The Palace Organization of the Ottoman State) (Ankara: Türk Tarih Kurumu, 1945), p. 3.
5. Sertoğlu, op. cit., p. 87.
6. L. Fekete, "Ueber Archivalien und Archivwesen in der Türkei," *Acta Orientalia* (Budapest) 3:3 (1953), pp. 179–205.
7. One measure of this is the very small number of documents concerning the United States, and the large number concerning other powers, in J. C. Hurewitz, ed., *The Middle East and North Africa in World Politics: A Documentary Record*, Vol. I: 1535–1914, 2nd ed. (New Haven: Yale University Press, 1975).
8. Sertoğlu, op. cit., barely mentions the Cevdet classification, pp. 70–71, but is fuller on the *Irade* classification, pp. 51–58.
9. Sertoğlu describes this classification while it was being reassembled, ibid., pp. 74–78; Stanford J. Shaw, "The *Yildiz* Palace Archives of *Abdülhamit II," Archivum Ottomanicum,* III (1971), pp. 211–237, is principally a listing in English translation of a substantial sample of the documents in this classification.
10. Some idea of the resources in European archives is given in Roderic H. Davison, "European Archives as a Source for Later Ottoman History,"

Report on Current Research on the Middle East (Middle East Institute, 1958), pp. 33–45. See also Daniel H. Thomas and Lynn M. Case, *The New Guide to the Diplomatic Archives of Western Europe* (Philadelphia: University of Pennsylvania Press, 1975).

11. See the description and references in John A. De Novo, *American Interests and Policies in the Middle East, 1900–1939* (Minneapolis: University of Minnesota Press, 1963), pp. 167–76.
12. James A. Field, Jr., *America and the Mediterranean World, 1776–1882* (Princeton: Princeton University Press, 1969), p. 327.
13. Robert Morris, *Freemasonry in the Holy Land. A Narrative of Masonic Explorations Made in 1868, in the Land of King Solomon and the Two Hirams* (LaGrange, Ky., 1879), p. 289.
14. Ibid., pp. 268, 269.
15. David Finnie, *Pioneers East* (Cambridge: Harvard University Press, 1967).
16. Leland Gordon, *American Relations with Turkey, 1830–1930* (Philadelphia: University of Pennsylvania Press, 1932).
17. James Field, *America and the Mediterranean World, 1776–1882, op cit.*
18. John DeNovo, *American Interests and Policies in the Middle East, 1900–1939, op. cit.*

Americans in the Holy Land, 1850-1900: A Select Bibliography

Yohai Goell
and
Martha B. Katz-Hyman

DAVID Finnie, in his *Pioneers East: The Early American Experience in the Middle East* (Cambridge, Mass.: Harvard University Press, 1967), appended a list of contemporary accounts by American travelers to the Middle East until 1850. Our bibliography supplements Finnie's list for the period 1850–1900. It is limited, however, to travelers to the Holy Land who published their descriptions in monograph form. Several manuscript diaries, recorded by the America–Holy Land Project, are not listed here.

The list is arranged by the name of the traveler, and, when known, includes pertinent data about each individual; the time actually spent in the Holy Land; and the pages of the published volume pertaining to the Holy Land. Also included are those Americans who decided to remain there, the most prominent being Simon Berman, Rolla Floyd, and Bertha Spafford Vester.

The nature of American interest in the Holy Land during the last half of the nineteenth century is shown by the biographical data collected to date. Of the 131 individuals who published the accounts listed below, 55 had some religious affiliation or identification, whether as clergy or missionaries; 25 were authors or publicists; 12 were United States government personnel; 18 are classified as miscellaneous; and for 23 biographical data could not be found.

Allen, Mary S. Dates unknown.

Traveled to the Holy Land in 1896.

From West to East, or the Old World as I Saw It, Being a Description of a Journey from California to the Holy Land and Egypt, by the Way of England, France, Switzerland and Italy. Chicago, 1898. Pages dealing with the Holy Land: 46–88.

Appleton, Thomas Gold, 1812–1884.

Essayist, poet, and artist; trustee of various cultural institutions in Boston. Traveled to Palestine in the spring of 1875.

Syrian Sunshine. Boston, 1877. Pages dealing with Palestine: 5–247.

Bacon, Leonard, 1802–1881.

Congregationalist minister; served at the First Church of Christ, New Haven, Conn. Traveled to the Holy Land in 1851.

A Letter from Rev. Leonard Bacon, D.D., to the Church and Congregation under his Charge. . . . Jerusalem, 1851. Entire pamphlet deals with the Holy Land.

Barclay, James Turner, 1807–1874.

Missionary in Jerusalem, 1853?–1856.

The City of the Great King: or, Jerusalem As It Was, As It Is, and As It Is to Be. Philadelphia, 1857. Entire book deals with Jerusalem.

Bartlett, Samuel Colcord, 1817–1898.

Professor of biblical literature, Chicago Theological Seminary, 1858–1877; President of Dartmouth College, 1877–1892; corporate member of the American Board of Commissioners for Foreign Missions. Traveled to the Near East and the Holy Land in 1873–1874.

From Egypt to Palestine through Sinai, the Wilderness and the South Country: Observations of a Journey Made with Special Reference to the History of the Israelites. New York, 1879. Pages dealing with the Holy Land: 185–511.

Bausman, Benjamin, 1824–1909.

Clergyman, German Reformed Church, ordained 1853; served

congregations in Reading, Pa., 1863–1909. Traveled to Europe and the Holy Land, 1856–1857.

Sinai and Zion: or, a Pilgrimage through the Wilderness to the Land of Promise. Philadelphia, 1861. Pages dealing with the Holy Land: 101–473.

Berman, Simon, 1818–1884.

Emigrated to the United States from Poland in 1852. Went to the Holy Land in 1870 to form a cooperative agricultural settlement.

Sefer Mas'ot Shim'on. Cracow, 1879. Pages dealing with the Holy Land: 71–80. Book written in Yiddish.

Bottome, Margaret, 1827–1906.

Author and longtime contributor to religious magazines on subjects pertaining to women; founded International Order of the King's Daughters and Sons, a Christian service organization.

A Sunshine Trip: Glimpses of the Orient. New York, 1897. Pages dealing with the Holy Land: 106–164.

Brooks, Noah, 1830–1903.

Author and journalist; in California 1859–1871; wrote for New York newspapers, 1871–1885; editor, *Newark (N.J.) Advertiser,* 1884–1894. Traveled to the Near East and the Holy Land in 1894–1895.

The Mediterranean Trip; a Short Guide to the Principal Points on the Shores of the Western Mediterranean and the Levant. New York, 1895. Pages dealing with the Holy Land: 105–120.

Browne, John Ross, 1821–1875.

Author and round-the-world traveler, 1842–1867. Traveled to the Holy Land in 1851.

Yusef, or the Journey of the Frangi: a Crusade in the East. New York, 1853. Pages dealing with the Holy Land: 319–409.

Bryant, William Cullen, 1794–1878.

Poet and journalist; editor of the *New York Evening Post,* 1829–1878. Traveled to the Holy Land in 1852–1853.

Letters from the East. New York, 1869. Pages dealing with the Holy Land: 102–185.

Burt, Nathaniel Clark, 1825–1874.

Presbyterian clergyman in Ohio. Toured Europe, Egypt, and Palestine in 1866–1867.

The Far East: or, Letters from Egypt, Palestine, and Other Lands of the Orient. Cincinnati, 1868. Pages dealing with the Holy Land: 205–340.

The Land and Its Story: or, the Sacred Geography of Palestine. New York, 1869. Entire book deals with the Holy Land.

Camp, Phineas, 1788–1868.

Poems of the Mohawk Valley, and on Scenes in Palestine. . . . Utica, N.Y., 1859. Pages dealing with the Holy Land: 127–176.

Carpenter, Mary Thorn. Dates unknown.

Probably traveled in the Holy Land in 1894.

In Cairo and Jerusalem; an Eastern Note-book. New York, 1894. Pages dealing with the Holy Land: 173–222.

Carradine, Beverly, 1848–?

A Journey to Palestine. St. Louis, Mo., 1891.

Champney, Elizabeth Williams, 1850–1922.

Author, traveled widely in Europe, contributed to *Harper's* and *Century* magazines.

Three Vassar Girls in the Holy Land. Boston, 1892. Pages dealing with the Holy Land: 105–247.

Clemens, Samuel, 1835–1910.

Humorist and novelist. Traveled to the Holy Land in 1867.

The Innocents Abroad, or, the New Pilgrim's Progress, by Mark Twain (pseud.). Hartford, 1870. Pages dealing with the Holy Land: 465–608.

Travelling with the Innocents Abroad. Mark Twain's Original Reports from Europe and the Holy Land, ed. by Daniel Morley McKeithan. Norman, Okla., 1958. Pages dealing with the Holy Land: 206–309.

Coleman, Henry Roush, 1834–?

Freemason. Traveled to the Holy Land in 1880.

Light from the East; Travels and Researches in Bible Lands in Pursuit of More Light in Masonry. Louisville, Ky., 1882. Pages dealing with the Holy Land: 51–380 and 415–564.

Cox, Samuel Sullivan, 1824–1889.

Member of the House of Representatives from Ohio, 1857–1865; from New York, 1869–1885. Minister to Turkey, 1885–1886. Traveled to the Holy Land in the summer of 1881.

Orient Sunbeams, or From the Porte to the Pyramids by Way of Palestine. New York, 1882. Pages dealing with the Holy Land: 271–360.

Crosby, Howard, 1826–1891.

Presbyterian minister and educator in New York. Traveled to the Holy Land in 1849(?).

Lands of the Moslem; a Narrative of Oriental Travel, by El-Mukattem (pseud.). New York, 1851. Pages dealing with the Holy Land: 134–325.

Cummings, Jonathan. Dates unknown.

Author and editor of millennial publications in Boston. Traveled to the Holy Land in 1889–1890.

A Tour to the Holy Land and Six Weeks in Jerusalem in the Interest of the Nation of Israel. Cambridgeport, Mass., 1890. Pages dealing with the Holy Land: 39–215.

Curtis, George William, 1824–1892.

Author and orator, traveled widely; associate editor of the *New York Tribune,* 1852–1857; editor, *Harper's Weekly,* 1863–? Traveled to the Holy Land most probably in 1850.

The Howadji in Syria. New York, 1858. Pages dealing with the Holy Land: 133–286. Book is based on letters to the *New York Tribune.*

Cuyler, Theodore Ledyard, 1822–1909.

Presbyterian clergyman, graduated from the Princeton Theological Seminary, pastor in Brooklyn, 1860–1890. Traveled to the Holy Land in 1881.

From the Nile to Norway and Homeward. New York, 1882. Pages dealing with the Holy Land: 78–129.

Dana, Charles Anderson, 1819–1897.

Newspaper editor of the *New York Tribune,* 1847–1862, and the *New York Sun,* 1868–1897, among others.

Eastern Journeys: Some Notes of Travel in Russia, in the Caucasus, and to Jerusalem. New York, 1898. Pages dealing with the Holy Land: 107–146.

De Forest, John William, 1826–1906.

Author and traveler. Spent two years in the Levant, especially Syria, years unknown.

Oriental Acquaintances; or, Letters from Syria. New York, 1856. Pages dealing with the Holy Land: 59–121.

De Hass, Frank S. Dates unknown.

U.S. consul in Jerusalem, 1873–1877.

Recent Travels and Explorations in Bible Lands. . . . New York, 1881. Pages dealing with the Holy Land: 90–403.

De Leon, Edwin, 1828–1891.

Author and editor. U.S. consul-general in Egypt, 1853–1861. Visited Jaffa at the time of attack on American colonists, 1858.

Thirty Years of My Life on Three Continents, 2 vols. London, 1890. Pages dealing with the Holy Land: vol. 1, pp. 246–290.

Dootlittle, George Curtis, 1867–1922.

Traveled to the Holy Land in 1899.

Forbidden Paths in the Land of Og; a Record of Travels of Three Wise and Otherwise Men to the East of the Jordan, by the Otherwise Man (pseud.). New York, 1890. Entire book deals with the region of the Jordan Valley.

Dorr, Benjamin, 1796–1869.

Episcopalian clergyman from Philadelphia. Traveled to Europe, Egypt, and the Holy Land in 1853.

Notes of Travel in Egypt, the Holy Land, Turkey, and Greece. Philadelphia, 1856. Pages dealing with the Holy Land: 138–283.

Dorr, David F. Dates unknown.

Traveled in the Holy Land in 1853.

A Colored Man Round the World, by a Quadroon (pseud.). (Cleveland?), 1858. Pages dealing with the Holy Land: 179–188.

Dulles, John Welsh, 1823–1887.

Apparently a Presbyterian clergyman. The "ride" took place in 1879.

The Ride through Palestine. Philadelphia, 1881. Pages dealing with the Holy Land: 19–377.

Eddy, Daniel Clarke, 1823–1896.

Baptist clergyman, longtime pastor of First Baptist Church, Brooklyn. Published two books of juvenile literature based on travels in the Holy Land. Traveled to the Holy Land in 1861.

Rip Van Winkle's Travels in Asia and Africa, by Rupert Van Wert (pseud.). New York, 1882. Also published under the titles *Van Wert's Travels in Asia and Africa,* by Rupert Van Wert (pseud.)., Chicago, 1884, and *Eddy's Travels in Asia and Africa,* Boston, 1893. Pages in 1884 edition dealing with the Holy Land: 111–206.

Edwards, Robert A. Dates unknown.

Pastor of the Church of St. Matthias, Philadelphia. Traveled to the Holy Land in 1889.

From Joppa to Mount Hermon; a Series of Narrative Discourses on the Holy Land Delivered in the Church of St. Matthias, Phila-

delphia, During the Autumn and Winter of 1889–1890. Second edition, revised and corrected. Philadelphia, 1890. Entire book deals with the Holy Land.

Eisenstein, Judah David, 1854–1956.

Encyclopedist, anthologist, and author. Visited the Holy Land in 1899.

Otzar Zikhronothai. New York, 1929. Pages dealing with the Holy Land: part 1, pp. 88–96. Book written in Hebrew.

Elliott, Charles Wyllys, 1817–1883.

New York merchant, philanthropist, and author. Appointed a planning commissioner for Central Park, 1857.

Remarkable Characters and Places of the Holy Land. . . Hartford, 1869. Discussion of Holy Land scattered throughout book. Several chapters were written by other authors.

Emerson, Jesse Milton, 1818–1898.

Traveled to the Holy Land in 1885–1886.

New York to Orient; a Series of Letters Written during a Brief Trip through Europe to Palestine. . . . New York, 1886. Pages dealing with the Holy Land: 71–120.

Fairbanks, Hiram Francis, 1835–?

A Visit to Europe and the Holy Land, 5th ed. New York, 1888. Pages dealing with the Holy Land: 110–237.

Field, Henry Martyn, 1822–1907.

Presbyterian clergyman, traveled extensively. Went to the Holy Land in 1882.

Among the Holy Hills. New York, 1884. Pages dealing with the Holy Land: 9–189.

On the Desert; a Narrative of Travel from Egypt through the Wilderness of Sinai to Palestine. New York, 1883. Pages dealing with the Holy Land: 38–330.

Floyd, Rolla. Dates unknown.

A former member of the Adams Colony in Jaffa, he became a

well-known guide in Palestine. He arrived with the Adams Colony in 1866.

Bible Witnesses from Bible Lands; Verified in the Researches of the Explorers and Correspondents of the American Holy-Land Exploration. . . . by Robert Morris, John Sheville, Rolla Floyd, and Samuel Hallock. New York, 1874.

Fogg, William Perry. Dates unknown.

Arabistan: or, The Land of "The Arabian Nights." London, 1875. Pages dealing with the Holy Land: 82–114.

Fort, Joseph Marstain. Dates unknown.

Traveled to the Holy Land in 1891 with Henry Marvin Wharton (see below).

The Texas Doctor and the Arab Donkey; or, Palestine and Egypt as Viewed by Modern Eyes. Chicago, 1893.

Freese, Jacob R., 1826–1885.

U.S. commissioner to the Paris Exposition, 1867. Traveled to the Holy Land in March–April 1867.

The Old World. Palestine, Syria, and Asia Minor. Travel, Incidents, Description and History. Philadelphia, 1869. Pages dealing with the Holy Land: 19–253.

Fulton, John, 1834–1907.

Presbyterian clergyman; professor of canon law at Divinity School, Philadelphia; editor of the *Church Standard.*

The Beautiful Land; Palestine As It Was and As It Now Is: Historical, Geographical, and Pictorial, along the Lines of our Saviour's Journeys. Chicago, 1891. Abridged edition published under the title *Palestine; the Holy Land As It Was and As It Is.* Philadelphia, 1900.

Gage, William Leonard, 1832–1889.

The Home of God's People. Hartford, 1873. Entire book deals with the Holy Land.

The Land of Sacred Mystery; or, The Bible Read in the Light of Its Own Scenery. Hartford, 1871. Pages dealing with the Holy Land: entire book except pp. 585–610.

Studies in Bible Lands. Boston, 1869. Entire books deals with lands mentioned in the Bible.

Gilder, Richard Watson, 1844–1909.

Poet, editor of the *Century.* Was in Bethlehem in 1896.

In Palestine and Other Poems. New York, 1898. Pages dealing with the Holy Land: 11–21.

Gillman, Henry, 1833–1915.

Scientist, U.S. consul in Jerusalem, 1886–1891.

Hassan: a Fellah; a Romance of Palestine. Boston, 1898. Entire book is set in the Holy Land.

Grant, Julia Dent, 1826–1902.

Wife of Ulysses S. Grant. Visited the Holy Land in February 1878, during the Grants' round-the-world trip.

The Personal Memoirs of Julia Dent Grant. Edited, with notes and foreword by John Y. Simon. New York, 1975. Pages dealing with the Holy Land: 232–236.

Gray, Albert Zabriskie, 1840–1889.

Episcopal clergyman.

The Land and the Life; Sketches and Studies in Palestine. New York, 1876. Entire book deals with the Holy Land.

Griswold, Louise M. Dates unknown.

Traveled to Palestine on the *Quaker City* excursion in 1867.

A Woman's Pilgrimage to the Holy Land; or, Pleasant Days Abroad. Being Notes of a Tour through Europe and the East. Hartford, 1871. Pages dealing with the Holy Land: 216–313.

Hale, Edward Everett, 1822–1909.

Unitarian minister in Boston and prolific author.

Hale, Susan, 1833–1910.

Sister of Edward Everett Hale; artist and author.

A Family Flight over Egypt and Syria. Boston, 1882. Pages dealing with the Holy Land: 240–334 and 362–366.

Hallock, Samuel. Dates unknown.

See entry under Floyd.

Harman, Henry Martyn, 1822–1897.

Professor of ancient languages and literature, Dickinson College, Carlisle, Pa. Traveled to the Holy Land in 1869–1870.

A Journey to Egypt and the Holy Land, in 1869–1870. Philadelphia, 1873. Pages dealing with the Holy Land: 102–217.

Harriman, Walter, 1817–1884.

Ordained a minister of the Universalist Church; military career officer; governor of New Hampshire, 1867–1868. Traveled to the Holy Land in 1882.

Travels and Observations in the Orient and a Hasty Flight in the Countries of Europe. New York, 1883. Pages dealing with the Holy Land: 90–265.

Holland, Frederick West, 1811–1895.

Unitarian clergyman; secretary, American Unitarian Association, 1847–1850. Traveled to Europe, Egypt, and Asia Minor in 1850–1851.

Scenes in Palestine, by a Pilgrim of 1851. Boston, 1852. Entire book deals with the Holy Land.

Holmes, T. Dates unknown.

Heart and Thought. Memories of Eastern Travel. Bolton, 1887.

Honeyman, Abraham Van Doren, 1849–1936.

Traveled to the Holy Land in 1899.

From America to the Orient. Plainfield, N.J., 1899. Pages dealing with the Holy Land: 75–163. Each chapter of the book is written by one of the people who accompanied Honeyman.

Howe, Fisher, 1798–1871.

Businessman and author. Traveled to the Holy Land in 1852.

Oriental and Sacred Scenes, from Notes of Travel in Greece, Turkey and Palestine. New York, 1854. Pages dealing with the Holy Land: 154–408.

The True Site of Calvary, and Suggestions Relating to the Resurrection. New York, 1871. Entire book deals with an investigation of where Calvary really was.

Hubbell, Nathan, ?–1905.

Methodist clergyman, served in New York, Brooklyn, and New Haven. Traveled to the Holy Land in the fall of 1889.

My Journey to Jerusalem, Including Travels in England, Scotland, France, Belgium . . . Turkey, Palestine and Egypt. New York, 1890. Pages dealing with Palestine: 212–270.

Hurlbut, Jesse Lyman, 1843–1930.

Methodist clergyman; editor and author. Traveled to the Holy Land about 1899.

Travelling in the Holy Land through the Stereoscope. New York, 1900. Pages dealing with the Holy Land: 1–185.

Hutton, Laurence, 1843–1904.

Author, essayist, and lecturer; editor of *Harper's Magazine,* 1886–1898. Traveled to the Holy Land most probably in 1894.

Literary Landmarks of Jerusalem. New York, 1895. Entire book deals with Jerusalem.

Jessup, Mrs. Henry Harris. Dates unknown.

Wife of a longtime missionary in Syria; left Beirut April 23, 1885, and returned May 18, 1885.

The Holy Land; Extracts from the Journal of Mrs. Henry H. Jessup. (31 pp.), published with the consent of Mrs. Jessup from her private journal; no pagination; mentions Binghamton, New York, 1885?

Johnson, Electa Amanda Wright, 1838–?

The Simple Story of an Uneventful Life. Milwaukee, 1924?

Johnson, Sarah Barclay, 1837–1885.

Daughter of James T. Barclay (see above.); in 1856 she married J. Augustus Johnson, then U.S. consul in Syria. She was probably in the Holy Land from 1853 to 1856 with her father.

Hadji in Syria, or Three Years in Jerusalem. Philadelphia, 1858. Pages dealing with the Holy Land: 26–303.

Jones, Eli (1807–1890) and Sybil (1808–1873).

Ministers of the Society of Friends from New England, who traveled on a mission to Palestine, 1867–1869.

Eastern Sketches: Notes of Scenery, Schools, and Tent Life in Syria and Palestine by Ellen Clare Miller. Edinburgh, 1871. Pages dealing with the Holy Land: 92–194.

Knight, Susan G. Dates unknown.

Author of juvenile books.

Ned Hardwood's Visit to Jerusalem. Boston, 1888. Pages dealing with the Holy Land: 9–228.

Knox, Thomas Wallace, 1835–1896.

Author, inventor, and traveler. Went to the Holy Land in 1873–1874, and in 1878.

Backsheesh! or, Life and Adventures in the Orient. Chicago, 1875. Pages dealing with the Holy Land: 329–361 and 367–439.

The Boy Travellers in the Far East; Part Fourth, Adventures of Two Youths in a Journey to Egypt and the Holy Land. New York, 1883.

Lawrence, Rosewell Bigelow. Dates unknown.

Traveled to the Holy Land in 1892.

Letters from Egypt and the Holy Land to the Medford "Mercury," February 13 to June 26, 1892. Boston, 1892. Pages dealing with the Holy Land: 43–55.

Lee, James Wideman, 1849–1919.

Methodist Episcopal clergyman in Missouri and Georgia. He was a member of an expedition to the Holy Land in 1894.

The Romance of Palestine: a History for Young People Containing over One Hundred and Fifty Original Photographs and Pen Pictures. . . . St. Louis, 1897.

Leech, Harry Harewood. Dates unknown.

Letters of a Sentimental Idler, from Greece, Turkey, Egypt, Nubia, and the Holy Land. New York, 1869. Pages dealing with the Holy Land: 304–445.

Lemley, John, 1843–?

The Land of Sacred Story. Albany, 1891. The book derives from letters first printed in *Zion's Watchman.*

Lent, William Bement, ?–1902.

Traveled to the Holy Land most probably in 1898.

Holy Land from Landau, Saddle and Palanquin. New York, 1899. Pages dealing with the Holy Land: 7–228.

McGarvey, John William, 1829–1911.

Ordained minister of the Disciples of Christ; pastor of various congregations in Missouri and Kentucky, 1851–1874. Professor of sacred history at Kentucky University, 1865–?

Lands of the Bible; a Geographical and Topographical Description of Palestine with Letters of Travel in Egypt, Syria, Asia Minor, and Greece. Cincinnati, 1880.

MacGavock, Randal William, 1826–1863.

A Tennessean Abroad; or, Letters from Europe, Africa, and Asia. New York, 1854. Pages dealing with the Holy Land: 237–283.

McKenzie, Alexander, 1830–1914.

Congregational clergyman, graduated from Harvard and Andover; from 1867 he was the pastor of First Church, Cambridge, Mass.

Some Things Abroad. Boston, 1887. Pages dealing with the Holy Land: 322–452.

Melville, Herman, 1819–1891.

Author. Traveled to the Holy Land in 1856–1857.

Clarel, a Poem and Pilgrimage in the Holy Land, 2 vols. New

York, 1876. Entire poem relies on his trip to the Holy Land for background.

Journal of a Visit to Europe and the Levant, October 11, 1856–May 5, 1857, edited by Howard C. Hornsford. Princeton, 1955. Pages dealing with the Holy Land: 124–161.

Mendenhall, James William, 1844–1892.

Echoes from Palestine, Cincinnati, 1883.

Merrill, Selah, 1837–1909.

Archaeologist and U.S. consul in Jerusalem, 1882–1885, 1891–1893, and 1898–1907. He was ordained into the Congregationalist ministry and was a member of the American Palestine Exploration Society.

East of the Jordan; a Record of Travels and Observations in the Countries of Moab, Gilead and Bashan during the Years 1875–1877. New York, 1881. Entire book deals with the Holy Land.

Morris, Robert, 1818–1888.

President of Masonic College, La Grange, Ky., and publisher of the Universal Masonic Library in 30 volumes. Traveled to the Holy Land in 1868.

Freemasonry in the Holy Land or, Handmarks of Hiram's Builders: Embracing Notes Made during a Series of Masonic Researches, in 1868, in Asia Minor, Syria, Palestine, Egypt and Europe, and the Results of Much Correspondence with Freemasons in Those Countries. New York, 1872. Pages dealing with the Holy Land: 239–545.

See also entry under Floyd.

Muhr, Fannie. Dates unknown.

One of several Americans who joined the pilgrimage organized by Herbert Bentwich for the "Ancient Order of Maccabeans" in 1897.

Fannie Muhr's Reminiscences of the Maccabean Pilgrimage, April 1897. Philadelphia, 1897. Pages dealing with the Holy Land: 11–25.

Newman, John Philip, 1826–1899.

Methodist Episcopal bishop, who was chaplain of the United States Senate from 1869 to 1874, and who served a congregation in New York, 1879–1884. He visited Europe, Syria, Palestine, and Egypt in 1860–1861.

"From Dan to Beersheba," or the Land of Promise as It Now Appears; Including a Description of the Boundaries, Topography, Agriculture, Antiquities, Cities and Present Inhabitants of the Wonderful Land with Illustrations of the Remarkable Accuracy of the Sacred Writers in Their Allusions to Their Native Country. New York, 1864. Entire book deals with the Holy Land.

Newman, Mrs. John Philip. Dates unknown.

The Flowery Orient: Temples and Shrines in Heathen Lands. New York, 1878.

Newton, Richard, 1812–1887.

Protestant Episcopal clergyman, who served several congregations in Philadelphia, 1840–1887. Traveled to the Holy Land in 1870.

Illustrated Rambles in Bible Lands. New York, 1875. Also published under the titles *In Bible Lands,* London, 1880, and *Rambles in Bible Lands,* Edinburgh, 1887. Pages in 1887 edition dealing with the Holy Land: 41–246.

Odenheimer, William H., 1817–1879.

Rector of St. Peter's Church, Philadelphia, 1841–1859, and Episcopal bishop of New Jersey, 1859–1879. Traveled to the Holy Land in 1851–1852.

Jerusalem and Its Vicinity: A Series of Familiar Lectures on the Sacred Localities Connected With the Week Before the Resurrection. Philadelphia: 1855. Entire book deals with the Holy Land.

Osborn, Henry Stafford, 1823–1894.

Presbyterian clergyman, graduate of the Union Theological Seminary, and professor of natural science in Virginia. Traveled to the Holy Land in 1857.

Palestine, Past and Present; with Biblical, Literary, and Scientific Notices. Philadelphia, 1859. Pages dealing with the Holy Land: 229–530.

Paine, Caroline. Dates unknown.

Tent and Harem: Notes of an Oriental Trip. New York, 1859. Pages dealing with the Holy Land: 254–300.

Palmer, Lucia A. Dates unknown.

From Park Hill-on-Hudson, New York.

Oriental Days. New York, 1897. Pages dealing with the Holy Land: 127–244.

Phelps, Sylvanus Dryden, 1816–?

Baptist clergyman, pastor of the First Baptist Church, New Haven, Conn., 1846–1874. Traveled to the Holy Land about 1861–1862.

Holy Land, with Glimpses of Europe and Egypt; a Year's Tour. New York, 1863. Pages dealing with the Holy Land: 191–368.

Also published as *Bible Lands, with Glimpses of Europe and Egypt.* Chicago, 1867.

Potter, Henry Codman, 1835–1908.

Protestant Episcopal bishop of New York from 1887. Traveled to the Holy Land most probably in 1876.

The Gates of the East: a Winter in Egypt and Syria. New York, 1877. Pages dealing with the Holy Land: 165–253.

Prime, William Cowper, 1825–1905.

Lawyer, journalist, and author; from 1884, professor of art history at Princeton. Traveled to the Holy Land about 1855–1856.

Tent Life in the Holy Land. New York, 1857. Pages dealing with the Holy Land: 25–406.

Randall, David Austin, 1813–1884.

Baptist clergyman in Ohio and editor of the *Christian Journal,* 1845–1858. Traveled to the Holy Land in 1861.

The Handwriting of God in Egypt, Sinai, and the Holy Land; the Records of a Journey from the Great Valley of the West to the Sacred Plains of the East. Philadelphia, 1862. Pages dealing with the Holy Land: 227–353 of part 1 and 18–332 of part 2.

Rhodes, Albert, 1840–?

Served as U.S. consul in Jerusalem, 1863–1865.

Jerusalem As It Is. London, 1865. Pages dealing with the Holy Land: 42–463.

Ridgaway, Henry Bascom, 1830–1895.

Methodist clergyman. He was one of a party of twelve, including eight Americans, who toured the Holy Land in 1873–1874.

The Lord's Land; a Narrative of Travels in Sinai, Arabia Petraea, and Palestine, from the Red Sea to the Entering In of Hamath. New York, 1876. Pages dealing with the Holy Land: 13–670.

Schaff, Philip, 1819–1893.

Church historian and professor of biblical learning at the Union Theological Seminary, 1870–1893. Traveled to the Holy Land in 1876–1877.

Through Bible Lands; Notes of Travel in Egypt, the Desert, and Palestine. New York, 1878. Pages dealing with the Holy Land: 133–360.

Schettler, Paul A. Dates unknown.

Member of the Mormon Church. Traveled to the Holy Land in 1873.

Correspondence of Palestine Tourists Comprising a Series of Letters by George A. Smith, Lorenzo Snow, Paul A. Schettler and Eliza R. Snow of Utah; Mostly Written While Travelling in Europe, Asia and Africa in the Years 1872 and 1873. Pages dealing with the Holy Land: 197–290.

Shepp, Daniel B. Dates unknown.

The Photographs of the Holy Land . . . A Complete Tour of Palestine . . . A Photographic Panorama of Sacred History. Chicago, 1894. Pages dealing with the Holy Land: 1–97 and 1–8 in section dealing with panorama of Jerusalem at the time of the death of Jesus.

Sheville, John. Dates unknown.

See entry under Floyd.

Smith, George Albert, 1817–1875.

A founder of Salt Lake City, Utah. He served the Mormon Church in many offices throughout his life. Traveled to the Holy Land in 1873.

See entry under Schettler.

Smith, Jerome Van Crowninshield. Dates unknown.

Physician and professor of anatomy in Boston and New York. Traveled to the Holy Land about 1852.

A Pilgrimage to Palestine, with Notes and Observations on the Present Condition of the Holy Land. Boston, 1853. Pages dealing with the Holy Land: 61–216 and 248–329.

Smith, Lee Stewart. Dates unknown.

Through Egypt to Palestine. Chicago, 1896.

Smith, William Alexander. Dates unknown.

From Occident to Orient; a Record of a Nine Months' Tour Through Europe, Egypt, Holy Land, Asia Minor and Greece . . . with an introduction by W. W. Barr, 2nd edition, revised and enlarged. Pittsburgh, 1897.

Sneersohn, Haym Zvee, 1834–1882.

A proto-Zionist, he settled in the Holy Land with his family in early childhood, but traveled widely on public missions on several occasions. He returned to the Holy Land as a citizen of the United States.

Palestine and Roumania, A Description of the Holy Land, and the Past and Present State of Roumania, and the Roumanian Jews. New York, 1872. Pages dealing with the Holy Land: 17–84.

Note: The book consists of a series of lectures given by Sneersohn while in the United States. Among the testimonials printed in the book is one from Brigham Young.

Snow, Eliza R., 1842–1887.

President of the Mormon Women's Relief Society, 1866–1887, and composer of several Mormon hymns. Traveled to the Holy Land in 1873.

See entry under Schettler.

Snow, Lorenzo, 1814–1901.

Founder of Brigham City, Utah. He was elected president of the Mormon Church, 1898. Traveled to the Holy Land in 1873.

See entry under Schettler.

Stewart, Robert Laird, 1840–1916.

Presbyterian clergyman and professor of theology and biblical archaeology; honorary secretary of the Pennsylvania section of the Palestine Exploration Fund.

The Land of Israel; a Text-book on the Physical and Historical Geography of the Holy Land Embodying the Results of Recent Research. New York, 1899. Discussion of Holy Land scattered throughout book.

Memorable Places among the Holy Hills. New York, 1902. Entire book deals with the Holy Land.

Stoddard, Charles Warren, 1843–1909.

Author and professor of English literature. Traveled to Egypt and the Holy Land in 1876–1877.

A Cruise under the Crescent; from Suez to San Marco. Chicago, 1898. Pages dealing with the Holy Land: 16–88.

Stoddard, John Lawson, 1850–1931.

Traveler and lecturer; promoted "Stoddard Lectures" in large American cities for nearly twenty years. In the late 1870s he traveled for two years in Greece, Palestine, and Egypt.

John L. Stoddard's Lectures, vol. 2; Constantinople, Jerusalem, Egypt. Chicago, 1897. Pages dealing with the Holy Land: 113–224.

Also published as: *Jerusalem. Illustrated and Embellished with One Hundred and Twenty-one Reproductions of Photographs.* Chicago, 1897.

Swift, John Franklin, 1829–1891.

Lawyer and diplomat. He was a regent of the University of California, 1872–1888, and United States ambassador to Japan, 1889. Traveled to the Holy Land in 1867.

Going to Jericho; or, Sketches of Travel in Spain and the East. New York, 1868. Pages dealing with the Holy Land: 190–311.

Talmage, Thomas DeWitt, 1832–1902.

Presbyterian clergyman and lecturer; editor of several magazines. Traveled to the Holy Land in 1889.

Talmage on Palestine; a Series of Sermons . . . in Which He Geographically Depicts What He Saw and What He Learned on His Recent and Noted Pilgrimage to the Holy Land. New York, 1890. Entire book deals with the Holy Land.

Taylor, Bayard, 1825–1878.

Traveler, correspondent, poet and translator. Traveled to the Holy Land in 1852.

The Lands of the Saracens; or, Pictures of Palestine, Asia Minor, Sicily and Spain. New York, 1885. Pages dealing with the Holy Land: 39–114.

Terhune, Albert Payson, 1872–1922.

Author and journalist for the *New York Evening World,* 1894–1916. Traveled through Syria and Egypt in 1893–1894.

Syria from the Saddle. New York, 1896. Pages dealing with the Holy Land: 103–318.

Terhune, Mary Virginia Hawes, 1830–1922.

Author and prolific writer on household management. In 1893 she was sent to the Holy Land by the *Christian Herald,* and was accompanied by her son, Albert Payson Terhune (see above).

Home of the Bible: What I Saw and Heard in Palestine . . . , by Marion Harland (pseud.). New York, 1896.

Also published under the title: *Under the Flag of the Orient.* Philadelphia, 1897. Pages dealing with the Holy Land: 121–401.

Thomas, Joseph, 1811–1891.

Lexicographer, associated with J. B. Lippincott and Co.; compiled gazetteers and medical dictionaries. Traveled to the Holy Land in 1852–1853.

Travels in Egypt and Palestine. Philadelphia, 1853. Pages dealing with the Holy Land: 69–140.

Thomson, William McClure, 1806–1894.

Presbyterian clergyman. He was a missionary in Syria and Palestine from 1832 to 1876.

The Land and the Book: or, Biblical Illustrations Drawn from the Manners and Customs, the Scenes and Scenery of the Holy Land, 2 vols., New York, 1859. The Holy Land is discussed throughout both volumes.

Tiffany, Francis, 1827–1908.

Unitarian clergyman, minister to congregations in Massachusetts, 1865–1882.

This Goodly Frame the Earth; Stray Impressions of Scenes, Incidents and Persons in a Journey Touching Japan, China, Egypt, Palestine and Greece. Boston, 1895. Pages dealing with the Holy Land: 312–334.

Tompkins, Edward Staats DeGrote. Dates unknown.

Through David's Realm. Troy, N.Y., 1889. Pages dealing with the Holy Land: 1–322.

Trumbull, Henry Clay, 1830–1903.

Congregational minister and army chaplain during the Civil War. He was an editor of the *Sunday School Times.* His trip to the Holy Land was made in 1881.

Kadesh-Barnea; Its Importance and Probable Site, with the Story of a Hunt for It; Including Studies of the Route of the Exodus and the Southern Boundary of the Holy Land. New York, 1884. Entire book deals with the site of Kadesh-Barnea.

Studies in Oriental Social Life and Gleams from the East on the Sacred Page. Philadelphia, 1894. The Holy Land is dealt with in some way in each chapter.

Turner, William Mason. Dates unknown.

Traveled to the Holy Land in 1859.

El-Khuds, the Holy; or, Glimpses in the Orient. Philadelphia, 1861. Pages dealing with the Holy Land: 13–75, 135–424.

Upham, Thomas Cogswell, 1799–1872.

Congregational minister, and professor of mental and moral philosophy and instructor in Hebrew at Bowdoin College, 1824–1867. Traveled to the Holy Land in 1852.

Letters, Aesthetic, Social, and Moral, Written from Europe, Egypt, and Palestine. Brunswick, Maine, 1855. Pages dealing with the Holy Land: 335–530.

Van Horne, David, 1837–1930.

Minister to Reformed (Dutch) congregations in New York, Ohio, Pennsylvania, 1867–1888. Was president and professor of systematic theology at Heidelberg Theological Seminary, Tiffin, Ohio, 1888–1916.

Tent and Saddle Life in the Holy Land. Philadelphia, 1885. Entire book deals with the Holy Land.

Vester, Bertha Spafford, 1878–1968.

Born in Chicago, she was brought to Jerusalem in 1881 by her parents, who were among the founders of the American Colony there.

Our Jerusalem: an American Family in the Holy City, 1881–1949. Garden City, N.Y., 1950. Entire book deals with the Holy Land.

Vincent, John Heyl, 1832–1920.

Methodist Episcopal clergyman who preached at Harvard, Yale, Cornell, Wellesley and other colleges. He was appointed bishop in charge of European work in 1900, and spent a year in Europe and Palestine, 1862–1863.

Earthly Footsteps of the Man of Galilee, Being Five Hundred Original Photographic Views and Descriptions of the Places Connected with the Earthly Life of Our Lord and His Apostles, Traced with Notebook and Camera. New York, 1893. Collection of 25 booklets, with booklets 1, 2, and 5–14 dealing in part or entirely with the Holy Land.

To Old Bethlehem. Meadville, Pa., 1892. Entire book deals with the Holy Land.

Wallace, Edwin Sherman, 1864–?

Presbyterian minister, and U.S. consul in Jerusalem, 1893–1898.

Jerusalem the Holy; a Brief History of Ancient Jerusalem; with an Account of the Modern City and Its Conditions Political, Religious and Social. Edinburgh, 1898. Entire book deals with Jerusalem.

Wallace, Susan Arnold Elston, 1830–1907.

Author, and wife of General Lewis Wallace, U.S. minister to Turkey, 1881–1885.

Along the Bosphorous, and Other Sketches. Chicago, 1898. Pages dealing with the Holy Land: 79–101 and 123–127.

The City of the King; What the Child Jesus Saw and Heard. Indianapolis, 1903.

Ward, Aaron, 1790–1867.

Lawyer and congressman. He represented New York in the House of Representatives, 1825–1829, 1831–1837, and 1841–1843. Traveled to the Holy Land in 1859–1860.

Around the Pyramids: Being a Tour in the Holy Land, and, Incidentally, through Several European Countries, and Portions of Africa, during the Years 1859–1860. New York, 1863. Pages dealing with the Holy Land: 121–215.

Warner, Charles Dudley, 1851–1900.

Editor and author, longtime contributor to *Harper's Magazine.* Traveled to the Holy Land in the winter and spring of 1875.

In the Levant. Boston, 1877. Pages dealing with the Holy Land: 1–153.

Warren, Henry White, 1831–1912.

Methodist Episcopal bishop, 1880–? Ministered to several congregations in Massachusetts, Pennsylvania, and New York, 1855–1880.

Sights and Insights, or, Knowledge by Travel. New York, 1874. Pages dealing with the Holy Land: 238–290.

Warren, William Wilkins. Dates unknown.

Traveled to the Holy Land in 1866–1867.

Life on the Nile, and Excursions on Shore between Cairo and Asouan. Also a Tour in Syria and Palestine in 1866–67. Paris, 1867. Pages dealing with the Holy Land: 115–140. The book was compiled from a series of letters to the Boston *Traveller.*

Waters, Clara Erskine Clement, 1834–1916.

Author and lecturer on art and travel.

A Simple Story of What One of Your Lady Friends Saw in the East. Boston, 1869. Pages dealing with the Holy Land: 41–78.

Wharton, Henry Marvin, 1848–1928.

Baptist clergyman in Luray, Va., and in Baltimore, Md. He led a party of thirty Americans to the Holy Land in the spring of 1891.

A Picnic in Palestine. Baltimore, 1892. Pages dealing with the Holy Land: 72–289.

Wilson, Edward Livingston, 1838–1903.

Photographer, editor, and owner of *Wilson's Photographic Magazine,* from 1864. He conducted several large photographic expeditions.

In Scripture Lands: New Views of Sacred Places; with One Hundred and Fifty Illustrations from Original Photographs by the Author. New York, 1890. Pages dealing with the Holy Land: 23–343.

Worcester, John, 1834–1900.

Boston clergyman, instructor in the New Church Theological

School, 1878–1881, and its president, 1881–? Traveled to the Holy Land in the spring of 1882.

A Journey in Palestine in the Spring of 1882. Boston, 1884. Pages dealing with the Holy Land: 1–89.

PART III

U.S. Government Resources

Records in the National Archives Relating to America and the Holy Land

Milton O. Gustafson

Early in the nineteenth century, the United States established a consulate in Manila, but after the army occupied the Philippine Islands in 1898, the records of that consular office disappeared. Someone claimed that the records were probably kept in the stack area in the National Archives called the "Philippine Room," an area filled with boxes of army records, many of them in Spanish and still unsorted. Unfortunately, as in the case of the Nazi intelligence files in the "Archives attic" or Robert E. Lee's long-lost amnesty oath, someone was exaggerating: there is no "Philippine Room."

There is also no stack area in the National Archives for records on America-Holy Land relations. The holdings of the National Archives, the permanently valuable records of the federal government, are organized into record groups according to their provenance, or administrative origins. Within each record group, the records are arranged, as far as possible, in the original order in which they were filed. Since the records were filed to facilitate the operations of an office, not the future research interests of scholars, they are rarely arranged in terms of subjects such as scholars pursue.

But two major research efforts of the National Archives have been helpful in identifying records relating to the Holy Land. The first is a "Reference Information Paper" compiled by Elizabeth Buck and published in May 1955 as "Materials in the National Archives Relating to the Middle East." It is organized by subject—government and politics, diplomatic relations, military affairs, geography, economic affairs, and social conditions—and thereunder by country. Thus, although there is discussion in general terms of records relating to Iran, Arabia, Iraq, Lebanon, Syria, and Turkey, there is also a section for Palestine under each subject. It is a useful beginning.

The second major research project, organized by Nathan Reingold, an archivist in the Industrial Records Division, was for a paper on records in the National Archives relating to American Jewish history for the annual meeting of the American Jewish Historical Society in 1958. Reingold asked all the branches of the National Archives to provide him with detailed information about records relating to American Jewish history, and these reports, which should be in the permanent reference file of each branch, are also helpful. One of his specific requests was for records relating to Jews as a group, Jewish issues, and Jewish organizations, and some of the replies in this category yield many good illustrations.

The description of records relating to America–Holy Land relations which follows is organized into broad time periods; within each period, I give a general description of some of the different record groups and series that contain relevant records, as well as examples of specific documents that I hope may stimulate researchers to further work.

The Period before World War I

Correspondence filed by the State Department (Record Group 59) for the period from 1789 to 1906 is divided into three major groupings: diplomatic, consular, and miscellaneous letters. The diplomatic correspondence consists of four separate subgroups: instructions to U.S. ministers and ambassadors, dispatches from them, notes to foreign legations, and notes from foreign legations; each arranged by country and thereunder chronologically, and all available on microfilm. Obviously, of most interest are the dispatches from the American minister in Turkey, for Palestine was part of the Turkish Empire. These dispatches for the period from 1818 to 1906 are on 77 rolls of M46, and registers listing each document by date and number, with a sentence or two about the subject, are also available on microfilm.

The consular correspondence also consists of a single series of instructions to consuls, arranged chronologically, and dispatches from them, arranged by city, and thereunder chronologically. There are also registers that serve as finding aids to the consular correspondence. Of central importance are the dispatches from the U.S. consuls in Jerusalem, available on 9 rolls of T471 for the period from 1856 to 1906. Dispatches from the U.S. consuls in Beirut from 1836 to 1906 are available on 23 rolls of T367.

Consular dispatches contain much routine administrative information: the appointment and replacement of consuls and their assistants; their arrivals at and departures from their posts; their accounts; requests for more stationery and more pay; and sundry other office matters. But there is also much other information, as the following examples from 1871, 1881, and 1891 indicate.

In 1871 Consul Richard Beardsley sent 51 dispatches to the State Department. He reported robberies perpetrated against a Mr. Welsch, Rolla Floyd, and C.J. Gangdon; the death of Oliver A. Ward; the visit of the U.S. frigate *Guerrieri* to Jaffa in June, with over 150 seamen and officers subsequently touring the Holy Land; the landing in August of the U.S.S. *Shenandoah* in Jaffa; and the arrival of former Secretary of State William H. Seward for a tour of the Holy Land. He also sent several reports on political and economic affairs, conditions in Palestine, the corruption of the courts, and the difficulties of reform.

Consul J.G. Willson sent 23 dispatches to the department in 1881. He reported on robberies committed against American travelers; on the suicide of Joshua W. Sharp; on conditions in the consular district regarding agriculture, commerce, and improvements; and on the arrival of eighteen people from Chicago, "under the influence of some strong religious impulse," who, despite their obvious culture and wealth, had peculiar religious views. Another visitor, a Mrs. Davis from Boston, hoped to start a colony of emigrants from New England in Palestine. Willson sought to discourage the establishment of religious colonies in a land so uncongenial to strangers. He reported also on Jewish immigration to Palestine, the Porte's restrictions on this immigration, and the possibility of Jewish immigration to other parts of Turkey, that were subject to Ottoman law. The harvest of 1880 had been good so the cost of wheat, flour, and barley was only half what it was the previous year. The price of petroleum had jumped by 50 percent, but soon returned to normal; there was no reason for its prohibitive cost "except the caprice of the grocers." As for American products in the market, he found "petroleum, corned beef, hams, and occasionally sewing machines, guns, and pistols."

In 1891 two consuls sent a total of 41 dispatches to the State Department, including reports on streets and roadways; the wreck of a Russian steamer at Jaffa and the rescue of American citizens through the heroism of Jaffa boatmen; the incidence of cholera; and Jews and Jewish colonies in Palestine. After Selah Merrill assumed charge of the office for a second term, he requested the appointment of David Feinstein as a second dragoman because "a large proportion of the United States subjects here are naturalized Jews from Russia or Poland. Many of these persons have never been in the United States and cannot speak a word of English." He needed someone who understood not only English, German, and Hebrew, but especially "Jewish Jargon," which he called "the barbarous language spoken by most of this class of our American subjects." Merrill reported that his predecessor, Henry Gillman, had been lax in registering American citizens. As of January 1, 1891, Gillman reported 317 Americans living in the Jerusalem district. One year later Merrill reported that there were 375 Americans, and he listed them by family, name, age, occupation, where born, where naturalized, and number and date of passport. For example, numbers 214 to 229 relate to the family of Louis Levy, 80 years old, born in Russia; his son Lazaros, age 38, a machinist, and his wife, Rachel, and their six sons, aged 2 to 17; another son and his wife and their three children; and a third son, 22, and his 18-year-old wife, who had no children. Among those listed was Furman O. Baldwin, the 15-year-old son of Edward Baldwin, who attempted suicide ten years later.

Besides the diplomatic and consular correspondence, the third major grouping of State Department files for the 1789–1906 period is for miscellaneous correspondence. The miscellaneous letters, bound in 1,533 volumes, consist of almost all letters received by the State Department and not filed with the diplomatic and consular correspondence. They are arranged chronologically, without regard to place, name, or subject, and are a major untapped resource. Although there is a printed calendar for the letters to 1820, no one has systematically gone through some 80 volumes of registers and indexes to find letters on a specific subject. The letters, often with enclosures, can provide some unexpected research surprises.

For 1840, there are several letters from J.C. Levy and others of Charleston, South Carolina, protesting the treatment of the "Israelites of Damascus and Rhodes." In 1876, the International Committee of the Society of Palestine for the Protection of Christians and Jews in the Holy Land, with headquarters in Paris, requested the United States and other powers to reach an international agreement to assure the security of Christians and Jews in Palestine, in all of their civil and religious establishments. There is no indication that any action was taken except to file the letter. For 1905, there is a letter from Julius Goldman to Oscar Straus, enclosing a letter from Narcisse Leven complaining about the activities of Ibrahim Sabbag, involved in a land dispute with the Jewish Colonization Association. Although it may be impossible to determine the facts today without other evidence, the letters contain much information about the land dealings of the Jewish Colonization Association. After Straus and Goldman visited the secretary of state, Sabbag was dismissed from his post as honorary dragoman of the U.S. consulate in Beirut.

In 1906 the State Department adopted a new filing system, a subject file called the Numerical File. In less than five years, almost 26,000 separate case files were established. Some files were so specific they contained only a single document; others were so general they contained thousands of documents. There are elaborate finding aids, created both at the time the documents were filed and later, to help find relevant correspondence, including internal memorandums of the department. The cards filed under Palestine in the card index provide references to documents in several dozen different numerical case files.

File 25487 consists of only one document, a four-page report (June 23, 1910) on the establishment of the Jewish Agricultural Experimental Station in Palestine, with Aaron Aaronsohn as managing director, and funding by Jacob Schiff, Julius Rosenwald, and others.

File 13653 is a report (April 15, 1908) on a motorcar tour of the Holy Land by Charles J. Glidden, an American, who traveled about 750 miles on Palestine's roads. The success of the trip indicated that there was a brand-new export market available for cars with a high road clearance. The report quoted an American missionary as saying that Glidden's arrival set off the wildest and most enthusiastic time "since the coming of King David as King of the Jews."

Many documents in different files relate to Selah Merrill, American consul in Jerusalem for sixteen years, from 1882 to 1885, from 1891 to 1893, and from 1898 to 1907. Shortly after Merrill was ordered to transfer from Jerusalem to Georgetown, British Guiana, in 1907, he finally resigned from the consular service. File 2931 contains numerous letters from people, both in the United States and Palestine, on Merrill's behalf against his transfer. Only one letter was critical of Merrill; Emil Guenther of Philadelphia rejoiced that Merrill's transfer to Georgetown would result in "the everlasting gratitude of the American colony in Jerusalem."

That colony of Americans, a group of Christian-socialist followers of Horatio Spafford, were bitter opponents of Consul Merrill, and their mutual antagonism is documented in several case files. One letter complained that the American citizens residing in the colony were the "victims of gross religious bigotry." Alexander Hume Ford wrote an article on the colony, critical of Merrill, which was published in *Appleton's Magazine*, and the State Department subsequently decided to transfer him from Jerusalem.

File 2985 concerns another project that Merrill supported, the export trade of the River Jordan Water Company. He reported that Col. Clifford E. Nadaud was establishing a new industry, "carrying thousands of tons of water from the Jordan, Palestine's sacred river, to distant America." Merrill's part in the project was to use the consular seal to certify the authenticity of the merchandise in the water casks. The Department of State objected, and Colonel Nadaud was unable to obtain an exclusive export monopoly on River Jordan water.

Besides the records of the State Department, there are records which were originally filed at each Foreign Service diplomatic or consular office, and later transferred to the National Archives (Record Group 84). In the nineteenth century, despite detailed instructions, record-keeping practices in the various consular and diplomatic posts varied widely, although the records of the legation (later embassy) in Constantinople are fairly well organized. Much in them duplicates State Department files, but certain series contain unique documents regarding America–Holy Land relations.

The 25 volumes of "Letters Received in the Legation from U.S. Consulates in Turkey" include seven volumes of letters from Beirut from 1832 to 1880; one volume from Jerusalem, containing letters dated 1845, 1854, 1857–1879, and 1882; and one volume containing letters from the consular agency at Jaffa, 1832–1836. Nineteen volumes of "Letters from Various Consulates to the Legation," written from 1890 to 1912, are arranged chronologically. The legation files also include one volume of correspondence from the Navy Department and naval officers on ships in the Mediterranean, 1831–1881, and 26 volumes of "Miscellaneous Correspondence Received" for the period from 1830 to 1911.

Records of the consulate general at Constantinople include eight volumes of correspondence with subordinate consuls in Jerusalem from 1879 to 1910.

These records, filed at the consular agencies at Haifa and Jaffa and at the consulate in Jerusalem, are not as well organized. The Haifa records, from 1872 to 1917, total only four feet, in 17 bound volumes, four boxes, and five envelopes. Jaffa records, from 1866 to 1917, also total four feet, in 30 volumes and one envelope. The Jerusalem records, extending from 1856 to 1935, total 72 feet and include correspondence with other consuls, the consulate-general and legation in Constantinople, and the State Department. There are miscellaneous letters from private citizens, five volumes of Consular Court records, and a variety of personal information in the form of wills, marriage certificates, passport applications, a register of visitors, and a register of children born to American parents.

Biographical information about the people who served as U.S. consuls in Palestine is found among the letters of application and recommendation for positions in the State Department and the Foreign Service (Record Group 59). Arranged alphabetically by name of applicant, each file includes letters from successful and unsuccessful applicants, letters and petitions supporting their appointment, and letters either opposing an applicant or complaining of his actions after his appointment.

The file for John Warren Gorham, the first American consul to serve in Jerusalem, who stemmed from an old and distinguished Massachusetts family, reveals that President Franklin Pierce requested the appointment and that Edward Everett recommended it. After two years, the resident American physician in Beirut reported that Gorham "was intoxicated nearly the whole time" on a visit there, "a circumstance that deeply humiliated all of his countrymen."

Henry Gillman, the consul in Jerusalem from 1886 to 1891, first wrote to the State Department in September 1885 to apply for the position as consul at Marseilles. He had been superintendent and librarian of the Public Library of Detroit. In April 1886, having received no reply to his application, he wrote again, using the excuse that he had read that someone had been arrested for stealing mail from the Washington post office and that his first letter had perhaps been lost. He added that he would even take on a good consular appointment in Japan, referring to himself as a lifelong Democrat. Three years after his appointment to Jerusalem, a "patriotic citizen," who failed to sign his name, wrote to President Benjamin Harrison that Gillman was "incapable and incompetent," and urged his removal. Selah Merrill was thereupon appointed to his second term as consul at Jerusalem, in 1891.

Another valuable source for biographical information about consular officers, and also for commercial and general economic conditions of their consular districts, is the consular inspection reports (Record Group 59). Beginning in 1906, Foreign Service inspectors regularly visited each post, and their reports included sections on personnel evaluations, administrative operations of the office, and the efforts of the consul in promoting trade expansion. Inspectors described the office, enclosed photographs and maps of the city, reported on record-keeping practices, evaluated the consul's relations with local officials and the business community, and described the personal habits of the consul. They analyzed the commercial, industrial, and political importance of each post. The consul was required to describe and provide statistics on the kinds and amounts of foreign goods imported into his district; the nationality of the carriers; the extent of trade between his district and the United States and other industrial nations; the number and names of export-import firms in his district; local banking facilities; possible opportunities for U.S. trade; the number of American citizens residing in his district and their businesses; the nature of foreign firms engaged in industry, mining, commerce, insurance, banking, and agriculture; and the cost of living in the consular district. The inspection reports are important for their descriptions of the social life of the consular district, and the personal and professional information they contain about each consul makes it possible to evaluate the reliability of his dispatches and other records.

For Jerusalem, there are three inspection reports between 1907 and 1913, and five others for the period from 1922 to 1931. There were three inspections of the consular agency at Haifa between 1907 and 1913, and three for the post at Jaffa between 1907 and 1912.

Among the Jerusalem inspection records is a report by Consul Merrill to the effect that only two American vessels had landed at his district in 1906, both small yachts loaded "with religious cranks who have a colony here." He reported that the principal business of his office was to help American citizens who had gotten into trouble. By 1910, the inspector found that conditions had deteriorated drastically under Merrill's successor, Thomas Wallace. He enclosed a list of American Jews who were not registered in the consulate as American citizens and suggested that the next consul would do well to go about registering them. By 1913, under the vigorous administration of William Coffin, conditions had improved so remarkably that Coffin was promoted to another post. He was succeeded by Otis Glazebrook, who served as consul in Jerusalem during the difficult years from 1914 to 1920.

In the nineteenth century, the U.S. Navy Department was the only other federal agency interested in the Holy Land. An American naval officer, Lt. William F. Lynch, was the first major explorer of the River Jordan and the Dead Sea. Lynch's original handwritten report of his expedition is among the miscellaneous records of the Naval Records Collection of the Office of Naval Records and Library (Record Group 45). In November 1847, Lynch sailed from Brooklyn to Constantinople, winning approval for the exploration project from the sultan. He landed at Acre, and after an overland voyage to the Sea of Galilee, he and his party rowed down the River Jordan to the Dead Sea. Lynch's report includes correspondence concerning the expedition, notes taken during the descent of the Jordan and the Dead Sea, and reports by members of the expedition on the bird and plant life of the region and its geology. Contained in the material are astronomical, thermometric, and barometric tables; an analysis of Dead Sea water; a table of meteorological observations; a map of the route and camps of the expedition; and sketch maps of the Jordan and the Dead Sea. More information about this early American expedition to the Holy Land may be found in Yehoshua Ben-Arieh's article in the Spring 1973 issue of *Prologue: The Journal of the National Archives.*

World War I and the Peace Settlement

The central file of the Department of State (Record Group 59) after 1910 is called the Decimal File, a subject file similar to the short-lived Numerical File, except that its subjects were predetermined according to a decimal classification scheme. The first digit represents the primary subject class; for example, 3 is for protection of interests, 6 for commercial relations, 7 for political and treaty relations, and 8 for internal affairs of states. Within each primary class, subjects are further defined and identified by a decimal number, and country numbers are used to identify subjects relating to the various countries. For example, 67 is the number for Turkey, and 67N is the number for Palestine; thus, file 867N.01 is for government of Palestine, and file 867.4016 is for race problems in Turkey. File 763.72, which is for political relations between Austria-Hungary (63) and Serbia (72), eventually turned into the subject file for World War I. Most of the documents relating to the war are in file 763.72, available on 518 rolls of microfilm (M367) for the period from 1910 to 1929. All of the records in the 867 and 867N files for the period from 1910 to 1929 are also available on microfilm (M353, 88 rolls).

Each document is identified by a decimal file number followed by a slash mark (/) and the specific document or enclosure number, numbered consecutively in each file from 1906 to June 30, 1944. The basic finding aid for the decimal file is the Purport Lists, lists of documents in each file, available on 654 rolls of microfilm (M973), but there are also card indexes which are useful in finding the relevant subject files.

Documents relating to the American response to the Balfour Declaration are in both the Termination of War file (763.72119) and the Government of Palestine file (867N.01). Another large file (367N.11) is for documents relating to the protection of American citizens in the Holy Land.

One of the largest and most important decimal files is the one for the government of Palestine (867N.01), containing about 300 documents through 1922. It consists mainly of reports from Jerusalem and Great Britain and much public mail regarding the proposed

The Colonial interest in and devotion to the study of Hebrew are demonstrated by the college seals of Yale, Columbia and Dartmouth.

Isa. 32. 5.

a nigardly-foole shall no more be called liberall, nor the churle said to be bountifull.

Isa: 62. 4.

It shall no more be said unto thee forsaken; neither shall it be said any more to thy land desolate; but thou shalt be caled Hephzi-bah, and thy land Beulah.

shall bow-downe to him, for a peece of siluer, and a morsell of bread. 1. sam. 2. 36

He shall be the head, & thou shalt be ye taile. deu. 28. 44

A page from the Hebrew exercise book of Governor William Bradford of the Massachusetts Bay Colony, denotes his respect for the Hebrew scriptures and language. Reproduced from Isidore S. Meyer, *The Hebrew Exercises of Governor William Bradford* (Plymouth, Mass., 1973).

Rabbi Raphael Haim Isaac Carigal of Hebron, one of a number of rabbis with whom Ezra Stiles, Congregationalist minister and President of Yale University, studied Hebrew and discussed the Bible, Talmud and Kaballah. Stiles was one of many American religious and cultural leaders steeped in Hebrew tradition and lore.

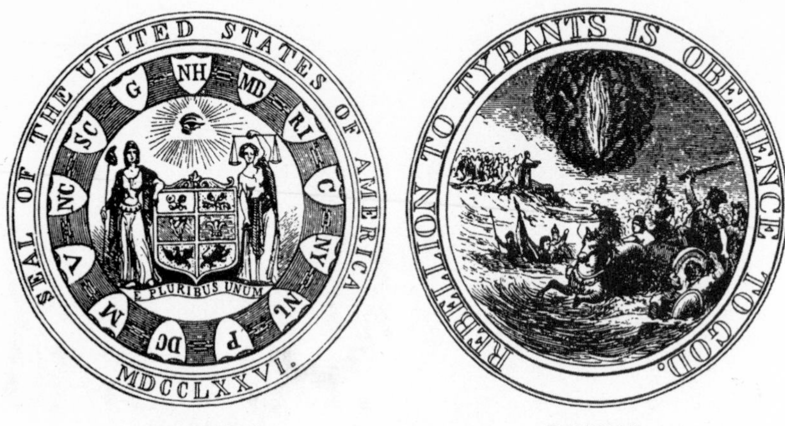

American revolutionaries equated their rebellion against England with the struggle of the Israelites against the Egyptian Pharoah. When the official seal for the United States was being created, a design was submitted by Thomas Jefferson, Benjamin Franklin and John Adams depicting the Israelites crossing the Red Sea with Pharoah in pursuit and Moses standing on the other side. Reproduced from Oscar S. Straus, *the Origin of Republican Form of Government in the United States of America* (New York and London, 1901).

Evidence of scientific, strategic and potential commercial interests of the United States in the Holy Land is illustrated by the U.S. naval expedition on the Naaman River, south of Acre, in 1848. Reproduced from W.F. Lynch, *Narrative of the United States' Expedition to the River Jordan and the Dead Sea* (Philadelphia, 1849).

These scenes of mid-nineteenth-century Jerusalem depict the American presence in the Holy City. Reproduced from James Turner Barclay, *The City of the Great King* (Philadelphia, 1857).

An American cemetery near Neby Daud.

The American Christian mission premises, on the Stronghold of Zion.

Travel through the Holy Land could be quite comfortable. These scenes are reproduced from John Welsh Dulles, *The Ride Through Palestine* (Philadelphia, 1881), and John Heyl Vincent, *Earthly Footsteps of the Man of Galilee* (New York, 1893).

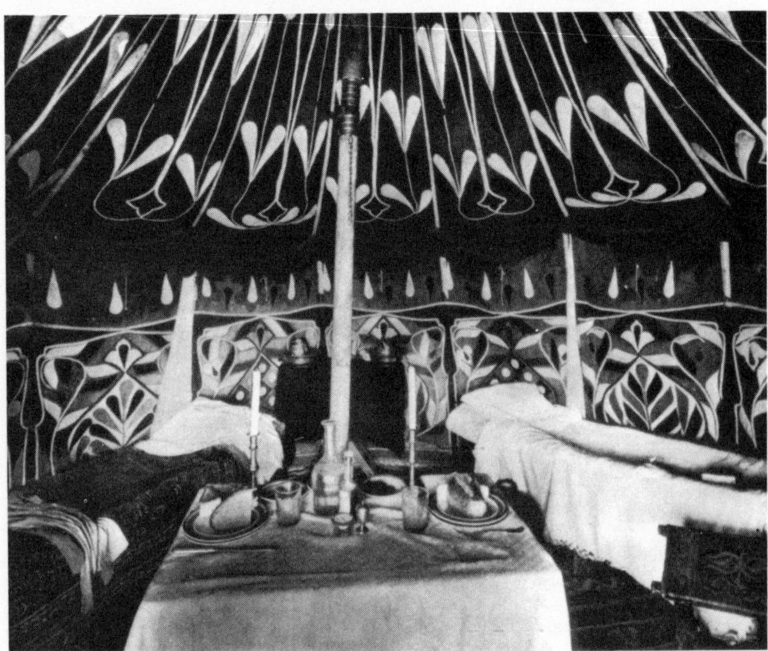

Living conditions could also be quite primitive as seen in this photograph of a midday meal in Palestine. Reproduced from John Lawson Stoddard, *John L. Stoddard's Lectures,* Vol. 2 (Chicago, 1897).

Mark Twain with his party of eight, traveling through the Holy Land in 1867. Reproduced from Mark Twain, *The Innocents Abroad, or, The New Pilgrim's Progress* (New York, 1899).

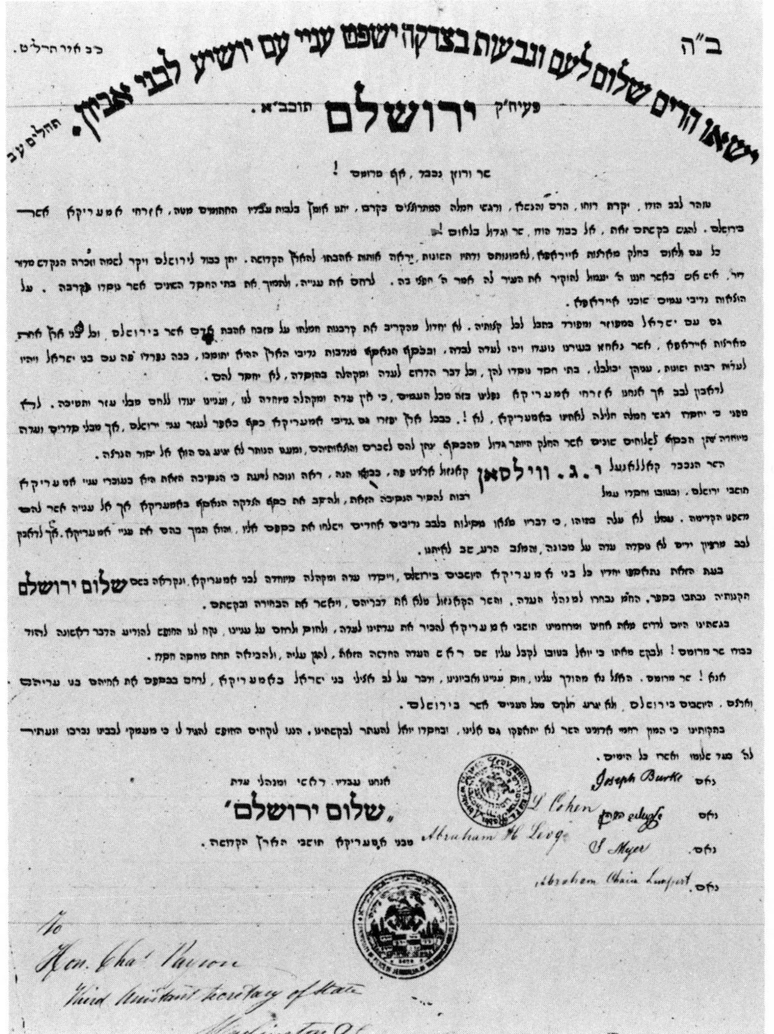

ב"ה

ישאו הרים שלום לעם וגבעות בצדקה ישפט עניי עם יושיע לבני אביון. תהלים ע"ב

פעיה"ק ירושלם תובב"א.

שלום ירושלם

Joseph Burke

L Cohen

Abraham H Levy

S Myer

To
Hon. Chas. Payson
Third Assistant Secretary of State
Washington D.C.

The Articles of Incorporation of Sholem Yerushalayim, an unsuccessful attempt to establish an American Kollel in Palestine in 1879. A "Kollel" was a formally organized group of Jewish immigrants in Palestine who originated from the same geographical location in the Diaspora and subsisted on donations sent from their place of origin.

Reverend Dr. T.D. Talmage baptizing an American pilgrim in the River Jordan ca. 1890. Reproduced from T.D. Talmage, *Talmage on Palestine* (New York, 1890).

A group of pilgrims before the Dome of the Rock. Reproduced from Henry Marvin Wharton, *A Picnic in Palestine* (Baltimore, 1892).

Members of the Maccabean party on their pilgrimage in April 1897. Reproduced from *Fannie Muhr's Reminiscences of the Maccabean Pilgrimage*, April, 1897 (Philadelphia, 1897).

Jerusalem as seen from the summit of (the new) Calvary. Reproduced from Edwin Sherman Wallace, *Jerusalem the Holy* (Edinburgh and London, 1898).

Albert Payson Terhune described himself "like something between an Arab and a cowboy." Reproduced from Albert Payson Terhune, *Syria from the Saddle* (New York, 1896).

The United States Consulate in Jerusalem, ca. 1898. Reproduced from Edwin Sherman Wallace, *Jerusalem the Holy* (Edinburgh and London, 1898).

Consular Guards

The International River Jordan Water Company collected, transported and sold bottled samples of the Jordan River in the United States ca. 1906. (U.S. National Archives and Records Service)

A July Fourth pageant in the American Colony in Jerusalem, ca. 1920. (Vester-Lind family albums)

Early settlers in Herzliya, on land purchased by the American Zion Commonwealth, June 1926. (Herzliya Municipal Archives)

The cornerstone-laying ceremony of the central building for "Agudath Achim Anshe America" fraternal society in Jerusalem, ca. 1933. (Central Zionist Archives)

Department of State
Washington, October 20, 1902.

Rev Marcus H Dubov
619 Bond. st,
Evansville, Indiana

למכתבך קבלתי, איש האלהים
ושמחתי כי מצא חן בעיניך מעשה
ידי אם בעד אחיך הנרדפים
במלכות רומעניע שלום לך ולעדתך
בני משה.

הנני שאל מן ה' אלהינו כי יברך
ברך את אנשי בריתך אשר בעוואנסוויל
בכל אשר תעשו הן בדבר שפתים
או במעשה ידים.. ואלהי השלום יהיה
עמכם לעולם. ואני אוהבך.

John Hay

Department of State
Washington, October 20, 1902

Rev. Marcus H. Dubov
619 Broad Street
Evansville, Indiana

"I received your letter, man of God, and I was happy that my efforts on behalf of your persecuted brethren in the kingdom of Roumania pleased you. Peace to you and your congregation Bnai Moshe.

I ask from the Lord our God that He bless the people of your covenant in Evansville, in all you do, both in word and deed. May the God of peace be with you forever. I am he who loves you.

John Hay"

The continued interest of prominent Americans in the study of Hebrew is expressed in this letter written by Secretary of State John Hay in the early part of the twentieth century.

British mandate for Palestine. Among the documents are a resolution from the Connecticut state legislature favoring development of Palestine as a Jewish state, and a request from Rep. Adolph J. Sabath for a copy of a report on the revolutionary movement for establishment of racial domination of the world by Jewish radicals.

Since American Zionists were involved not only in the movement for the establishment of a Jewish state in Palestine, but also in activities on behalf of their coreligionists in Russia, records relating to Zionism are located in other decimal files. The file for political affairs in Russia includes an amazing report called "Bolshevism and Judaism" (861.00/5399), which cites the spurious "Protocols of the Elders of Zion" as evidence and reports that recognition of a Jewish state in Palestine, the achievement of a Jewish state in Russia under the Bolsheviks, and the imminent success of Jewish states in Germany and Austria are simply the first steps toward worldwide Jewish rule.

Other intelligence and investigative records relating to Zionism are found among the records of the Office of the Counselor and the Chief Special Agent of the Department of State (Record Group 59). Separate subject files include, for example, a set of the reports from Special Agent William Yale, dated from October 1917 to March 1919, on his travels throughout the Middle East, particularly in Syria, Palestine, and Arabia. A separate file contains several copies of the "Protocols of the Elders of Zion."

Records kept at the consular post in Jerusalem after 1912 (Record Group 84) were also filed by subject according to a modification of the State Department's decimal filing system. The primary subject classes—the first digit—are the same in both systems, but the country number is omitted from the post records. Thus, file 800 is for political affairs and file 801 is for the government of Palestine. Documents in the post files were arranged and bound on a yearly basis. There are a total of 35 volumes for the period from 1914 through 1921, including 8 volumes for 1916, 3 each for 1917 and 1919, and none for 1918 because the consular office in Jerusalem was closed.

Soon after the United States entered the war, Edward M. House, at the request of President Wilson, organized a group of experts to gather data on geographical, ethnological, historical, economic, and political problems in Europe and other areas of the world in preparation for the anticipated peace conference. This group of experts, known as the Inquiry, conducted a number of investigations, many of which related to the Middle East, and assembled a large quantity of material on national boundaries.

The largest group of Inquiry records is a series of Special Reports and Studies (Record Group 256). A list of these is in appendix 2 of the inventory for *Records of the American Commission to Negotiate Peace*, compiled by Sandra K. Rangel and published in 1974. Among the Inquiry documents relating to Palestine are: "Report on the Geography, History, Ethnology, Religions, Economics, Domestic Life, and Government of the Land of Palestine" by Lewis Bayles Paton; "Palestine" by David Magie; "Palestine and Jewish Nationalism" (no author given); and "The Boundaries of Palestine" by Aaron Aaronsohn. Among the other reports of interest is "A Report on Zionism" by O.J. Campbell, a professor at Princeton.

The correspondence files of the Inquiry are arranged alphabetically by the name of the correspondent. In the file for Campbell, for example, there is an anonymous critique of his report on Zionism which concludes that the report should be discarded and that Campbell should be suspended "from all and any connection with the Inquiry." The correspondence in the folder for the Zionist Committee consists of letters between Isaiah Bowman and Nellie Straus, secretary of the Zionist Organization of America.

In December 1918, the Inquiry was absorbed into the Intelligence Division of the American Commission to Negotiate Peace, and twenty-three members of the Inquiry staff accompanied President Wilson and the other American delegates to the Peace Conference in Paris. The records of the American Commission at the Peace Conference (Record Group 256) consist of 537 bound volumes, also available as a microfilm publication (M820). The records are arranged according to a decimal classification scheme devised by the Department of State. The essential finding aid for these records is a card index prepared years later by the Peace Conference Section of the State Department's Division of Communications and Records. There is a card for each document (sometimes each paragraph of some of the minutes of meetings), which gives the subject, the decimal file number, the date, the type of document, and a digest of the document.

There are 90 cards filed under Palestine. Many of them are for documents in file 185.5137, the file designation for "Turkish Peace

Treaty; Political Clauses; Syria, Mesopotamia, Palestine," which is bound in three volumes. To illustrate the detailed card index, file 180.03101/48 is the document for the minutes of the meeting of the Big Five on February 27, 1919, at which representatives of the Zionist Organization presented the Zionist case. File 180.03401/101 is the minutes of the meeting of the Council of Four on March 20, 1919, at which the question of Palestine was discussed (on page 5 paragraph 1, page 7 line 9, and page 9 paragraph 1).

File 185.112/1 contains the final recommendation of the Intelligence Section of the American delegation regarding Palestine: that a separate state of Palestine should be established and placed under Great Britain as a mandatory of the League of Nations, that "the Jews be invited to return to Palestine and settle there," and "that it will be the policy of the League of Nations to recognize Palestine as a Jewish state as soon as it is a Jewish state in fact."

File 867N.00 includes an anti-Zionist petition, signed by 299 prominent American Jews, which rejected the idea that Palestine should be a Jewish state. In a memo about the petition, W.L. Westermann concluded that the argument of the petitioners against Zionism was not very strong, and that the views of the Zionists and the non-Zionists about the future of Palestine were not very different. The real issue, he thought, was the fact that the Balfour Declaration infringed upon the rights and desires of most of the Arab population of Palestine, who did not want their country to be made a homeland of the Jews.

Records of the King-Crane Commission to investigate conditions in Palestine and Syria are in file 181.91. The file includes correspondence relating to the mission, reports, and cross-references to related documents in other files.

When President Wilson returned to the United States during the middle of the Peace Conference, he met with a Jewish delegation headed by Judge Julian W. Mack of Chicago. The delegation asked him to clarify his statement implying that the American government and people were agreed that the foundation for a Jewish commonwealth should be laid in Palestine. Wilson's statement had aroused consternation in Paris, according to the minutes of the meeting of the other American commissioners, Robert Lansing, Henry White, and Tasker Bliss, on April 12, 1919 (184.00101/49). It had been published in the Egyptian press, and the American delegates wanted to issue a strong denial of Wilson's statement because they felt it went much further than the Balfour Declaration. Wilson replied that he had not used the exact words attributed to him, and that no one had said that he did, but he did say them in substance, and what he meant was that the United States agreed with the British position. Faced with that ambiguous reply, the other American delegates at their meeting on April 18 decided that it would be best not to make any additional comment on the matter.

Because of American involvement in World War I, records of other agencies of the federal government for this period include records relating to the Holy Land. Among military records, for example, the intelligence (G-2) files of the American Expeditionary Force General Headquarters, which are part of the records of the AEF (Record Group 120), include intelligence reports on Syria and Palestine. The presence of the U.S. Navy in the eastern Mediterranean is graphically illustrated by a navy film among the holdings of the Audiovisual Archives Division. "Our Navy in the Near East," released in 1922, shows U.S. destroyers visiting ports in the area and crew members visiting mosques and temples in Bethlehem and enjoying camel races in Damascus.

Zionism was a subject of interest to the Department of Justice. Its central files (Record Group 60), for example, contain a letter from Judge Mack to the attorney general, dated November 18, 1918, protesting against a document that made serious charges against the Zionist organization in the United States. Without describing the document, Mack contended that "the Russian original is a barefaced forgery." Presumably, he meant the "Protocols of the Elders of Zion." The attorney general replied that he had no idea what Mack was referring to and asked for more information.

The holdings of the Cartographic Archives Division include well over 1.5 million maps and charts and about 2 million aerial photographs. Besides a published *Guide to Cartographic Records in the National Archives,* the division's unpublished finding aids include a reference folder listing Middle East maps.

One of the most significant instances in which the expertise of geographers and cartographers was employed in the conduct of United States foreign policy was the Versailles Peace Conference of 1919. The records of the Inquiry include more than 1,100 maps, researched and compiled by a distinguished group of social scientists.

The maps exhibit virtually every mappable phenomenon that was considered potentially relevant to the postwar territorial restructuring of the world, with particular emphasis given to ethnic, religious, and linguistic distributions, and to political boundaries, existing and proposed. Among the maps relating to the Holy Land are annotated base maps showing proposed boundaries for a Jewish state, and one showing boundaries of the proposed Jewish and Syrian states and the location of Jewish agricultural colonies.

Another large group of maps is the War Department Map Collection (Record Group 77). This collection includes a military map showing successive lines of advance in Palestine from October to December 1917, as well as road maps dated 1918 for Haifa, Nazareth, and Jaffa.

Mandate Period

During the period from 1922 to 1939, the Decimal File of the Department of State (Record Group 59) is again the most important group of records relating to Palestine. Although the records in each decimal file are numbered consecutively, each file was divided at the end of 1929 and 1939 to facilitate the transfer of records to the National Archives.

All of the documents in the 867N file for the period through 1929 are on rolls 79 to 88, and the purport lists are on roll 3 of M353. The largest segment of the file, Government of Palestine (867N.01), contains 509 documents on the Zionist movement, British mandate policy, and the Anglo-American Palestine mandate convention of 1924. When the British mandate was established in 1922, reports from the consulate in Jerusalem, mostly filed under Political Conditions in Palestine (867N.00), indicated that there was an "absence of expected rioting attending the ratification of the mandate." Later, a separate file (867N.404 Wailing Wall) was established for correspondence regarding clashes between Jews and Muslim-Arabs over incidents and disturbances at the Wailing Wall in Jerusalem.

For the 1930–1939 period, decimal file 867N is contained in 22 boxes. Some of the larger segments of the file are: Political Affairs in Palestine (867N.00), 500 enclosures; Government of Palestine (867N.01), 117 enclosures; Race Problems of Jews and Arabs in (867N.404 Wailing Wall), 52 enclosures; Jewish Colonization in

Palestine (867N.52), 8 enclosures; Immigration into Palestine (867N.55), 183 enclosures; and 179 enclosures in the Public Press file (867N.9111), which includes bimonthly reports consisting of a review of the local press in Jerusalem, interviews with local officials, and personal observations. The purport lists for file 867N for the period from 1930 to 1939 are microfilmed on rolls 418–419 of M973.

The records of the consular office in Jerusalem (Record Group 84) for the period from 1922 to 1935 largely duplicate the records kept in the central file in Washington, but there is also a great deal of correspondence with private citizens relating to trade promotion which is not duplicated anywhere. The records of this fourteen-year period are bound in 110 volumes, ranging from 4 volumes for 1923 to 17 volumes for 1934. The confidential correspondence for the entire period from 1920 to 1935 was bound in 6 volumes. Finally, there are 5 volumes of miscellaneous correspondence and documents relating to estates and consular court cases from 1891 to 1935.

Beginning in 1925, the Division of Commercial Affairs of the Department of State began to keep a separate file of consular trade reports (Record Group 59). These records, for the period from 1925 to 1950, are arranged chronologically by year, and thereunder alphabetically by consular post. There are 691 feet of records for the period from 1925 to 1942, and 681 rolls of microfilm for the period from 1943 to 1950. For the year 1939, for example, there are two thick folders of commercial reports from the consulate in Jerusalem, including fortnightly economic reports, about three pages each, based on government reports, local press, and personal observations, and an annual review of commerce and industry in the consular district. Among the special reports are such items as "Market for Office Machines and Equipment in Palestine in 1938" and "Living Costs for Americans in Palestine."

A similar series of consular political reports covers the period from 1925 to 1935. They are also arranged chronologically by year, and thereunder alphabetically by consular post. Reports from Jerusalem for 1929 include "Palestine Disturbances of August 1929," "Political Crisis in Palestine," and "General Arab Strike."

For this period, there are also many military intelligence documents relating to the Holy Land. Army intelligence documents, part of the records of the Military Intelligence Division, War Department General Staff (Record Group 165), consist primarily of reports from the military attachés in Turkey and Great Britain. The general file designations 2657-HH, Political Conditions in Palestine, and 2658, General File on Palestine, however, also include intelligence reports on India. There is also a regional file, 1933–1944, for Palestine, filed in 16 boxes, consisting of declassified intelligence reports, arranged by subject according to a G-2 decimal filing system. Naval intelligence documents, part of the records of the Office of the Chief of Naval Operations (Record Group 38), are arranged by an alphanumeric number, and thereunder by serial number. There is no subject index, but there are lists of documents in different files. File C-10-F 20402, for example, contains reports on political conditions in Palestine and the partition problem, 1930–1938.

The records of the United States Senate (Record Group 46) and the House of Representatives (Record Group 233) form a unique body of records in the National Archives. As records of the legislative branch of the government, they fall under different rules than the other records in the National Archives, which are records of agencies in the executive branch. For example, all records of the House of Representatives that have not been published are restricted; no one may examine them without the permission of the Clerk of the House.

In 1922 Congress approved a joint resolution favoring the establishment in Palestine of a National Home for the Jewish People, and the records of the Senate Foreign Relations Committee include a bundle of petitions on this subject. For example, the Rotary Club of Sault Ste. Marie, Michigan, sent a copy of its resolution to the Senate opposing persecution of Jews in foreign countries, while Palestine National League organizations in Chicago, New York, Youngstown, St. Paul, and Milwaukee all sent messages opposing the adoption of the congressional resolution.

Even the Agriculture Department was interested in the Holy Land. In 1939 and 1940, Walter C. Lowdermilk, the chief of the Research Section of the Social Conservation Service, traveled extensively and made observations of land use and soil and water conservation in Palestine, Transjordan, and Syria. In one of his letters (Record Group 114), he described his interest in examining "the problems of climactic change and agriculture, ancient and modern, in this part of the world." He hoped to determine the "fate and future of agriculture" in Palestine, but conditions were difficult.

> All of our field trips have been carried out under guard. An armored car fitted with machine guns and sharp shooters with army rifles, have impressed us with the seriousness of the situation in Palestine, although we have chafed at being hindered in making many examinations in the field that we wanted to do. You would be amused to see us covered by two men with rifles, as we have tried to get a soil sample or a picture of a bench terrace.

The records of the Bureau of Reclamation (Record Group 115) include a reference file of background material on Palestine, useful in terms of a comparison of American projects with the Palestine experience. It includes a copy of a report dated December 1927 entitled "Agricultural Colonization in Palestine" by an advisory commission chaired by Elwood Mead and a report by A.T. Strahorn, "Soil Reconnaissance of Palestine," dated 1927, which included several photographs, now in the custody of the Audiovisual Archives Division, showing harvesting, dairy barns, irrigation canals, and pumping stations in Palestine. There are also clippings from various American newspapers and periodicals about irrigation and reclamation in Palestine.

Finally, among the records of the United States Shipping Board (Record Group 32) are correspondence and memos of the 1920s relating to the proposed sale of the *Mount Clay*, the *President Arthur*, and the *President Fillmore* to the American Palestine Line, Inc., for the purpose of landing Jews in Palestine and for the coastal trade.

World War II and After

For the period from 1940 to 1944, decimal file 867N of the Department of State (Record Group 59) is filed in 13 boxes. The largest segments of the file are Political Affairs in Palestine (867N.00), 113 enclosures, including a report dated May 31, 1944, by William Yale on the early presentation of Palestine documents to the postwar programs committee; Government of Palestine (867N.01), 695 enclosures, listed on 87 pages of purport lists; and Regulations on Residence, Trade, and Travel in Palestine (867N.111), 54 enclosures. One of the documents in this file, for example, is a cross-reference to a telegram from Tehran in another file (890G.111/46), reporting that Iraqi authorities had refused transit visas to 700 Polish Jewish children and 100 adults to go from Iran to Palestine; it was suggested that the U.S. government furnish air transportation at commercial rates so that they could fly direct from Iran to Palestine. Other large files in the 1940–1944 period are Military Affairs in Palestine (867N.20), 165 enclosures, mainly concerned with the formation of a Jewish army in Palestine; Race Problems of Jews in Palestine (867N.4016), 50 enclosures; and file 867N.55, Immigration into Palestine, 70 enclosures. The purport lists for file 867N for the 1940–1944 period are microfilmed on rolls 597 and 652 of M973.

In the decimal file for the 1945–1949 period, records relating to Palestine are found in two main files. File 867N is contained in 38 boxes, mostly relating to the Arab-Zionist controversy over the future status of Palestine. File 501.BB Palestine, comprised of documents relating to the Palestine question at the United Nations, is contained in 15 boxes. Needless to say, these records are extremely active; researchers must place their name on a waiting list to examine them. The National Archives hopes, in the near future, to microfilm all of the records in the 867N file from 1930 through 1949.

Records of the consular posts of the State Department located in Palestine (Record Group 84) are few in number and scattered for the war period and after. Although there are records for the office in Beirut dated from 1936 to 1949, the records for Haifa, Tel Aviv, and Jerusalem are dated only from 1948. The records for the Jerusalem office, for example, for the period from 1948 to 1953 total only seven feet.

During World War II, the Office of War Information (Record Group 208) formulated and carried out programs to disseminate information in the United States and abroad about the progress of the war and American policies, activities, and objectives. Among the records of the Overseas Operations Branch are scattered outpost reports and a variety of other propaganda material relating to Jewish resettlement and American opinion on the Palestine issue. Among the records of the Domestic Operations Branch, which took over many of the functions of the Office of Government Reports and the Office of Facts and Figures, is a massive file of clippings from several hundred newspapers throughout the country.

Another wartime agency, the Office of Strategic Services, created a complex card index to catalogue its records (Record Group 226). There are over 900,000 cards arranged by country, and thereunder by subject number: 0-general, 1-political, 2-economic, 3-military, 4-naval, 5-aviation, 6-social and psychological, propaganda, press, population movements, etc., 7-subversive activities. Each card contains a good summary of the document and lists the number of pages and its date. OSS records reflect the hopes and fears of both Jews and Arabs in relation to Palestine. For Palestine, there are several thousand cards available to researchers, but they cannot be copied; the records must be reviewed individually to see if they can be declassified. OSS intelligence reports include a wide variety of data on individuals, groups, political activities, economic information, and social and psychological subjects.

One reference card in file 1.1 under Palestine refers to document 26607 C, a nine-page memorandum on the Arab-Jewish and Palestine question by Francis Kettaneh, dated January 12, 1943, summarized as follows:

> The Moslems are friendly to the United States, but German propaganda has convinced them that the United States, dominated by Jews, is backing the Zionist movement in Palestine. England's attempt in the last war to appease the Jews and Arabs merely antagonized both. The Zionist project of a Jewish Palestine, and Gibbs' project of a federation of Arab states, are unfeasible. Palestine's geography unfits it for large populations, and both Moslems and Christians oppose control of their holy places in Palestine by a Jewish state. It would be better to give the Jews an African colony, where they would dispossess nobody.

Document 77600 C is a report of a conversation with Moshe Shertok of the Jewish Agency in Palestine, June 1, 1944, which notes:

> Shertok felt that the British use the war as an excuse to delay settlement in Palestine. Responsible Jews will not press an issue now and will do all possible to aid Allies, but they do desire unlimited immigration. Should an Arab federation ever materialize, Palestine would join if her status as a Jewish State were recognized. He discounted Russian interest in Palestine, indeed, seemed to fear it. He also denied strongly that many Jews would wish to leave Palestine for their previous homes after the war.

Document 61726 S, a 56-page report entitled "Status and Prospects of the White Paper on Palestine," dated March 2, 1944, is summarized as follows:

> The White Paper of 17 May 1939 was a compromise which satisfied neither the Jews nor the Arabs. . . . British prestige with the Arabs is high, but no Arab leaders endorse British policy—Jewish opposition is

vehement. A revision in the form of a trilateral agreement will be needed at the close of the war.

Document 32990 C, a four-page report dated April 9, 1943, predicts that "Civil War may be expected in Palestine after the present war is over. Jews and Arabs are both heavily armed, and are making preliminary feints. British and U.S. relations to the question are discussed."

The Research and Analysis Branch of the OSS prepared thousands of reports during the war on a multitude of subjects, arranged in numerical order by the number of the report. After the war, its personnel were transferred to the Department of State, and the series of numbered reports it prepared as the Office of Intelligence and Research through 1961 have been transferred to the National Archives (Record Group 59.) A card index, arranged by country and subjects, serves as a finding aid. Among the reports are "Status and Prospects of the White Paper on Palestine" (1666), dated March 2, 1944; "Problem of Jewish Immigration into Palestine" (2409), October 4, 1944; "The Objectives and Activities of the Irgun Zvai Leumi" (2612), October 13, 1944; and "Aims and Activities of the Stern Group in Palestine" (2717), December 1, 1948.

Military records for the World War II period are voluminous, and records relating to the Holy Land can be found in many different files. The records of the Army Staff (Record Group 319) include records of the Office of the Assistant Chief of Staff, G-2, Intelligence, 1939–1945, totaling over 8,500 feet and over 1,000 rolls of microfilm. The intelligence document, or ID, file, 1942–1954, includes scattered intelligence reports on the Palestine problem. A card index to the file, which is still classified, serves as the basic finding aid. Each card lists one to twenty intelligence reports by title, date, and source (one of various intelligence agencies).

Among the records of the Operations Plans Divisions of the War Department General Staff (Record Group 165) is an 091 file for Palestine, 1942–1945, which includes reports from various sources on the following subjects: "Joint Statement by the American and British Governments Regarding Palestine"; "Emergency Committee to Save the Jewish People of Europe"; "Strategic Engineering Study No. 70—Palestine and Trans-Jordan"; and "Request for permission for officers and men to take all or portion of rotation leave in Palestine."

The records of Secretary of the Navy James V. Forrestal include a general correspondence file for 1940–1947, with a subject card index as a finding aid. File 81-2-45, for example, contains a request dated April 25, 1947, from Forrestal to his staff. He wanted a brief summary report giving him factual background information on Palestine. He knew there were many books and lengthy reports on the subject, but he wanted something brief, which would specifically cover the Balfour Declaration and "the Grady statement." The result was a six-page memo by Rear Adm. Edmund T. Wooldridge, and one might surmise that it was the only document that Forrestal ever read sympathetic to Jewish interests in Palestine.

The records of the Office of the Secretary of Defense (Record Group 330) include a numerical file of the Correspondence Control Section of the Administrative Secretary. That file contains correspondence and memorandums written in the summer of 1948 about the possible courses of action should the United States become militarily involved as part of a United Nations truce force in the Middle East.

Among the records of the United States Senate in the National Archives (Record Group 46), the files of the Foreign Relations Committee include much correspondence of the 78th and 79th Congresses, 1942–1946, relating to a proposed Senate resolution sponsored by Senators Robert Taft and Robert Wagner favoring the restoration of Palestine to the Jewish People.

Newsreels are no longer produced, but one can relive history through the newsreels made by several companies on a semiweekly basis, and now deposited in the National Archives, for the period from 1929 to 1967. Included in the highlights of world events are stories on Jewish refugees attempting to evade British warships and enter Palestine in 1946, and on the various Arab-Israeli wars. Audiovisual records also include a *March of Time* film entitled "Palestine Problem," made in 1945, which attempts to provide a history of the movement for the establishment of a Jewish state in Palestine from World War I.

Among the sound recordings in the National Archives Gift Collection (Record Group 200) are speeches by President Eisenhower at the American-Jewish Tercentenary Dinner on October 20, 1954; on the Egyptian crisis, October 31, 1956; on the Middle East, January 5, 1957; and on the Middle Eastern problem, February 20, 1957.

Also of interest are a speech by Golda Meir at the National Press Club, March 1, 1974, and interviews with Abba Eban, then Israeli ambassador to the United States, on September 21, 1953, and March 14, 1955. In addition, there are videotape recordings of the "CBS Evening News" from April 1, 1974, to the present.

In the Cartographic Archives Division, one of the largest collections consists of maps produced by the State Department's Office of the Geographer. The Isaiah Bowman collection has a Palestine series, which includes the following maps: Jewish Land Holdings, 1937; Palestine, Character of Agriculture Land, showing Hills, Waste Land, Plains, and the Population of Jerusalem and Haifa by Religion, 1943; Annual Rainfall in Palestine, 1943; Palestine: Proposals of the Partition Commission, 1938; and others. Among the maps in the collection of the Office of Strategic Services are maps of the Near East in general, and specific maps of Palestine showing political subdivisions.

One of the lot files, or separately maintained office files of the State Department accessioned by the National Archives, contains the International Organization files of Herbert A. Fierst, subject files of the Special Assistant to the Director of the Office of United Nations Affairs (Record Group 59). A box list of folder labels serves as a finding aid. One folder, "Emigration to Israel," contains a single document, which should be in the central file. It is a memo written by Robert McClintock on June 3, 1948, pointing out that under the Security Council Resolution of May 29 on Palestine, the United States should prevent the emigration to Palestine or other countries of people who are potentially "fighting personnel." Thus, he advised instructing General Clay in Germany not to permit the departure of such people from displaced persons camps. The Fierst file also includes four folders on the Combined Anglo-American Committee on Palestine.

Another State Department lot file of special interest in the study of America–Holy Land relations consists of the 11 boxes of the Rusk-McClintock file for 1947–1949. During this period, Dean Rusk and Robert McClintock were responsible for the Palestine question at the United Nations. The reference file each kept consists of copies of correspondence, memos, telegrams, drafts, and miscellaneous material relating to the Palestine question, all arranged in chronological order. Included, for example, is correspondence with Judge

Joseph M. Proskauer, President of the American Jewish Committee.

Also in this file is an excellent example of the brief internal notes or memos that are often more informative than the formal letters to which they are attached. On March 1, 1948, Judge Proskauer presented his views on the question of partition to Under Secretary of State Robert Lovett. The tone of his letter is illustrated by the following brief exerpt:

> Assuming, arguendo, that the Security Council cannot use force to implement partition, it still remains true that it can use force to stop the violence of those who are using force to block partition. Assuming, arguendo, that no United Nations force can coerce a Palestinian Arab into agreeing to partition, it can surely, nonetheless, stop him and his fellow Arabs from using violence that threatens world peace. I know there is a headache in this thing, but the only way to get rid of that kind of headache is to face up to the situation and act boldly.

With the draft reply, McClintock added a short poetic note for Lovett which tells us much more than the reply about what they really thought of Proskauer's advice.

> Subject: Same Old Thing.
> Assuming, arguendo,
> That a headache is an ache
> Which will throb diminuendo
> Once partition's not at stake,
> Will there be no fresh crescendo
> of Proskauerings to take
> Assuming, arguendo,
> One can keep and eat the cake.

Comments on Dr. Gustafson's Paper

Wayne S. Cole

IMPORTANT as the Department of State's role is in American foreign affairs, it is not the whole story—and it never has been. Today virtually every department of the administrative branch of the government is involved in one way or another in American foreign affairs, and so are countless subordinate and independent agencies of the government. Both houses of Congress and multifarious committees are concerned actively with foreign affairs (including those between America and the Holy Land). Furthermore, though Department of State records eventually find their way to the Diplomatic Branch of the National Archives, many thousands of letters and documents on American foreign affairs are to be found in other depositories.

I suspect that every branch of the National Archives includes some letters, papers, and documents relating to America and the Holy Land. Outside the Diplomatic Branch, my own research has concentrated particularly on legislative materials—especially those created during the years of Franklin D. Roosevelt's presidency, 1933 to 1945. The House Foreign Affairs Committee records here were not particularly rich or fruitful for my purposes, while I found the records of the Senate Committee on Foreign Relations to be uneven but valuable—whether the chairman of that committee happened to be William E. Borah of Idaho, Key Pittman of Nevada,

Walter George of Georgia, Tom Connally of Texas, or Arthur H. Vandenberg of Michigan. Among the many topics treated in those files were Jewish matters, immigration, and Palestine. Other legislative committees (both standing and special) in both houses of Congress create records that relate to military, economic, religious, and social concerns of America in the Holy Land.

The Legislative Branch in the National Archives also has what it calls papers supporting Senate and House bills and resolutions. Those are organized by house, by Congress, by session, and by the specific number of the bill or resolution. From my own experience, using this category of materials seems to be a needle-in-the-haystack activity. Sometimes one finds nothing; other times one finds only a print of the bill or resolution. But sometimes one finds uniquely valuable correspondence. As far as I know, these materials are little used (or at least little cited), but they can be extremely valuable.

Furthermore, there has never been a clear, sharp line between official legislative committee records that go to the National Archives on the one hand, and the personal papers of committee chairmen and members on the other. Consequently, the scholar may find important letters and records relating directly to the Senate Foreign Relations Committee in the personal papers of former chairmen of that committee, including the papers of Borah, Pittman, and Connally in the Library of Congress Manuscript Division, and the papers of Vandenberg in the William L. Clements Library at Ann Arbor, Michigan. Similarly, the private papers of minority party members of committees may be as valuable on particular subjects as the private papers of committee chairmen (especially if those minority party legislators were ranking committee members, or if their constituents felt strongly on the particular subject). For example, the papers of Borah in the Library of Congress, of Hiram Johnson in the Bancroft Library in California, and of Vandenberg in Michigan are as rich on Foreign Relations Committee concerns of the Roosevelt era as the papers of the chairmen for those years, Senators Pittman, George, and Connally. Senator Robert F. Wagner's papers at Georgetown University and Senator Theodore F. Green's papers in the Library of Congress are especially rich on Jewish matters, refugee problems, immigration, and Palestine.

Just as the distinction between official and personal legislative papers has never been clearly drawn, so, too, the distinction between official Department of State records and the personal papers of diplomats and State Department officials has sometimes been less sharp than one might expect. Consequently, many items important in American foreign affairs may be found outside the National Archives in the personal manuscript collections of former American diplomats and Department of State officials. The manuscript collections of former Secretaries of State Charles Evans Hughes and Cordell Hull in the Library of Congress, of Frank B. Kellogg in the Minnesota State Historical Society Library, and of Henry L. Stimson in the Yale University Library all contain letters concerned with America and the Holy Land. And when Edward R. Stettinius, Jr., moved out of his offices, he came close to gutting the Department of State's central files; for his tour as secretary of state, one must turn to his so-called "personal" papers at the University of Virginia in Charlottesville. As far as I know, no other secretary of state in the twentieth century defined his "personal papers" so broadly as Stettinius did. But the papers of James F. Byrnes at Clemson University in South Carolina; George C. Marshall at the Marshall Library at Lexington, Virginia; Dean Acheson at the Truman Library at Independence, Missouri; and of John Foster Dulles at Princeton University in New Jersey, all contain pertinent materials.

Similar generalizations apply to the personal manuscript collections and diaries of diplomats and subordinate Department of State officials, including the papers of William E. Dodd, Norman H. Davis, and Breckinridge Long in the Library of Congress; the papers of Hugh R. Wilson in the Herbert Hoover Presidential Library in West Branch, Iowa; those of R. Walton Moore and Adolf A. Berle at the Franklin D. Roosevelt Library in Hyde Park, New York; and those of William Phillips and Jay Pierrepont Moffat at Houghton Library at Harvard University. Personally, I found two kinds of communications in such manuscript collections to be particularly fascinating and helpful. First, President Roosevelt encouraged diplomats to write directly to him rather than limiting their communications officially to the State Department. Many took him at his word. Dodd, for example, wrote long, detailed letters to Roosevelt during his service as ambassador to Germany, and they included many observations on Nazi persecution of the Jews, on Dodd's reactions, and on his policy recommendations. Second, over the years career foreign service officers (like career military officers) developed personal ties and camaraderie among themselves. In personal correspondence with each other, those serving in Washington often tried to keep their friends who were assigned to diplomatic posts abroad informed on the latest State Department gossip and on their impressions of recent appointees and policies in an administration. Such letters often include valuable and candid inside information for the researcher. I found this to be the case, for example, when using the Moffat papers at Houghton Library and the Norman Davis papers in the Library of Congress.

But if the distinction between official and personal papers of legislators, diplomats, and State Department officials was unclear, there was almost no distinction at all made for the papers of former presidents until the recent controversies surrounding the Richard M. Nixon administration. Former presidents or their heirs considered presidential papers to be their personal possessions and took them when they departed the White House. Papers of early American presidents were deposited in various places and were subject to widely varying restrictions. Many of them eventually went to the Manuscript Division of the Library of Congress, which has microfilmed them and made them available for sale to researchers and libraries.

With the creation of the Franklin D. Roosevelt Library at Hyde Park, New York, in the 1940s, however, a new kind of research institution became a fixture on the American scene. Beautiful edifices in West Branch, Iowa; Hyde Park, New York; Independence, Missouri; Abilene, Kansas; and Austin, Texas, now house the papers of presidents Herbert Hoover, Franklin D. Roosevelt, Harry S. Truman, Dwight D. Eisenhower, and Lyndon B. Johnson. Such an edifice is in process for the John F. Kennedy papers in Massachusetts, and is a continuing center of controversy as far as the papers of the Richard M. Nixon administration are concerned. In each instance private funds paid for the construction of the library building; in each instance the former president or his heirs donated his papers under certain restrictions to the United States government to be administered by the National Archives under the General Services Administration and in each instance the library staff also gathered the manuscripts of other individuals who served in public life during the administration of that particular president. There is no real consistency on just where the papers of high administration officials may eventually be deposited. For example, among Franklin D. Roosevelt's cabinet members, Secretary of the Treasury Henry Morgenthau, Jr.'s papers and diaries went to the Roosevelt Library; the papers of Secretary of State Cordell Hull, Secretary of the Interior Harold L. Ickes, and Secretary of the Navy Frank Knox went to the Library of Congress; Secretary of War Stimson's papers and diaries went to Yale University; and most of Secretary of Agriculture Henry A. Wallace's papers went to the University of Iowa in Iowa City. The papers of presidential counselors and assistants Samuel I. Rosenman, Clark M. Clifford, and George M. Elsey at the Truman Library are particularly valuable for research on United States policies toward Palestine and Israel.

Governments act to serve the needs and interests of individuals and groups, and one finds expressions of those concerns in various depositories on the governmental level. But one could and should extend one's research still further, to the papers of the private individuals and groups whose expressions of their needs and interests help to move the government to action on domestic and foreign affairs. The possibilities for that further extension of one's research perimeters are limitless. Of obvious importance for the subject of America and the Holy Land are the papers of Felix Frankfurter, which are divided among the Library of Congress, Harvard University, and the Central Zionist Archives in Israel; and those of Rabbi Stephen S. Wise at the American Jewish Historical Society at Brandeis University. Though he was not a focal point for my own research, I found correspondence of Dr. Wise in most of the nearly one hundred manuscript and archival collections I researched over the years.

I shall mention just one additional way of "working outward" from the National Archives in one's research on America and the Holy Land. I have in mind research in the foreign office and diplomatic records of other countries, particularly in the British Foreign Office records in the custody of the Public Records Office in London. Diplomats assigned to Washington report, of course, to their home governments on the policies and policymakers of the United States. Research in British Foreign records provides both inside information and distinctive perspectives that the researcher may be unable to find elsewhere. I single out the British records for several reasons: Britain's deep involvement in Palestine and the Middle

East; the generally excellent quality of British diplomatic reporting; the intimacy of Anglo-American diplomatic relations; and the simple fact that, unlike most governments, Great Britain (like the United States) makes its diplomatic records available to researchers comparatively early and freely. Most British Foreign Office records through the end of World War II in 1945, are open for research, and they are extremely valuable for many subjects in the history of American foreign affairs.

Comments on Dr. Gustafson's Paper

Jules Davids

DR. MILTON GUSTAFSON'S inventory of the records in the National Archives on America and the Holy Land offers a useful guide to scholars who are concerned with investigating the diplomatic materials relating to this field of study. Three things strike me in considering Dr. Gustafson's inventory. The first is the massive quantity of materials that can be found in the National Archives; the second is the fact that much of this data is still largely untapped; and the third is the opportunity that this vast reservoir of archival documents offers to scholars to produce significant studies on America and the Holy Land. To be sure, a great deal has been written on the Middle East, particularly on contemporary issues and problems. Yet, it can be said that as a specific field of study, America and the Holy Land has not been adequately dealt with by American diplomatic historians. Dr. Gustafson's inventory may help to remedy this deficiency. Certainly, the consular material, especially before World War I, could be explored more extensively. Although numerous studies have been made on Palestine during World War I and the mandate periods, much more could be done in examining the relationship between the United States and Palestine. The archival materials are also enormously rich on the periods of World War II and the post-war years. One of the sources that especially invites attention is the intelligence data that can be found in the Army, Navy, and OSS records, much of which has only recently been declassified.

The War Department records include Army Intelligence documents (G-2) and a regional file (RG 165) on Palestine for the years 1933–1944. The latter consists of 16 boxes of documents containing intelligence reports, all declassified and arranged by subject according to the G-2 filing system. In Record Group 165, there are also numerous reports from American military attachés in Turkey and Great Britain. General File designations 2568 and 2657-HH in this collection contain reports on Palestine and the political conditions in Palestine. Supplementing this data are the records of the Chief of Naval Operations (RG 38), which include the documents of Naval Intelligence. Although there is no subject index to this material, there are lists of documents in different files, and file C-10-F has a sizable number of reports on political conditions in Palestine and on the partition problem from 1930 to 1938.

Worth exploring, too, are the central files of the Justice Department. These are organized by subject in a numerical classification system. They cover the years 1870 to 1947, with a name index of persons for the period from 1917 to 1933 and a subject index for the records before 1920. The intelligence data that has been least tapped is that of OSS (RG 226). There are over 900,000 cards in the OSS files, arranged by country and by subject under each country. Several thousand cards are on Palestine, and there are numerous reports on individuals, groups, political activities, economic affairs, and social and psychological subjects.

Other records in the National Archives that pertain to America and the Holy Land are those of the United States Senate (RG 46) and the House of Representatives (RG 233). These contain significant information on resolutions and other matters relating to Palestine. Of special interest is the material of the Senate Foreign Relations Committee, which includes reports of the 78th and 79th congresses, covering the years from 1942 to 1946, on a proposed Senate resolution sponsored by Senators Robert A. Taft and Robert Wagner supporting the restoration of Palestine to the Jewish People.

Dr. Gustafson's inventory survey, while obviously helpful to scholars, is, however, only a first step toward nurturing the development of diplomatic studies on America and the Holy Land. What is needed is not simply a description of the records and their location in the National Archives, but some assessment of their content and quality. Another problem that confronts the scholar is the accessibility of the archival material. Most of the documents have not been microfilmed, so it is necessary to go to Washington, D.C., to read them. To "plow through" the raw data, whether on microfilm or in the National Archives, is tremendously time-consuming, and this clearly limits their availability. It was partially in realization of this fact that I tried to develop a new methodology with regard to the compilation of archival documents and to their use. This was undertaken in the collation and organization of the documentary materials in the National Archives on China.

The results of my efforts led to the publication in 1973 of the first series of 21 volumes of the *American Diplomatic and Public Papers: The United States and China* on "The Treaty System and the Taiping Rebellion, 1842–1860." Nine series of volumes are projected to cover the period from 1842 to 1945. All documents are photo-facsimiled and organized topically and under each topic, chronologically. Each volume contains a calendar and a précis of the documents, together with an introduction that provides a guide to the documentary materials. A complete index to the documents in all the volumes was also set up. A key feature of the compilation is the attempt to develop an integration and continuity of the correspondence and dispatches, not only of the United States, but those of China, as well as England, France, Russia, and other countries. In addition, selected supplementary documents were included from manuscript papers and private letter collections when they were deemed to be helpful. The purpose of the compilation was to present a larger dimension to the diplomatic interaction between the United States and China than could be found in the annual volumes of the *Foreign Relations Papers of the United States.*

I believe this methodology can also be applied to the assemblage of documents in the National Archives on America and the Holy Land. In this regard, Dr. Gustafson's inventory could be an excellent starting point. The China project has had the full cooperation of the National Archives, without which it could not have been undertaken. I am confident that the diplomatic branch under Dr. Gustafson would support and provide the assistance needed on a similar program dealing with America and the Holy Land. The China volumes, together with my cataloguing and indexing of source materials on Sino-American relations until World War II, have already assisted graduate students at Georgetown University in the completion of three doctoral dissertations: one dealing with the period from 1842 to 1847, a second on the 1880s, and a third on World War II. Each has contributed toward modifying generally accepted historical interpretations. I am sure that a documentary program on America and the Holy Land would also provide a stimulus to the writing of dissertations and monographs in this field of study.

The task of bringing order and direction to the massive amount of materials in the National Archives on America and the Holy Land will not be easy, but it can be done. A major problem that faces the American diplomatic historian is the difficulty of confining his attention solely to the relations between the United States and Palestine or, after 1948, between the United States and Israel. Because of the rivalries of the Great Powers, it is virtually impossible to divorce either Palestine or the State of Israel, particularly in the twentieth century, from the power politics that has largely dominated the Middle East. Indeed, the region we designate as the Middle East has been the fulcrum of conflict for centuries. This, of course, is no less true today than it was in the past. Although a focus can be placed on America and the Holy Land, the interplay of the Great Power rivalries and the sources of tension between Arabs and Jews, and among the Arab states themselves, cannot be ignored. Since this is so, a compilation of documents will necessarily have to take into account not only Dr. Gustafson's inventory of the records on America and the Holy Land, but the summary of Materials in the National Archives Relating to the Middle East (Reference Information Papers, no. 44, May 1955).

Herbert Hoover and the Holy Land: A Preliminary Study Based upon Documentary Sources in the Hoover Presidential Library

W. D. Blanks

To THE average observer, the Herbert Hoover Presidential Library and Archives may not seem a fruitful source of materials for the relationship between America and the Holy Land. This is so because Hoover did not hold public office during the period of marked Jewish immigration into Palestine or during the decade of controversy that led to the establishment of the State of Israel in 1948. Often forgotten, however, is the fact that Hoover remained a very active public figure almost until his death in 1964. During most of the period from his entrance into public life until approximately 1962, he maintained a prodigious correspondence on topics relating to both foreign and domestic affairs. Even a cursory examination of his Post-Presidential Papers staggers the average reader, not only with the extent and variety of his interests but also with the number of persons and organizations seeking his aid and guidance on many subjects and problems.

Among the numerous issues occupying his interest during his years as president of the United States (1928–1932) and through the establishment of the State of Israel in 1948 was his concern for Palestine as the Jewish homeland and later for the fate of the Palestine Arabs. The former interest began in 1929, and the latter took the form of the so-called "Hoover Plan" for the rejuvenation of the irrigation system of the Tigris-Euphrates Valley and the resettlement of the Palestine Arabs in Iraq (to make way for the settlement of displaced Jews in Palestine). This "Hoover Plan" was first proposed in 1945, although there is some indication that Hoover had explored this topic earlier.[2]

This paper emphasizes two topics: Hoover's attitude toward the establishment of Palestine as the Jewish homeland and the "Hoover Plan." No attempt is made to include all statements submitted upon request to various American Jewish organizations, such as the Jewish War Veterans, on this subject.

Hoover and Palestine as the Jewish Homeland

The occasion for Hoover's first public expression pertaining to Jewish activities in Palestine was in 1929 when A. Tannenbaum of the Zionist Organization of America requested a statement regarding the massacre of Jews and Arab rioting in Hebron. Expressing confidence in the vigorous action taken by the British authorities to restore order in Palestine, Hoover went on to say (in an attached memorandum):

> I have watched with keen interest and sympathy the splendid work for the upbuilding of Palestine, in which so many American Jews take an important part, in behalf of their less fortunate brethren abroad. It is a historic task that the Jewish people is meeting with unexampled perseverance, sacrifice, and hard work. The Holy Land, desolate and neglected for centuries, is being rebuilt not only as an inspiring spiritual center, but also as a habitable and peaceful land that will in the near future harbor a large population with increased opportunities for prosperity among the farmers, the industrialists, the laborers and the scholars.[3]

This statement met with an immediate response from the Arab world. The very next day a cablegram was received from the Executive Committee of the Syro-Palestine Congress in Cairo. As translated for the President, it made three points:

> First, Palestine has been purely Arabian for 14 centuries; Second, it is dangerous and illogical to make it Jewish again before exterminating its population of 800,000 persons surrounded by 30 million Arabs and 300 million Mussulmans. Which is unjust and impossible. Third, to make Palestine [a] Jewish fatherland is to make perpetual disorders therein.

Mr. Hoover was further urged to consider the contents of this cablegram and to "study [the] question exhaustively."[4]

In 1931, President Hoover reaffirmed his support of the establishment of a Jewish homeland in Palestine in a message he addressed to the chairman of the Conference on American Palestine Campaign. His feelings are expressed in two of the four paragraphs that form the letter:

> The fact that the Conference is being held under the auspices of the Jewish Agency, representing a union of entire American Jewry on behalf of the Jewish national home in Palestine, offers the best assurance of the success of the Conference and of the effort to follow.
>
> I have on a number of former occasions expressed my deep interest in the cause in which you are engaged—a cause embodying a nobility, courage, and idealism that deserves not merely the sympathy, but admiration and fullest measure and support of all mankind.[5]

Just prior to his leaving the White House, Hoover wrote the chairman of the American Palestine Campaign commending the fact that a conference was being held in New York

> to plan for the continued maintenance in the Jewish homeland of those institutions into whose establishment has gone so much of material assistance, labor, and sacrifice. Your efforts hold universal significance to Jewry, even as the Jewish people have made a world contribution to spiritual advancement. . . .[6]

The next statement relating to the Holy Land appears to have come in 1943 after a lapse of eleven years. In a message to the National Conference for Palestine of the United Jewish Appeal, Hoover wrote that "in these days of tyranny and persecution Palestine looms as a shining symbol of strength and hope to Jews, not only in Europe but throughout the world."[7]

From such statements—and further research may disclose still more—it is evident that Hoover had viewed the establishment of Palestine as a Jewish homeland well before the beginnings of Nazi persecution in Germany. As far as has been ascertained, however, he had not yet expressed himself on the problem of the Arab population of Palestine, which would either have to coexist with or be displaced by Jews immigrating to that country.

To this problem, and indeed to the problems of the Arab population of the whole "Fertile Crescent," he turned his attention in november 1945, both as an engineer and as a humanitarian. The result became known as the Hoover Plan, or the Hoover Plan for Iraq and Palestine.

The Hoover Plan for Resettling Palestinian Arabs in Iraq

The first public statement of the Hoover Plan appeared in the New York *World-Telegram* on November 19, 1945. It was headlined "Hoover Urges Resettling Arabs to Solve Palestine Problem" and subtitled "Says Irrigation Could Provide Good Iraq Land" and "Believes Migration Would End Conflict over Jewish Refuge."[8]

The newspaper observed that "there is a sane and practical solution of the Palestine problem in the opinion of former President Herbert Hoover." The plan, which came in response to an inquiry by the *World-Telegram,* "approaches the problem from an engineering standpoint," an approach which hopefully would lead to a subordination of the racial and political aspects of the problem and "to a process by which both Jews and Arabs might benefit materially."[9]

Because of its importance, Hoover's complete statement as printed by the paper and in his published writings is here included.

> There is a possible plan of settling the Palestine question and providing ample Jewish refuge. It at least is worth serious investigation for it offers a constructive humanitarian solution.
>
> In ancient times the irrigation of the Tigris and Euphrates Valleys supported probably ten million people in the Kingdoms of Babylon and Ninevah. The deterioration and destruction of their irrigation works by the Mongol invasion centuries ago and their neglect for ages are responsible for the shrinkage of the population to about 3,500,000 people in modern Iraq. Some 30 years ago, Sir William Willcocks, an eminent British engineer, completed a study of the restoration of the old irrigation system. He estimated that about 2,800,000 acres of the most fertile land in the world could be recovered at a cost of under $150,000,000. Some progress has been made under the Iraq Government, but their lack of financial resources and the delays of the war have retarded the work greatly. Some years ago it was proposed that this area should be developed for settlement by Jewish refugees. This did not, however, satisfy the Jewish desire for a homeland.
>
> My own suggestion is that Iraq might be financed to complete this great land development on the consideration that it be made the scene of resettlement of the Arabs from Palestine. This would clear then Palestine completely for a large Jewish emigration and coloniza-

> tion. A suggestion of transfer of the Arab people of Palestine was made by the British Labor Party in December, 1944, but no adequate plan was proposed as to where or how they were to go.
>
> There is room for many more Arabs in such a development in Iraq than the total of Arabs in Palestine. The soil is more fertile. They would be among their own race which is Arab speaking and Mohammedan. The Arab population of Palestine would be the gainers from better lands in exchange for their present holdings. Iraq would be the gainer for it badly needs agricultural population.
>
> Today millions of people are being moved from one land to another. If the lands were organized and homes provided, this particular movement could be made the model migration of history. It would be a solution by engineering instead of by conflict.
>
> I realize that the plan offers a challenge both to the statesmanship of the Great Powers as well as to the good-will of all parties concerned. However, I submit it and it does offer a method of settlement with both honor and wisdom.[10]

Response was not long in coming from Zionist, Iraqi, and Christian sources.

On November 21, the American Zionist Emergency Council mailed Hoover a copy of its official reaction, which was to be published in the *World-Telegram.* In substance this statement argued that "the Zionist Organization has never advocated the transfer of Palestine's Arabs to Iraq or elsewhere. On the contrary, we always maintained and still maintain that within the boundaries of Palestine there is room enough for its present population, Jew and Arab, and for several million more Jewish settlers." Developments of the last twenty years amply proved this; nevertheless, "when all the long accepted remedies seem to fail it is time to consider new approaches."[11] Editorial comment in the American Jewish press was very favorable, however, according to the same letter to Hoover from Eliahu Ben-Horin.[12]

The Iraqi response was relayed to Hoover by Ben-Horin, who quoted from the Jewish Telegraphic Agency report from Cairo. According to this information, Bagdad had urged a boycott of all American goods, and the Iraqi papers called the Hoover Plan a "Devilish American Plan" and a "New Zionist Scheme."[13]

On December 13, Ben-Horin notified Hoover that Representative Christian A. Herter of Massachusetts had inserted his proposal in the *Congressional Record.*[14]

But the American press coverage was not outstandingly favorable, according to clippings in the Hoover Library. The *New York Times,* for example, ignored the proposal completely. In a letter to Elisha Friedman on November 25, Hoover stated, "I am convinced the plan has great merits," and expressed the hope that "a strong letter to the *New York Times* (who have not deigned to notice it) might help for a start."[15] Friedman prepared two drafts of an article which he apparently submitted for publication in the *Times.*[16] Likewise he prepared an article on the plan, which he sent to *Harper's Magazine,* but it was rejected by the editor.[17] Despite these rebuffs, Hoover apparently did not give up. Several days later, he wrote to Friedman: "Supposing I could find a publisher, I am wondering if you would be interested in writing a short book on the plan that I have suggested for Palestine." He also offered to supply engineering data that he had in his possession.[18] One positive note was struck by radio commentator Elmer Peterson of Station KFI, Los Angeles, in a broadcast in favor of the plan. According to a partial transcript of this broadcast, the estimated sum of $100,000,000 could be financed by a loan from the United Nations.[19]

A substantial portion of the technical information had been supplied by F. Julius Fohs of Houston, Texas, a noted engineering consultant on irrigation matters. In December, Fohs wrote Hoover that he was working on a memorandum "covering data on Irak [*sic*] and the Middle East, which will be sent to you from Houston as soon as completed."[20]

Work now continued rapidly on the engineering aspects. In a letter dated January 15, Friedman noted that "the Zionist organization officially takes the position that there is room in Palestine for all the present population, and an additional number from Europe." But he did suggest an approach which might help accomplish the purpose of the plan. This would be to gather "a responsible group of scientists, technical men, and distinguished citizens" who would "undertake this proposal quite independently of any existing organization."[21]

On January 20, Fohs wrote Hoover a letter in which he made five suggestions. These included the following: to begin to form a technical committee, to raise $25,000 "to get the matter started," and to make further examination of irrigation and hydroelectric possibilities in the area.[22] The first meeting of the technical committee took place on the evening of February 4, at the home of William Fondiller, vice-president of the Bell Research Laboratories. Plans were made to invite several scientists to a future meeting, and hope was expressed that funds might be obtained from the Refugee Economic Corporation.[23]

The next—and apparently final—step along this line is contained in the "Minutes of Meeting at N.Y. Faculty Club, March 4, 1946."[24] The purpose of this meeting, of which Fondiller was chairman (the names of the other participants are listed in the minutes), was to form a "Committee to work with Mr. Herbert Hoover along the lines of his proposal to solve the Palestine Program by re-settling the Palestine Arabs in Iraq." After a briefing submitted by Ben-Horin and the reading of the technical reports prepared by Fohs, it was decided that Col. J. R. Elyachar of the U.S. Army Intelligence Corps would take steps to gather additional information, and that the committee would hold an early meeting with Hoover "to learn what information he had gathered on his own investigation."[25]

Unfortunately this memorandum is the last reference among the materials kept in the Hoover Library which pertain to the implementation of the Hoover Plan. The plan is mentioned again, but only in later correspondence, dated after the United Nations Partition Plan went into effect and after the establishment of the State of Israel (with the consequent flight of many of the Arabs from areas of Palestine controlled by Israeli forces).[26] Especially interesting is a note written by Ben-Horin in May 1949, reporting his continuing efforts on behalf of the plan. In it he mentions receiving a letter from Eleanor Roosevelt which states, "I think your plan is excellent and I have sent it to the President." The letter continues with the observation that it has become obvious that any further efforts to implement the plan should be made through the White House rather than through the State Department.[27]

With this correspondence, references in the Hoover Library both to the Hoover Plan and to Palestine as a Jewish homeland come to an end. There is obviously much additional data regarding the Hoover Plan which should be available in archival sources and in private papers, both in the United States and abroad. It is the hope of the writer that someone will undertake to write a definitive monograph on the Hoover Plan, from its early development to its full national and international impact.

Notes

1. This paper is intentionally a "preliminary study" for the following reasons: First, research has been limited to only those documents and archival sources located at the Herbert Hoover Presidential Library, West Branch, Iowa. There has been no attempt to locate and examine those sources which may be available elsewhere. Secondly, it is the intent of this paper merely to suggest topics upon which further research may be justified.

   The author expresses his appreciation to Mr. Robert Wood, assistant director, and to the staff of the Herbert Hoover Presidential Library for their continuing help and hospitality.
2. Although no specific documentation dated before 1945 was found, this assumption is based upon the following: First, the existence of an undated note mentioning that the presence of the Arab population in Palestine constitutes a barrier to the settlement of Jewish refugees. This problem "can be solved," the note continues. The note appears in the file immediately following a letter dated 1939 from Hoover to Lewis L. Strauss. This letter expresses appreciation for a memorandum—also located in the file—regarding the problem of locating a place for Jewish refugees to settle. Herbert Hoover to Lewis L. Strauss, August 28, 1939. "Admiral Lewis L. Strauss" folder, Post-Presidential Individual File, Hoover Library (hereafter, "Hoover Library").

   Second, Mr. Hoover's apparent personal habit of never making a public statement of this formal nature without extended consideration of the idea and careful study. Some indication of this process is found in the following note to Mr. Eliahu Ben-Horin thanking him for a booklet ("Irrigation in Iraq") dated shortly before the announcement of the "Hoover Plan." "Many thanks for the booklet. I have now gone over some fifteen books! I am trying to boil a statement down to 200 words." Herbert Hoover to Eliahu Ben-Horin, November 14, 1945. "Jewish-Zionist" folder, Post-Presidential Subject File.
3. Herbert Hoover to the Zionist Organization of America, August 29, 1929. "Countries—Palestine" folder, Presidential Papers, Foreign Affairs File.
4. Cablegram from the Executive Committee of the Syro-Palestine Congress to President Hoover, August 30, 1929. "Countries—Palestine" folder, Presidential Papers, Foreign Affairs File.
5. Herbert Hoover to Dr. Cyrus A. Adler, January 25, 1931. "Countries—Palestine" folder, Presidential Papers, Foreign Affairs File.
6. Herbert Hoover to Morris Rothenberg, January 12, 1932. "Jewish—Zionist" folder, Post-Presidential Subject File.
7. As reported in the *New York Times,* May 1, 1943. "Jewish—Zionist"

folder, Post-Presidential Subject File.

8. "Hoover Urges Resettling Arabs to Solve Palestine Problem," New York *World-Telegram,* November 19, 1945. "Jewish—Zionist" folder, Post-Presidential Subject File.
9. Ibid.
10. Herbert Hoover, *Addresses upon the American Road, 1945–1948* (New York: D. Van Nostrand Company, Inc., 1949), pp. 16–17. In this book, the plan is titled "On the Palestine Question."
11. Eliahu Ben-Horin to Herbert Hoover, November 21, 1945. "Jewish—Zionist" folder, Post-Presidential Subject File. Mr. Ben-Horin was long associated with the American Zionist Emergency Council.
12. Ibid.
13. Eliahu Ben-Horin to Herbert Hoover, November 27, 1945. "Jewish—Zionist" folder, Post-Presidential Subject File.
14. Eliahu Ben-Horin to Herbert Hoover, December 13, 1945. "Jewish—Zionist" folder, Post-Presidential Subject File. The location of the statement in the *Congressional Record* is Page A5551 of the *Congressional Record,* Appendix, dated November 28, 1945, according to Mr. Ben-Horin.
15. Herbert Hoover to Elisha M. Friedman, November 25, 1945. "Jewish—Zionist" folder, Post-Presidential Subject File.
16. Elisha M. Friedman to Herbert Hoover, December 12 and 31, 1945. "Jewish—Zionist" folder, Post-Presidential Subject File. The second draft, prepared on December 31, was in part a reply to a criticism of the Hoover Plan by Khalil Totah printed in the *New York Times* on December 24. According to the letter cited below, the second draft was printed by the *Times* as a "letter to the Editor."
17. Eliahu Ben-Horin to Herbert Hoover, January 8, 1946. "Jewish—Zionist" folder, Post-Presidential Subject File.
18. Herbert Hoover to Elisha M. Friedman, January 14, 1946. "Jewish—Zionist" folder, Post-Presidential Subject File. Nothing was found in the library to indicate that a publisher was ever found or even that a manuscript was ever prepared.
19. Eliahu Ben-Horin to Herbert Hoover, January 18, 1946. "Jewish—Zionist" folder, Post-Presidential Subject File.
20. F. Julius Fohs to Herbert Hoover, December 20, 1945. "Jewish—Zionist" folder, Post-Presidential Subject File. An undated copy of the technical report can be found in this folder in the Hoover Library.
21. Elisha M. Friedman to Herbert Hoover, January 15, 1946. "Jewish—Zionist" folder, Post-Presidential Subject File.
22. F. Julius Fohs to Herbert Hoover, January 20, 1946. "Jewish—Zionist" folder, Post-Presidential Subject File.
23. Elisha M. Friedman to Herbert Hoover, February 5, 1946. "Jewish—Zionist" folder, Post-Presidential Subject File.
24. William Fondiller to Herbert Hoover, March 6, 1946. "Jewish—Zionist" folder, Post-Presidential Subject file.

25. Ibid.
26. Cf. letters from Eliahu Ben-Horin to Herbert Hoover, February 9 and August 6, 1948. "Ben-Horin, Eliahu" folder, Post-Presidential Individual File.
27. Eliahu Ben-Horin to Herbert Hoover, May 11, 1949. "Ben-Horin, Eliahu" folder, Post-Presidential Individual File.

PART IV

Illustrative Texts: Documents Reflecting American Interest in the Holy Land

Christian Attitudes

1. Pliny Fisk: Sermon before Holy Land Pilgrimage (1819)
2. "Visit to Bethlehem" by Pliny Fisk and Jonas King (1823)
3. Clorinda Minor: "Letter from Palestine" (1854)
4. William M. Thomson: "Nazareth" (1857)
5. Philip Schaff: "Religion in Jerusalem" (1877)

6–7. Christian Zionism: I. M. Haldeman's "Signs of the Times" (1914) and A. A. Berle's "World Significance of the Jewish State" (1918)

8. Ezra Taft Benson's "The Jews Return and Fulfill Prophecy" (1950)

Jewish Concern

9–10. Charles Rhind's proposal to President Andrew Jackson on American-Turkish Friendship Treaty (1829), and introduction to "Our brothers of the House of Israel" in Turkey and Russia (1829)

11. The Society for Holy Tithings (*Hebra Tarumot Hakodesh*) Circular (1846)
12. Isaac Leeser's vision of the Holy Land rebuilt
13. Correspondence on the Pilgrim Dwellings near Jerusalem (1869)
14. Emma Lazarus: *An Epistle to the Hebrews* (1882–1883)
15. Solomon Schechter: *Zionism: A Statement* (1906)
16. Richard J. H. Gottheil: "Zionism and the Western Jews" (1914)
17. Henrietta Szold: Letters from Eretz Yisrael (1920–1921)

Governmental Sources

18–20. The Adams Colony: Correspondence of the colonists, consuls, and Secretary of State Seward (1867–1871)

21–22. Consul Selah Merrill: East European immigration to the Holy Land (1891) and the Jordan Water Scheme (1906)

23. Consul Thomas R. Wallace describes the first motor car in the Holy Land (1908)
24. Recommendations on Palestine for President Woodrow Wilson prepared by the Intelligence Section (1919)

Biblical Place-Names

25. Master list of biblical place-names, compiled by Lottie K. Davis (1954)

Christian Attitudes

1.

PROMINENT among American Christians who traveled and lived in the Holy Land and who became important sources of information about it were the missionaries. The first of the major American missionary societies, the American Board of Commissioners for Foreign Missions, determined in 1818 to launch a mission in Palestine, primarily to witness to the Oriental churches and secondarily to the Muslims. Among the first missionaries to be sent was Pliny Fisk; his sermon on the eve of departure indicated why Christians were drawn to the Holy Land, and expressed the characteristic confidence of nineteenth-century Protestantism in the importance of their own missionary role as witnesses to the Scriptures and to "real Christianity," even before other churches. Selections from the first two parts of his six-part sermon follow.

Reference: Pliny Fisk, *The Holy Land as an Interesting Field of Missionary Enterprise. A Sermon, Preached in the Old South Church, Boston, Sabbath Evening, Oct. 31, 1819, just before the Departure of the Palestine Mission* (Boston: Samuel T. Armstrong, 1819).

Acts xx, 22.

And now, behold, I go bound in the Spirit unto Jerusalem, not knowing the things that shall befal me there.

You are aware, my hearers, that the determination was some time since formed to attempt a mission to Jerusalem and the surrounding country. You are also aware, that he who now addresses you, expects soon to embark, with a colleague, on the proposed mission. You will not, therefore, deem it unsuitable, that on this occasion, I should endeavor to explain the design, and the nature, of the contemplated undertaking. . . .

I. The mission is destined to an interesting land. It is destined to Judea, having at the same time particular reference to Asia Minor on the north west, where were the seven churches addressed in the Revelation, and also to Armenia on the north. In ancient days, it was 'a land flowing with milk and honey, the glory of all lands.' With a temperate and salubrious climate, with a soil naturally luxuriant, producing in the greatest abundance the means of support for man and beast, this country is capable of supporting, under a favorable government, and with favorable customs and laws, a very numerous population. This was the spot selected from all the surface of the earth by the Creator, to be the residence of that people, whom he loved above all other people. Here the Lord their God gave them 'a good land, a land of brooks of water, of fountains, and depths that spring out of vallies and hills; a land of wheat and barley and vines and fig trees and pomegranates; a land of oil olive and honey; a land, wherein they might eat bread without scarceness and not lack any thing; a land, in which they might build goodly houses and dwell therein, and in which their herds and flocks and gold and silver might be multiplied, that they might bless the Lord God for the good land which he had given them.' It would seem, that the country was originally a favored portion of the earth; or else that a peculiar blessing was granted, that it might be a suitable dwelling for the people of God.

This land is rendered almost sacred in the eyes of every Christian, by a thousand religious associations. Near this place, probably, was the first residence of man,—Paradise with all its innocence and all its bliss. Here, certainly, was the scene of almost all that is interesting in sacred story. On one of these mountains, Abraham manifested his faith: here Jacob wrestled with God; and here the Israelites found liberty and rest after all their cruel bondage and perilous journeyings. Here David breathed forth those pious sentiments, which have so much assisted, purified, and exalted, the devotions of millions; and here Solomon prepared for the world those wise sayings, which have so enlightened and guided millions in seasons of darkness and doubt. It was here, that Isaiah triumphed in such enrapturing visions of future holiness and peace for the people of God; that Jeremiah poured forth his pious lamentations, on account of prevailing wickedness and the prospect of national ruin; that Nehemiah, and his faithful associates, manifested such undaunted courage, religious hardihood, and persevering industry, in rebuilding the walls of Jerusalem;—that all the prophets taught, and labored, and bore reproach. It was in the wilderness of Judea, that John came to announce the Savior's approach and prepare his way before him. In one of these villages Jesus was born; on one of these plains the shepherds were watching their flocks, when a choir of angels came from heaven and sung in their hearing, *Glory to God in the highest, and on earth peace, good will to men.* In the waters of one of these streams our Redeemer was baptised; and it was in these villages that he went about teaching and preaching, healing the sick and raising the dead. On this ground was the garden which witnessed his agony, the stupidity of his faithful followers, and the treachery of the apostate; and on one of these hills stood his *cross,* the wonder of the universe, the only hope of a ruined world. This ground has been enriched with the blood of innumerable martyrs, and is the repository of unnumbered bodies, which are to be revived in the form of the Savior's glorious body. This is the spot, from which burst forth that heavenly light, that is to illumine every corner of the earth, and guide to glory all the elect of the Messiah.

But though all these associations may awaken curious inquiry, and inspire the imagination, yet the heart of piety will be more deeply affected by considering the character and condition of the people, who dwell in this land.

II. Judea is inhabited by several interesting classes of men. The principal of these are Mahommedans, and Jews; and Roman Catholic, Greek, Armenian and Syrian Christians.

The Mahommedans, who are masters of the country, who possess most of its wealth, and who have the exclusive management of political concerns, are, as you well know, the followers of that artful impostor, who arose in Arabia, about the commencement of the seventh century. Their religion was first propagated, and is still defended, by the sword. Cruelty and blood are among its most prominent characteristics. Mahommedan piety consists very much in fasts, ablutions, pilgrimages to Mecca, and the persecution of infidels and heretics. Mahommedans believe that Moses and Jesus were true prophets; that Jesus was the greatest of prophets except Mahommed; that the Pentateuch, the Psalms, the Prophets, and the Gospels were revelations from God, but have been so much corrupted by Jews and Christians, as to deserve but little credit. They assert the unity of God, the immortality of the soul, and future rewards and punishments. They have, indeed, much of truth in their system: but their customs, established by the usage of centuries, the despotic nature of their government, the prominent articles of their faith, and the very genius and spirit of their religion, shield the Mahommedans almost impenetrably from the influence of Christianity. To make spiritual conquests from them will require the most vigorous efforts of the Christian church. Let the Gospel prevail among them, and some of the strongest fortresses of error and sin will be taken. . . .

All the inhabitants of the country believe in one God, and the leading facts recorded in the Old Testament. Here are no gods of brass or wood; no temples to Juggernaut, or the Grand Lama; no funeral piles; no altars stained with the blood of human victims. Every where you see a faint glimmering of light, through the gross and almost impenetrable darkness.

Nor are the inhabitants of this region sunk in such entire stupidity and such brutal ignorance, as are the Hindoos of India, and the Hottentots of Africa. Here is intellect, enterprise, and some degree of literature and science. Here several classes of men are among the most interesting that dwell on the earth, and are worthy of the prayers and the attentions of all those, who desire to see influence, learning, talent, and strength of character consecrated to Christ.

2.

THE EARLY missionaries to Palestine kept a journal which was published serially in the American Board's periodical, *The Missionary*

Herald. In this typical entry concerning their first visit to Bethlehem, Pliny Fisk and his colleague Jonas King reveal something of the religious meaning that their experiences in and around the place of Jesus' birth had for them.

Reference: The Missionary Herald, XX (1824), p. 67.

Visit to Bethlehem
[April 30, 1823]

The next day they visited Bethlehem. The journal continues;—

We went out at Jaffa Gate, crossed the valley west of Mount Zion, ascended a steep rough hill, and then came to a tolerably level road, leading S.S.W. In an hour and a quarter, we came to the Greek convent of the prophet Elias. Thence the road to Bethlehem is a little nearer south. In half an hour from the convent we came to Rachel's tomb; or, at least, to the place which Jews, Mussulmans and Christians, all visit as such. Instead of a simple pillar, which Jacob erected, (See Gen. 55:20.) there is now a stone building, evidently of Turkish construction, which terminates at the top, in a dome. Within this edifice is the tomb. It is a pile of stones covered with white plaister, about 10 feet long, and nearly as high. The inner wall of the building, and the sides of the tomb, are covered with Hebrew names, inscribed by Jews.

West of this place, at a little distance, is a village, now called Ephratah, which has been called by some, Rama. If this were one of the ancient Ramas, it would be easy to see the force of that glowing description of the scene which transpired at Bethlehem, when Herod sent, and destroyed the young children. The lamentations and wailings of bereaved mothers were so great, that they were heard even in Rama, and Rachel sympathized with them, and wept in her grave.

In half an hour from this tomb, we came to the city, where was born, 1800 years ago, "a Savior who is Christ the Lord," where "the day spring from on high" first visited our world, where the Savior incarnate was first adored by man. As we entered the city, a multitude of little children, dirty and ragged, came out to meet us, and, holding up their little hands to receive alms, they began to sing, "Pilgrims go in peace," "Pilgrims go in peace." The Greek, Catholic and Armenian convents are together, a little east of the village, and encloses the supposed place of our Savior's Nativity.

Here they were introduced by a letter from the Greek convent at Jerusalem. Having passed through the church, they were conducted to the spot, sacred as the birth-place of our Lord, and to the manger, in which he is said to have been laid. A great number of lamps were burning over these venerated places, and the whole wore an appearance of splendor, widely different from that of a stable.

The field of the Shepherds.

From this place a Greek priest accompanied us to the Shepherd's field. It is twenty minutes ride from Bethlehem, a little south of east. The way to it is rough and stony. Bethlehem itself is on a hill, which seems like a pile of rocks, with here and there a patch of verdure. Between the rocks, however, where it is cultivated, vines, figs and olives appear to grow in luxuriance. On our right as we descended the hill, was a little mean looking village, in which it is believed that the Shepherds lived.

We rode along among the rocks and cliffs, reflecting how David here once tended his flocks, and learned to sing the praises of Jehovah; and how the Prophet Samuel came to anoint him king, and how the Son of David here made his appearance in our world;—when, all at once, a delightful valley, covered with green fields, opened to our view. Its beauty was heightened by the barren rocky hills all around it. As we entered it and rode along, it was delightful to imagine how a multitude of the Heavenly Host, came flying down from heaven upon the tops of the mountains, and, hovering over this verdant spot, where the flocks were resting, sung, "Glory to God in the highest, and on earth peace, good will towards men." Near one side of the plain is a field of olives, enclosed by a wall, with a subterranean Church in the centre of it. This is pointed out as the very spot where the Shepherds were, when the angel announced to them our Savior's birth. Our guide told us that the Greeks and Catholics had a long dispute about the possession of this place. The case was carried before the Grand Signore, and the Greeks, by dint of money, gained their cause. In this church the Christian Arabs now assemble for worship. Over this church, are the ruins of another church, and of a convent, which stood above ground. Under an olive tree near by, we sat down, and read Luke 2d: sung, "While Shepherds watched their flocks by night," and Hymn 3d, book 1st, and then united in giving thanks to the God of heaven, for the glad tidings which were here announced, and which had come to our ears in a far distant land, and to the ears of our dear christian friends, who were also at this time remembered by us. After this season of devotion we gathered some flowers in the field, and returned to Bethlehem. Many maps and geographies place Bethlehem south-east of Jerusalem. It is in fact west of south.

3.

CLORINDA Minor (1808–1855) was at first a devotee of William Miller, who preached that time would end in 1843. Disappointed with the failure of Miller's prognostication, she turned to Seventh-Day Adventism. She then became obsessed by the conviction that Christians should go to the Land of Israel to help prepare for the Jews' return. Leading the first known group of American colonists to the Holy Land, in 1851, Mrs. Minor established "Mount Hope Colony" in the "Plains of Sharon, three miles north of Jaffa." She remained dedicated to the development of a productive economy in the Holy Land, a commitment which created an affinity of approach with Isaac Leeser.

Reference: Clorinda Minor, "Letter from Palestine," *The Occident, and American Jewish Advocate,* XII (July 1854), pp. 200–206.

LETTER FROM PALESTINE

PLAINS OF SHARON, three miles north of Jaffa, April 4, 1854.

TO THE EDITOR OF THE OCCIDENT:

Dear Sir—I have to-day had the pleasure of receiving the February number of the Occident, and have perused the article on Palestine, with an interest more heartfelt than I can here express. A rainy day keeps my attached young Hebrew learners and myself from the gardens, and I improve the moment, to send a hasty reply to two points expressed in the following sentence; it is a misunderstanding as it regards ourselves, or the chief Rabbins here, with whom we are acquainted. The sentence is this: "It may be difficult to persuade the Elders in Palestine to look with any favor on missionaries, of whatever kind, no less than to induce these to do nothing but giving material aid, without attempting to *preach* their doctrines on every fitting opportunity."

First, with regard to the Elders here. After we were forcibly driven from our favorable site and newly-erected house in Artas, by the unprovoked and unjust persecutions of the English Consul and *his friends* in Jerusalem, and were waiting in that city until we could complete arrangements to remove to this vicinity, several Elders and the chief Rabbi and President of the German Jews visited us repeatedly, and assured us of their perfect knowledge of our course and affairs, and of their approbation of the same, and earnestly requested to be connected in effort with us, and that they would furnish any amount of laborers, so soon as we should be prepared to receive them; that they would engage to do something toward sustaining them, and replace any of whom we should disapprove with better men; that they had reason to hope for assistance from their friends abroad, if they were really at *work* under our protection. We accordingly engaged an intelligent member of their congregation, who came down with us, in company with another Jew and his family. We hear by our employed Jews frequently that they are still waiting for our enlargement. We meanwhile have continued here on a small scale, with most flattering success. . . .

. . . Like yourself, we do not think so meanly of the piety or intellect of the Jews here, as to suppose that they are acting blindly and unwisely toward us, without any regard to the security of their conscientious faith in God. No; they have seen our sufferings and sacrifice for this object; they *know* that we are not as missionaries, or persons sent and supported by others, that we do not labor for *hire*. Their old and their young men have been daily with us, and they have in all things enjoyed the same liberty of conscience as we would righteously claim from others for ourselves,—in obedience to the commands of which conscience, enlightened by the promises of God to Israel and quickened by his indwelling spirit, we are here—to labor, to suffer, and, after spending our all, if God will, to perish, in the attempt to rouse an ease and profit-seeking world to emancipate from worse than American slavery the half-covered, starving, imprisoned, spirit-crushed Hebrew captives of Palestine. I speak what I know, what I daily see and hear, and on which account my heart unceasingly cries to the God of Abraham, of Isaac, and of Jacob. . . .

. . . You are doubtless aware that it is strictly an individual and providential effort, originating with a few pious friends and myself in Philadelphia. Some ten years since, through the devout study of Hebrew Scriptures, we became convinced that the appointed time of the Gentiles' treading down the Sanctuary and the Host of Israel, spoken of in Daniel viii. 13, 14, was accomplished—that the times of the Gentiles were expiring, and the set time to favor Zion had come. We saw the multitudinous divisions, sects, and parties, among Jews and Gentiles, and the wide and general departure of most men from the holy teachings of the Law and the Gospel; and we read with hope and faith the promises of God to gather and restore and purify Israel, and that in the seed of Abraham all the nations of the earth should be blessed. We saw, according to Ezekiel xxxiv, and xxxvi., that God himself must do this work, and lost all confidence in human ability—Jew or Gentile—to accomplish. We saw, by Ezekiel xxxvi., that God would first turn to the desolate *land*—it should be tilled and sown, and yield food for his people, in preparation for their being "at hand to come." Afterward (verses 24–26) the Lord himself will gather them, and *"then"* sprinkle and change and reform their great departure from his will; and then (35th verse) the land that was desolate becomes like the garden of Eden. . . .

Before I close, I must not forget to mention that the state of the country is still so uncivilized and unsettled, and the Jews have been so long oppressed, that, unless they are known to be in connection with us, or under some special foreign protection, they are liable to insult in their new occupation in the country. It is, therefore, a present necessity that others should co-operate with them, for their safety, and the success of this enterprise. The rains the past winter have been regular, seasonable, and abundant, and the present season and harvest promise to be the most fruitful enjoyed here in many years, according to the testimony of old Arab farmers. Our winter grains and vegetables are very fine, and the latter rain has been falling freely the last five days. The extensive wheat and barley flats present a lovely scene of waving verdure. The orange, lemon, apricot, almond, peach, and apple trees, in the extensive Bianahs [sic] near our house, are in bloom, and the air is filled with their delicious perfume. The climate is delightful, and in our vicinity we have the constant and invigorating sea-breeze. We enjoy excellent health, with a few exceptions, from our constant exposure and open rooms, in winter, and the universal fruit diet of summer, both of which an improved state of things would remedy. We are truly attached to the young men now with us; they are active and ambitious to learn, and express toward us the most grateful affection. We desire to prepare them for teachers of labor and business. This week our sisters are preparing their new clothes for the Passover, and presents for their friends in Jerusalem. They will take with them, also, a camel-load of vegetables, for themselves and their poor friends. They leave us next week and will return after ten days. They express much anxiety lest, in this busy season, we shall need them. They are truly happy. I must close.

Dear sir, believe me, as ever, the humble and devoted friend of Israel.

C. S. MINOR.

4.

MANY American Christians have written books about their travels in the Holy Land; the most popular of them, one that sold nearly 200,000 copies, was by a member of the Syrian mission of the American Board of Commissioners for Foreign Missions, Dr. W. M. Thomson. Something of the flavor of his massive two-volume work comes through in this account of his visit to Nazareth in 1857.

Reference: W. M. Thomson, *The Land and the Book; or, Biblical Illustrations Drawn from the Manners and Customs, the Scenes and Scenery of The Holy Land* (New York: Harper & Bros., 1859), vol. 2, pp. 129–32.

March 29th

"CAN there any good thing come out of Nazareth? Come and see," as Philip said to Nathaniel.

Why not? It appeared really charming last night as we came down the mountain from the northeast with the grateful shadows of evening falling softly around it. The vale is small certainly, but then the different *swellings* of the surrounding hills give the idea of repose and protection; and, for my part, I would infinitely prefer to have the home of Mary and her divine Son in such a quiet seclusion, than to be obliged to force my way to it through the dust, and confusion, and hard worldliness of any crowded city.

I most emphatically accord with that opinion, or rather *feeling;* and there is a sort of latent beauty and appropriateness in the arrangement by which He who made all *things out of nothing* should himself come forth to the world *out of a place that had no history.* The idea here tempts one to linger upon it and expatiate, but this would throw us quite off our present track, which is to go "round about" and describe this city of Nazareth and her neighbors.

It is certainly remarkable that this place, dearest to the Christian heart of all on earth except Jerusalem, is not mentioned in the Old Testament, nor even by Josephus, who was himself on every side of it, and names the villages all about it, but seems yet totally ignorant of its existence. It was probably a very small hamlet, hid away in this narrow vale, and of no political importance whatever. And, so far as its subsequent history can be gathered from Eusebius, Jerome, and other ancient records, it never rose to distinction until the time of the Crusades. It was then made the seat of a bishopric, but long after this it was an insignificant village, and remained such through many a dark age of lawless violence. Within the last hundred years, however, it has gradually grown in size and risen into importance, until it has become the chief town of this district. It is now larger and more prosperous than in any former period in its history, and is still enlarging. The present population must exceed three thousand, but it can never become a great city. The position is not favorable, and there is a distressing want of water. Even at this early season there is an incessant contest for a jar of it around this fountain of the "Annunciation," which is the only one in the village. The present growth of Nazareth is mainly owing to the unchecked inroads of the Arabs from beyond Jordan, which has rendered it unsafe to reside in Beisan and on the great plain of Esdraelon. Most of the villages have been recently deserted, and this work of destruction is still going on; and the villagers from the plains are here in Nazareth, at Jennin, and still farther in toward the sea-board. Should a strong government again drive these Arabs over the Jordan, the population and importance of Nazareth would decline at once. It must, however, always be a spot sacred to the whole Christian world, for here our blessed Saviour passed the greater part of his life while on earth. But what a profound silence rests upon those thirty years of mysterious existence! We only know that here the child Jesus grew up from infancy to childhood and youth, increasing in stature as other children do, and in knowledge, and in favor both with God and man, as none ever have done. Here, too, he spent the years of his ripening manhood in humble labors and in sinless communion with God. How natural the desire to lift the veil that shrouds all this period in impenetrable darkness! Hence the spurious gospel of the "Infancy of Christ," stuffed with puerile or profane fables.

Let any one, curious to see what weak, uninspired man makes of the history of Jesus, turn to the First and Second Gospels of the Infancy, or the "Gospel according to Nicodemus," and he will be devoutly thankful to know that they are miserable forgeries, so foolish that they are rejected by all; and, so far from desiring to have the veil which covers the early life of the incomprehensible God-man lifted, he will adore the wisdom and the kindness that has thus concealed what we could not rightly appreciate nor even understand. Infinite wisdom decided that it was not well to encourage such inquiries, and has taken effectual care that they should never be answered. *There remains not one acknowledged anecdote of his life during all these years.* And, farther, I am most happy to believe that there is not a fragment of the ancient Nazareth itself which can be identified. It is nearly certain that every stone of the small hamlet where the Saviour of the world spent so many years has long ago dissolved back into the white marl of the hills from which it was quarried. This kind of rock disintegrates with great rapidity, and, as the place was often almost or quite destroyed and forsaken, the soft stones thus exposed would not last fifty years.

Well, thus I would have it. I like to feel assured that the *church* of annunciation, the *cave,* the *kitchen* of Mary, the *work-shop* of Joseph, the *dining-table* of our Lord and his apostles, the *synagogue* where he read the Prophet Isaiah, and the *precipice* down which his enraged fellow-villagers were determined to cast him headlong, *as now shown,* are all fabulous, aprocryphal, and have no claims to my veneration or even respect. The eye rests on nothing with which our Lord was familiar except his own glorious works. These remain the same. This narrow vale, on the side of which the village is built, climbing up the steep mountain back of it, is very much now what it was then. To this fountain the young Jesus came for water just as these fine healthy children now do with their "pitchers." Shut in on all sides by *fourteen* swelling eminences on the circling mountains, as Dr. Richardson counts them, Nazareth must have been always, as at present, very hot, particularly in the early part of the day. It was also wanting in prospects and distant views. Hence, no doubt, our Saviour would often climb to the top of this western hill, which rises at least five hundred feet above the bottom of the wady. There he could behold the distant sea, and breathe its fresh breeze. From thence, too, his eye would rove delighted over a vast expanse of sacred scenery. We can do the same, and in the doing of it hold converse with his spirit, and enjoy what he enjoyed, without one doubt to trouble, or one fable of meddling monk to disturb. Let this suffice. God does not admit impertinent curiosity behind the veil of his own privacy. . . .

5.

AMONG the Americans to travel in the Holy Land have been many prominent clergymen and scholars. One of the most famous of such visitors was Dr. Philip Schaff, a church historian and professor of biblical learning at Union Theological Seminary in New York. Like so many visitors before him, he spent considerable time in and around Jerusalem and reported on the religious situation he found there.

Reference: Philip Schaff, *Through Bible Lands: Notes of Travel in Egypt, the Desert, and Palestine,* (London: James Nisbet & Co., 1878?, pp. 240–52.)

EASTER FESTIVITIES

I witnessed in the Church of the Holy Sepulchre the solemnities of the Latin and Greek Easter festivals, which in 1877 were divided by one week, the former falling on April 1, the latter on April 8. I saw none of the disgraceful fights between the rival communions which are said sometimes to dishonor the Christian name on the very spot of the Crucifixion, and to call for the intervention of the

Mohammedan soldiers who are present in large force and look on with stolid indifference and sovereign contempt.

I cannot say that I have been favorably impressed. I would gladly recognize piety and devotion to Christ even under the crude and distorted forms of superstition. But I could not restrain the feeling that this is not the worship "in spirit and in truth" which our Saviour demands. In point of taste and art the solemnities of the holy week are far inferior to those of St. Peter's in Rome, and not to be compared with the Passion play at Ober-Ammergau, which I witnessed in 1871. The singing is miserable, and the only good music I heard in Jerusalem was in the Russian church and in the Protestant service. The Orientals seem to have no idea of music. The crowd in the Church of the Holy Sepulchre is almost crushing during the services. I saw a wooden Christ carried about and embalmed, on the Latin Good Friday, and heard seven sermons, good, bad, and indifferent, in as many languages. I saw the feet-washing on Greek Maundy Thursday, and the wild struggle of the people for the branches of the olive-tree, which are thrown among them at the close of the ceremony. I witnessed, on the Greek Easter eve, the scandalous fraud of the Holy Fire, and the tumultuous eagerness with which the superstitious people light their tapers at the sacred flame—said to be miraculously sent from heaven, but in fact kindled by the priests within the chapel of the Holy Sepulchre. It seems to have been originally a symbolical representation of the light of the Resurrection or the pentecostal fire. On Good Friday all the lamps were extinguished; on Easter they were relighted. But in the course of time the innocent symbol was turned into a lying miracle to feed the superstition of the ignorant people and to fill the pockets of the priests. The Latins, who formerly shared in it, now denounce it without mercy. Even the Armenian patriarch is said to have preached against this pious humbug, and yet he countenances it in practice together with the orthodox Greeks.

Before I left for the East, Dean Stanley, with his characteristic broad church charity, told me that he found it very beautiful to see the various Christian sects uniting in the worship of Christ under the same roof. But Protestants are excluded, and the old sects hate each other more than they do the Protestants. The jealousy and rivalry between the Greeks and Latins, though it may not break out openly, is as great as ever, and is one of the saddest aspects of Eastern Christianity.

The Old Churches

The Greek Church is the strongest in Jerusalem as to number, wealth, and influence, and is backed by the power of Russia. Its native members are Arabs, and speak Arabic; its clergy are mostly foreigners from the Greek islands, and speak modern Greek. It owns several monasteries. The "Great Greek Monastery," or Patriarcheion, near the Church of the Holy Sepulchre, is the residence of the patriarch, and has a valuable library. The "Monastery of St. John the Baptist" can accommodate five hundred pilgrims at Easter. A rich Greek priest built a beautiful summerhouse on the road to Jaffa, with a garden abounding in trees and flowers.

The Russians erected, from 1860 to 1864, several imposing and conspicuous buildings on an eminence west of the Jaffa gate. They consist of a consular residence, two hospices, one for men, one for women, and a beautiful church. The orthodox Church of Russia is undoubtedly the most vital and hopeful part of the Oriental Church, but is regarded with some jealousy by the Greeks..

The Latin communion, though smaller, is more active and derives its chief support from France and Italy. It is governed by a rival patriarch. It numbers several convents (called the *Terra Santa* convents), schools, and charitable institutions. The Casa Nuova of the Franciscans is a commodious and exceptionally clean hospice near the Jaffa Gate, and affords accommodation to travellers for a very reasonable sum (five francs a day, while the hotels charge twelve francs or more). Protestants are freely admitted as well as Catholics, and find hospitable treatment.

Both the Greek and Latin churches have been lately stirred up to new zeal by the educational labors of the Protestants.

The Oriental Schismatics are likewise represented in Jerusalem. The Armenians have a fine church, dedicated to St. James, a convent, and a hospice, near Mount Zion, and look intelligent and prosperous. Their spiritual ruler is called Patriarch of Jerusalem. The Copts and Abyssinians are poor and insignificant.

The Protestant Institutions.

The Protestants form the smallest of the Christian communities, but are growing in influence, and seem to be respected by the Mohammedans, who abhor the other Christians as idolaters.

The Church of England and the Evangelical Church of Prussia have been at work here for the last thirty or forty years. They are aided by the Chrischona Institute of Basle and the Deaconnesses' Institute at Kaiserwerth. There are now three Protestant congregations in Jerusalem, an English, a German, and a native Arab, all in nominal connection with the bishopric of St. James; but the English congregation, which consists mostly of Jewish proselytes, is under the direction of the London Jewish Missionary Society, the Arab congregation under the care of the English Church Missionary Society, and the German congregation under the care of the Prussian Oberkirchenrath. . . .

I cannot conclude without directing attention to the fact that America, which has done so much for the exploration of Palestine through Dr. Robinson and others, has done little for reviving primitive Christianity in this city, from which we received the greatest blessings. While the American Presbyterians have flourishing missions in Syria, and the Congregationalists in Turkey, there is not a single American mission church or mission school in all Palestine. It would indeed be wrong for any denomination to interfere with the good work of the Anglican Church, the Evangelical Church of Prussia, the Chrischona of Basle and the Deaconesses of Kaiserswerth. But the usefulness of their churches and schools already established might be largely increased by the aid and cooperation of American contributions and laborers.

The Jews

A word about the Jews. They have four holy cities in Palestine: Jerusalem, Safed, Tiberias, and Hebron. They still look forward to the restoration of their race and country. Their number in Jerusalem is growing rapidly and amounts fully to one third of the whole population. They are divided into three sects—the *Sephardim,* of Spanish and Portuguese origin, the *Askenazim,* from Germany, Hungary, Poland, and Russia, and a small number of *Karaites,* who adhere strictly to the letter of the written law and discard the rabbinical traditions. There are no reform Jews or rationalists in Jerusalem. They are all orthodox but mostly poor and dependent on the charity of their brethren in Europe. Many come to be buried on holy ground, and outside of the Eastern wall on the slopes of the valley of the Kedron, which are covered with tombstones. The Jewish quarter is squalid and forbidding. It ought to be burned down and built anew. The Polish Jews look dirty and shabby, and wear curls, which give them an effeminate appearance. The Hebrew language is used in Jerusalem as a conversational language, and there only. The Spanish and Portuguese Jews, whose ancestors emigrated after their expulsion from Spain under Isabella I (1497), still speak a Spanish patois. The German, Austrian, Polish, and Russian Jews speak a corrupt German. Baron Rothschild and Sir Moses Montefiore have done much for them by building hospitals and lodginghouses. They ought to buy Palestine and administer it on principles of civil and religious liberty.

Every traveller ought to visit the "Wailing Place of the Jews" at the cyclopean foundation wall of the temple, just outside the enclosure of the mosque El Aska and near "Robinson's Arch." There the Jews assemble every Friday afternoon and on festivals to bewail the downfall of the holy city. I saw on Good Friday a large number, old and young, male and female, venerable rabbis with patriarchal beards and young men kissing the stone wall and watering it with their tears. They repeat from their well-worn Hebrew Bibles and Prayer-books, the Lamentations of Jeremiah and suitable Psalms (the 76th and 79th). "O God, the heathen are come into thine inheritance; thy holy temple have they defiled; they have laid Jerusalem on heaps. . . . We are become a reproach to our neighbors, a scorn and derision to them that are round about us." . . .

The keynote of all these laments and prayers was struck by Jeremiah, the most pathetic and tender-hearted of prophets, in the Lamentations—that funeral dirge of Jerusalem and the theocracy. This elegy written with sighs and tears, has done its work most effectually in great public calamities, and is doing it every year on the ninth of the month of Ab (July), when it is read with loud weeping in all the synagogues of the Jews, and especially at Jerusalem. It keeps alive the memory of their deepest humiliation and guilt, and the hope of final deliverance. The scene at the Wailing Place was to me touching and pregnant with meaning. God has no doubt reserved this remarkable people, which, like the burning bush, is never consumed, for some great purpose before the final coming of our Lord.

6–7.

MUCH discussion concerning the Holy Land in the twentieth century has focused on the Zionist movement. Zionism evoked many and varied responses from Christians; some were opposed to the movement, others were neutral or indifferent, while considerable support for the Zionist cause came from certain Christian sources. There were many variations in this last group; two quite different positions underlie the following excerpts. The first, by a Fundamentalist Baptist pastor, I. M. Haldeman, a dispensationalist who expected the imminent return of Christ, welcomes Zionism as a sign of that return—and of the final conversion of the Jewish remnant. The second, by a liberal Congregationalist minister, A. A. Berle, welcomes Zionism and the prospective Jewish state for what it could do for Jews, for Christianity, and for the world.

Reference: I. M. Haldeman, *The Signs of the Times,* 5th ed. (New York: Charles C. Cook, 1914), pp. 450–55.

The cities have been waiting for their inhabitants.

The houses are ready to resound to the voices of men and women, to the songs of bride and bridegroom, and the laughter of children.

The streets, with here and there a gleam of paving stone, look up through moss and lichen, ready to welcome the rhythmic tread of the hurrying multitude.

The Word of God declares that before the final and distinctive restoration, great numbers of the Jews will return, go back as colonists, as speculators, and that land shall be bought and sold at the gates of Jerusalem.

That prophecy is being fulfilled to-day.

There are more Jews in Palestine than at any time since our Lord was crucified. Land is being bought and sold on speculation at the very doors of the city. Colonists have taken up land in the old, historic places, and are farming, by means of modern machinery, with satisfying success.

The climacteric sign of the restoration is with us to-day.

That sign is the organized movement known as—Zionism.

Zionism is a movement on the part of the Jews throughout the world to go back to Palestine and reconstitute themselves as a nation, rebuilding Jerusalem, erecting the temple, and restoring the faith of the fathers. The movement is no longer detached, or merely sentimental. It is organized, corporate and universal. Branches, committees and headquarters are established all over the earth. It has its literature and an oral advocacy. Men are writing and speaking in its behalf. Children are taught to repeat the word Zion as never before, and to set their faces thitherward. Moneys are raised, colonies are sent out, established and sustained. Multitudes of Jews among all nations, peoples, kindreds and tongues, are mentally asking their way to Zion and are setting their faces "thitherward."

It is a movement that can neither be denied nor ignored.

It is making itself known with increasing volume of assertion and assurance.

Blind, utterly blind, even to the word of the prophets, blind to the full meaning of the movement itself, impulsed by natural and selfish motives, whether national or individual, there are thousands of Jews to-day who, in attitude if not in actual fact, are homeward bound, and are repeating softly to themselves the magic word, "Zion."

The recent revolution in Turkey has accelerated the movement. The ban upon the Jew has been removed. He is now invited to become a citizen. The doors of the Turkish Parliament stand open, the day of Jewish citizenship in their own land is made possible. Already, representative and wealthy Jews may be found standing in the shadow of the Sublime Porte. Jewish synagogues are planned for the hill of Zion. By day and by night there are here and there devout Jews who are studying the plans of the temple laid down by the prophet Ezekiel, plans so wonderful that Sir Inigo Jones, the great English architect, has said that if the temple were really built along its lines it would, indeed, fill the whole earth with its glory—putting to shame the half-remembered splendors of ancient times.

Zion and Zionism are in the air.

All these things are verifications of the Word of God. Every accent is a witness that God speaketh the truth and that his Word is settled in heaven forever.

But this Zionist movement is a witness that the Coming of the Lord to rule and reign as king is not far away. Holy Scripture teaches in plain and unmistakable language that the Jews are to return to their own land, as many are doing now, in a state of unbelief and atheistic godlessness. The scriptures testify that the nations of Europe, and some in Asia, will be unified under a great and final head, known in Holy Writ as the Antichrist, the Man of sin and the Beast, but hailed in the political world as the Coming Man, the arbiter of nations, the maker and keeper of peace, the world's accepted king of kings and prince of peace. The scriptures teach that this man will be the prime factor in bringing the Jews back, as a body, into their own land; that he will be the power that shall make Zionism a success; that through him the nationalism of the Jews shall be accomplished. He will make treaties with them, sustain them, be to them as though he were the very Messiah, the Christ, receiving from them support and acclamation. At the last he shall trample all his treaties with them under foot, rob them, spoil them, and put them into a furnace blast of persecution unparalleled by anything that has gone before; a time of tribulation, a tribulation which our Lord defines as "the tribulation, the great one," and concerning which he says, the like of it has never been before, nor ever can be again; a stress and durance spoken of by Jeremiah specifically as the time of "Jacob's Trouble"; a sorrow and horror, and down sweep of pain and tragedy so great that, unless the Lord, we are told, should shorten the trial, no flesh could live, actually could exist.

This man, the world's great Coming Man, the pre-eminent persecutor of the Jews, will fill Jerusalem with anguish, enthrone himself on the necks of the Jews, direct his hatred and wickedness with unlimited vengeance, particularly against the remnant of Jews who shall, under the faithful preaching of divinely sent messengers, turn their faces toward the true Messiah of Israel, and beseech him to appear unto them. It is in the midst of this woe, and in answer to the despairing cry of the remnant, that the Lord will descend from heaven in the panoply of his power and glory; then it is that repentant and sore-smitten Judah shall turn to him and own their crucified Lord at last.

This Zionistic movement, its antecedents and accessories, are clear evidence that the *time* of Jacob's sorrow and the *hour* of the Lord's appearing are drawing nigh.

But the Zionist movement is, in itself, the quickening and warning sign of a more immediate event.

It is a sign that the secret rapture of the church is, indeed, imminent. Scripture teaches, and teaches it in figure, in type, in symbol, parable, and open statement, that before the Lord appears in glory to end Gentile rule, and bring in the rule of Israel according to the Abrahamic covenant, he will come secretly, without warning, into the air (He will come into the air and halt there, before he comes down to the Mount of Olives), and with a shout, with the voice of the archangel, and the trump of God, snatch his church (the dead raised, the living changed) out of the world, and from the way of the coming woe, and gather her to himself as the bridegroom receives his long awaited bride.

By so much, then, as the Zionist movement is a climacteric sign and witness in these times that the day of the Lord is at hand, by just so much it is a witness that "at any moment" the "door in heaven" may be opened, the Lord may speak, and all those who own his name be bidden to rise and meet him, see him face to face, and share his glory.

This is the deeper meaning of Zionism.

Every footstep Zionward, every face set "thitherward," every accent and song that repeats the name of Zion, should be a warning and an exhortation to the church, to the individual Christian, to watch, to wait and, with uplifted foot on the threshold of any circumstance, be ready, as though the Master had already said, "Come up hither."

"For ye know neither the day nor the hour wherein the Son of man cometh."—Matthew 25:13.

Reference: A. A. Berle, *The World Significance of a Jewish State* (New York: Mitchell Kennerley, 1918), pp. 13–17.

We may, for the present, leave to the Zionists, and the Jews as a whole, the discussion of what the erection of such a state may or may not mean to them. But there is another significance to the foundation of such a state, which interests the rest of the world, and in some respects hardly less than the Jews themselves. Would it mean anything, or nothing in particular, to the rest of the world, to have a Jewish social state called into being in Palestine? Would it be, to the rest of the world, just one more "small state" to dicker about, in the councils of the great powers? Would it be just the realization of the dream of a few Jewish enthusiasts and fanatics, to be looked at with kindly tolerance of patronizing friendly interest? It is likely that the vast body of Christians have never thought about this matter at all, considering it purely visionary, and entirely outside the bounds of practical discussion. But, supposing it did come within the sphere of practical disposition,—and the present writer believes that it has,—then what is the significance to the non-Jewish world of such a state, and what would its establishment mean to Christianity and Christian ideas and ideals? These are questions which have for the Gentile world both a political, sentimental, and religious significance. If such a state is established, it will be a unique commonwealth—one which admits of political possibilities far beyond anything of which the world has hitherto dreamed, and which may become the political instructor of the entire world. It will be socialized by its very constitution to a degree which would not be possible in any other state. The world will not be able to ignore the results which must ultimately flow from this community, if it develops normally and according to natural expectation. Then again, it will be in custody and control of the land and places out of which the entire Christian religion has emerged. It can hardly fail to have at least a deep sentimental interest to the Christian world that this is the case. The entire Christian church, in its variety of branches, as it teaches its own history and origins, will be compelled, side by side with this instruction, to teach the history and development of the nascent Jewish state. No commonwealth on earth will start with such a propaganda for its exploitation in world thought, or with such eager and minute scrutiny, by millions of people, of its slightest detail. The value of this to such a state can only be conjectured. But that it will give impetus to it, that it will aid it and upbuild it, goes without saying. Think what it would mean to any enterprise to have millions of Sunday-school children studying about it every Sunday in the year! To have its ideas and ideals expounded in thousands of Christian pulpits, to have its aims and practices discussed from a thousand different angles! Think of the possibilities of religious instruction contained in such an opportunity! If this House of Israel is reestablished in Palestine again, it will begin with an opportunity of world instruction in the religion of Israel which has never been vouchsafed to any other cult in the history of mankind! One of the very first and important results of all this will be, that the religion of Israel will be understood—and what may not that mean both for Israel and for Christendom—and therein lies a possibility of modification of the religion of the whole world! If no single other result were to be looked for, this itself would be a sufficient reason for the enlistment of all Christendom in the work of securing Palestine for the Jews, and the building up therein, on a secure foundation, a Jewish state.

8.

Reference: One Hundred Twentieth Annual Conference of the Church of Jesus Christ of Latter-Day Saints (Salt Lake City, 1950) pp. 71-79.

EZRA Taft Benson (1889-), elder in the Mormon Church, was secretary of agriculture in the Eisenhower administration. His address delivered at the 120th Annual General Conference (April 8, 1950), after the establishment of the State of Israel, is based on reports from members of the church who visited Israel. Speaking in Mormon idiom, he directs himself to all Christians in describing the unfolding miraculous drama in the Holy Land, recapitulating the historic position of the Mormon Church toward Jewish Restoration.

THE JEWS RETURN AND FULFILL PROPHECY

. . . *A Miraculous Drama*

I should like to speak with reference to a rather miraculous drama that is taking place today before our very eyes. In large measure it is unobserved, particularly by spiritual leaders, and yet it has been predicted by prophets anciently thousands of years ago, and in modern times has been referred to frequently by Latter-day prophets during the past one hundred and twenty years. . . .

This great event of which I speak is one of the signs of the times, and is very important, it seems to me, particularly to all Christian people. It is transpiring in a small strip of country about one hundred and ten miles long and fifty to sixty miles wide, in an area about the size of the state of Vermont. . . .

The number of Jews has multiplied in recent years in this area, in a rather remarkable manner. Plans are underway for the incorporation of about a million and a half more during the immediate months ahead, and projected plans call for an eventual population of some four million in this small area. . . .

The Jewish Problem

While in Europe in 1946, when mention was frequently made in the European papers of the Jewish problem, I received a comment from one of our great industrial leaders in this country who is a student of this particular problem, in which he said the only salvation the Jew has is to be as good a citizen as he possibly can of whatever country he is a resident.

Then later, one of our prominent business leaders quoting a high church authority whose church numbers into many millions in the South American countries, stated that the Jewish people would do their cause much more good if they attempted to move their people from places where they are not wanted to places where they are wanted, for example, South America, where there is ample room.

As Latter-day Saints, familiar with the ancient and modern prophecies, we of course do not agree that some other more suitable place should be and will be found for the descendants of Judah. We believe in the over-ruling power of Providence in the affairs of men and nations. We believe that the Old Testament prophets clearly predicted the dispersion and scattering of Israel and the eventual gathering of Judah in the land given to their fathers. . . .

. . . *Lack of Wisdom*

. . . In 1949, about a year ago, the *United States News and World Report* commented on the miscalculations of government officials and military experts with reference to the outcome of the struggle then being waged in Palestine, and reported that the "prophecies of the military experts, in particular have had to be revised." Then it continued by outlining the predictions of military authorities in our own country and in Great Britain particularly, to the effect that it was only a matter of a very brief time until the Jews would be overcome and be wiped out and "the Arabs would win quick control of Palestine. Now," the article continues "these official but private forecasters are in a state of confusion," and the "U.S. and Britain, as a result have to adjust their diplomacy, their military strategy to this fact of a strong Israel in the midst of Arab weakness."

It seems as though this probably is one more evidence of the fact that the wisdom of the wise shall perish. The prophecies of economists, would-be statesmen and military experts fail, while those of the Lord through his prophets are vindicated.

An interesting sidelight on this recent development is the fact that most of the descendants of Judah who have assembled in Palestine seem to look upon the events of the last few months as being nothing short of miraculous. It is a common comment among them that victory, in their eyes at least, was a miracle which cannot be explained in purely military terms. Some of our recently returned missionaries from Europe who have visited that land bring back the same report. . . .

Dedication of Palestine

As Latter-day Saints, from the very inception of this latter-day work, we have had a deep interest in this group of our Father's children, the descendants of Judah. One hundred and ten years ago, at this very conference, two of the elders of the Church, Elders Orson Hyde and John E. Page, were called to go to the land of Palestine and dedicate that land for the return of the descendants of Judah.

Ten years before, the Prophet Joseph had predicted on the head of Orson Hyde that in due time he should go to Jerusalem, the land of his fathers, and be a watchman to that people. History tells us that Elder Hyde did go and dedicate the land in 1841, and in 1873, Elder George A. Smith went to that land and again dedicated it for the return of Judah. . . .

Return of the Jews

So today, my brothers and sisters, in fulfilment of these ancient and modern prophecies, a great drama is being enacted in Palestine. The Jews are returning as one of the events of the last days. Resources are being built up through reclamation, rehabilitation and modernization.

I read the other day of one authority who stated that there is more scientific "know how" concentrated today in Palestine than in any similar area upon the face of the earth. I wonder if there isn't purpose behind it. I noted too, in the report of the Anglo-American Commission which was made of their study in 1946, that they commented that considerable numbers of the Jews are being converted to Christianity and that their attitude toward the Christ as the Redeemer of the world is rapidly changing. There has been much confusion over the Palestine question—much talk of division of the land, of quotas, import restrictions—but out of it all I can't help but feel that we will see a complete fulfilment of the prophecies which have been made regarding this people. These prophecies are in rapid course of fulfilment before our very eyes today. . . .

Jewish Concern

9–10.

CHARLES Rhind a successful merchant and active Republican in New York City, was intimately involved in the successful negotiation of a treaty of friendship and commerce negotiated with Turkey in 1830. The following letter was addressed by Rhind to President Andrew Jackson, indicating the course he would pursue in negotiating such a treaty.

Reference: Microcopy 639, roll 20. Letters of Application and Recommendation during the Administration of Andrew Jackson, 1829–1837, United States National Archives.

Sir

The Honble Mr. Van Buren yesterday requested me to send in a Memorial pointing out the mode by which I thought it most likely we might secure an arrangement with the Porte. I have accordingly addressed a Note this morning to The Hon. Secretary, and now do myself the honor of enclosing a copy thereof for the perusal of your Excellency.

With profound respect
I have the honor to be
Your Excellency's
obd. hlst.
Chas Rhind
Washington 21st July 1829

His Excellency
Andrew Jackson
President of the United States

(Duplicate)

Sir

Soliciting the favor of your reference to the Letter and other Documents which I had the honor of presenting to you yesterday, I avail myself of your polite suggestion to state the means by which I think a negotiation can be cheaply and expeditiously effected with Turkey for a passage thro the Dardanelles.

Having been so long connected in Commerce with that Country, and devoted so much attention to the extension of our Trade to that quarter, and being acquainted with the different modes most likely to obtain the object in view, after much reflection, I feel persuaded it could be accomplished by the means I propose.

The Agents hitherto sent out to that quarter (Messrs. English and Bradish) were certainly not calculated to promote a negotiation of this Kind. Mr Offley is undoubtedly the best selection yet made, and it was with a view to this very object, that I exerted myself to procure his present appointment, which I accomplished thro my Friend Mr. Colden and other members of Congress. Mr. Offley could not with propriety address me since he became the Diplomatic Agent of Government and altho I am acquainted with all the measures previously adopted I am consequently ignorant of the result of his late attempt, excepting what has appeared in the newspapers—but on seeing the first paragraph— (in Feby last) announcing that he was in Constantinople for the purpose of negotiating a Treaty, I had a conversation with Mr. Noah (who is perhaps the best informed person on that subject in the Ud States) and predicted a failure. He coincided with me in opinion, for it was obvious that if the European Powers once knew that we were endeavoring to obtain this privilege they would oppose us with all their might. From my own experience and many years reflection on the subject—the only means by which this object can be obtained at a cheap rate is the following.

Let Government give plenary powers to the Commodore commanding in that station, to conclude a Treaty. A Merchant of intelligence (and if possible one known in that quarter) then to be selected, who would proceed in his private capacity to Constantinople, and thro one of the first Jewish Bankers commence a negotiation with the Reis Effendi, more as a business matter than a Diplomatic one. When this Agent—(thro the Banker) had brought the negotiation to a point comporting with the instructions furnished him by Government, he would then proceed to the Commodore, who at a moments notice might proceed to Constantinople and consummate the business, before it was even suspected by the Ministry of European Powers. And if a final Treaty could not be effected, there cannot be a doubt but that we might obtain permission for five years, which in fact would be the same as perpetual.

I am persuaded that the proper time to effect this, is before the return of the French and English Ministers, for I am well aware that not only those Nations, but all the other Maritime Powers of Europe, are jealous of our obtaining this privilege, and will prevent it if they can, consequently it must be done privately and in the way I point out.

The Jewish Bankers are men of the highest standing in that Country, and at the present moment, when, by their means alone, the Sultan is supplied with the sinews of War, they could operate with more effect than at any other time. It would be easy for me to obtain such introduction to those Gentlemen as would secure their cordial co-operation.

Altho my objects are purely Commercial, and I ask for no Office of emolument (the Consulship of Odessa being entirely for personal security and to give efficiency to my Commercial operations) it would not be consistent with my interest to have an employment—as Agent of Government, further than for the temporary purpose of aiding in the accomplishment of this great object. Yet I freely offer my humble Services until it can be accomplished.

I am aware that there are applications for this appointment emanating however from very different motives than those by which I am governed. It has been known for some years that I have contemplated Commercial operations & Establishments at Constantinople and the Black Sea, and from my experience I have the vanity to think, there are but few who possess the advantages I have acquired.

I respectfully submit these ideas for your consideration
and have the honor to be

Sir
Your obt. hbe Sert
Chas Rhind
Washington 21 July 1829

The Honorable
M. Van Buren

THE FOLLOWING letter of introduction on behalf of Charles Rhind was written by Mordecai M. Noah and Naphtali Phillips to the Jewish communities in Russia and Turkey. It was designed to assist him as consul at Odessa in his main objective—to negotiate a treaty between America and Turkey.

Reference: Phillips Family Papers (P–17), American Jewish Historical Society. The original text is in Hebrew.

PEACE UNTO ISRAEL

To our brothers of the House of Israel:

We who have signed below have come to bear witness for the one who bears this document whose name is Charles Rhind, who is being sent from our country America to Russia to be a Consul there. It is known to you that he is a great and honorable prince from a family of honorable princes and from among the righteous of the world who has a good name and loves Israel. Therefore we have come to ask from all our brothers of the house of Israel in general, both those in Turkey, and Russia, or other countries which this prince will pass through among our brothers in Israel, that they should welcome him and befriend and honor him in every way possible for the sanctification of God's name specifically and for the sanctification of Israel who live here in America and for the sanctification of our brothers of Israel who live in other countries to publicize the kindness and names of our brothers in Israel in general.

Signed Mordecai ben Menahem [Noah]
Signed Naphtali ben Jonah [Phillips]
Friday, 17 Marheshvan (Nov. 13, 1829)

11.

THE EARLIEST contacts between American Jewry and the Holy Land were philanthropic in nature. At least three organizations were established during the nineteenth century to help alleviate the conditions of the Jews in Palestine. One of these was the *Hebra Tarumot Hakodesh* (Society for Holy Tithing). Established in London in 1824, an American branch was founded in 1832. The following announcement, issued in 1846, indicates the scope of the society's program and the manner in which it functioned.

Reference: Hebra Tarumot Hakodesh Papers (I–33), American Jewish Historical Society.

HEBRA TARUMOT HAKODESH.

EXTRACT FROM THE CONSTITUTION—SECTION 5.

"The money raised by this Society shall be remitted, at stated times, to some responsible Agent in Europe or Asia, to be distributed by him, fairly and equitably, amongst the different Congregations in the Holy Land; but in no instance whatever to be paid to any Messenger or agent of any of the Congregations there who may be sent here to collect the same."

The Hebra Tarumot Hakodesh has received recent intelligence that our Brethren in the Holy Land are suffering from the horrors of Famine, the consequence of the continued drought for near two years. They appeal to the sympathies of their more prosperous Coreligionists.

This Society has just received the acknowledgment of their last remittance made to Mr. HERSCH LEHRENS, and other gentlemen in Amsterdam, composing the Distribution Committee, and calling on us for all the additional aid in our power. With this view, the Hebra has appointed MESSRS. SOLOMON I. ISAACS, J. B. KURSHEEDT, and SIMEON ABRAHAMS, to solicit aid from all well-disposed Yehudim, in this city and elsewhere: the amount collected to be sent in accordance with the above Extract from the Constitution with the names of the donors, and the amount subscribed by each individual.

J. B. KURSHEEDT, PRESIDENT.
N. PHILLIPS, CLERK.

NEW-YORK, 18 Kislef, 5607.

12.

ISAAC LEESER (1806–1868), a pioneer spiritual leader in American Judaism, slowly embraced the conviction that the dream of Return can be a practical reality. Beginning as a practitioner of charity for the needy in the Holy Land, he began to consider the two-fold goal later to be defined as Zionism: the regeneration of the Land of Israel and its dedication to the spiritual and cultural rebirth of the entire Jewish People. The following citation from the *Occident* can be seen as a companion piece to Clorinda Minor's letter.

Reference: The Occident and American Jewish Advocate, vol. 11, no. 10 (January 1854), pp. 477–83.

PALESTINE.

Whatever the reasons may be, whether sought for in the marvellous or in natural causes, the fact is undoubted, that Palestine has ever been the land of affection to all believers in the Bible. The Mahomedan has his Al-Charim; the Christians possess their various churches and shrines; and they all no less than we, attach the highest earthly sanctity to the spots consecrated by the remarkable events of patriarchal and biblical history. It may be a fanatical error, as some would characterize it, for Jews to cluster round these places, where formerly they were the lords, but now little better than slaves and beggars, and subject to overbearing and tyrannical masters. But so they have been from the day the Temple fell a sacrifice to the flame, whether the ruler were the Normans, the Arabs, the Crusaders, the Egyptians, or the Turks. At no time for eighteen centuries, and even before the emblem of our national glory fell, were we otherwise than aliens on our own soil; still Palestine was the land of our hope, the country of our desire. But let those who blame the devout for this feeling, tell us why it should not be so? Are we so well treated in more civilized countries? Are we regarded as equals in many lands? How many Americas are there in the world? how many Hollands, Belgiums, and France? Tell us where are all the liberties which our deniers of a Messiah have obtained in Germany, Italy, Hungary and Poland? Where? dissipated to the four winds of heaven; and the partial light which dawned six years ago, and which promised to be the harbinger of a brighter day, has left us in greater obscurity, and the loosening of the chains of political and religious slavery, has caused us to feel the tightening of the bonds with a thousand-fold redoubled painfulness. Yes, dreamers, where is your Messiah's reign? where your universal freedom? where the lying down of the lamb and the wolf together? The wars of oppression against freedom still continue, and the wolf yet gnashes his teeth against the unoffending lamb, that is unable to brave his fury. Let us go where we will, excepting in countries where there live in all less than half a million of our brethren, the badge of political slavery and degradation is still ours; we are yet excluded from all places of profit and preferment, and even the right to a share in the possession of the land of our birth, is denied us in many countries. Oh! what a freedom this is! What a state that is, to satisfy the longing of the Jewish patriot for happier days—for a time when the land of Israel is again to be ours, to be occupied by the sons of freedom and industry, sitting each under his own vine and under his own fig tree, with none to make him afraid! Whatever others may do, we do not blame the oppressed, not even the free, in all lands, who look toward their ancient home as the true country of Israel, where the religion promulgated through Moses is ultimately to stand forward as the light and life of the world, guiding all mankind to universal freedom teaching them all a perfect, pure, universal faith, and a love, undying in the spirit for the Creator of all things.

Hence, we say, could a numerous agricultural population be drawn to Palestine, we should not only contribute towards the permanent relief of those residing there already, but we should open an asylum for many who now know of freedom only as a traditionary word, recorded in Scripture, as once their own in ancient days, of which they and their fathers before them have lost the true signification. If it could be accomplished, that the surplus of unemployed Israelites of Poland, Russia, Galicia, Hungary, and Turkey, should be planted in agricultural colonies in the valleys of the land of Israel, under the protection of the present energetic Sultan, Abdul Medjid, with full liberty to organize municipal corporations, permitted to bear arms, and fully empowered to use them in case of an attack from without, we should do much to ameliorate the abject condition of European communities, who now are daily exposed to insult and contumely of their arrogant and proud oppressors. If his home should become intolerable to an Israelite, he would know whither he could resort and find the means of self support, without the danger of being led away from the path of duty, which now, alas! is too often the case with those who go to England, France, and America, from other countries, simply to follow the only pursuit which seems to promise them a speedy return, namely, trading, in one of its many shapes, all other employments being inaccessible to a stranger who is unacquainted with language and customs of the lands he just arrives in. But were Palestine once open to receive Jewish immigrants; were its agricultural wealth once more accessible to our people; were its fields once more fertile and its cities rebuilt anew: not alone that many could unite themselves to its inhabitants to cultivate the soil, sure of a speedy and rich return for their labor; but those who have the genius and tact for business, could carry on profitable commerce with all parts of the world, in exchange for the varied products of the field and vineyards, and perhaps the many rich mineral resources which now lie unused and unknown, against whatever is raised from the soil and produced by skill and labor in every other country. This is no mere dream, the realization of which is beyond the range of possibility; but the same spectacle was witnessed in ancient times, when the harbors of Tyre and Zidon contained the commerce of the world; when Jerusalem was filled with the wares of all climes, and when prosperity and elegance smiled in every city of our prosperous commonwealth. If we revert to the description of Isaiah and Ezekiel, of the prosperity and elegance of Tyre and Jerusalem, we may indeed wonder at the awful desolation which now presides over these seats of ancient civilization and refinement; but at the same time, it leads us to the conviction that under similar circumstances similar results may be witnessed at some future, if even distant, day. If the waste places should be built up; if the broken cisterns should be repaired; if the now dry aqueducts should be restored; if the indolence of the inhabitants should be converted into thrift and industry: it cannot be otherwise than that the articles of export would be multiplied beyond calculation. The pastures in the wilderness of Syria and Judea would afford food for millions of sheep, whose fleece could readily rival and excel, perhaps, under the happy sky, which smiles serenely on that eastern fairyland, the best Merinos of Spain and Saxony; the silk-worm could readily be made to weave its shroud of the finest fibre after being abundantly fed "till the day of his changeful state," with the healthful leaves of the white mulberry, which will grow there in abundance, if only the commonest care be taken; the hills of the north could yield the abundant supply of the purest olive oil, for which they were anciently famous; the mountains of Judah could again be laden with the fruit of the vine, and the valleys of Jezreel and Sharon, and Carmel and Tabor, and the plains of Jericho and of the Great Sea, would again be burdened with the immense harvests, the hundred-fold yield, which anciently distinguished them. Cotton, too, and hemp, and fruits of various kinds, the Indian corn, the potato, the yam, the banana, and other products anciently unknown in Palestine, could be readily introduced, and yield their increase in unexampled plenty, if the laborers were once there to prepare the soil for their reception. And can it be doubted that so many articles, which in their raw or manufactured state would find a ready demand in other countries, should not soon enrich their producers, and elevate them as successful commerce always does, to a high state of refinement and elegance?

The ruinous cities would soon be rebuilt; the hovels of the timid tillers of the soil, who now fear to work, dreading the assault of the marauding Bedouin, would soon make place for comfortable farmhouses; the pastures now desolate, would resound at evening, with the bells of the returning flocks and herds, led home by the blithe and gay shepherds as in ancient times; the ports which are now rarely visited by the ships of foreign nations, because there is so little for them to carry away, would again be filled with vessels displaying the flag of every country; and the roads on which now painfully toils the camel of the caravan in its slow progress, would be made noiseful by the thundering steam car in its impatient boundings to reach the place of its destination; and all because industry once more would have breathed life and vigor into the listless, indolent few, that now vegetate, not live—starve, and not enjoy life, in a land which formerly nourished its millions of men and cattle, and now produces scarcely enough to feed its handful of persons, coming, as they have done, from many climes, without concert of action, without any cohesion or unity of purpose. . . .

There is no conceivable reason why Palestine and Asia Minor should be given over to sterility and desolation, when to former ages they were not alone the nursery of mankind, but the seat whence knowledge and religion were scattered all over the earth. Egypt may have been the home of early architecture and of the priests who guarded a secret knowledge of a purer philosophy than the majority of the people possessed; but it was nevertheless from the inhabitants of the first-mentioned lands that the religions which now govern the world were derived; and though Moses taught at first in Arabia, it was only from Palestine that his religion advanced under various guises as the conquering system, destined to overcome all others in its resistless march to universal dominion. . . . We will not at present enter into a discussion of the prophecies bearing on this topic; nor investigate how far we should rely on a sudden development of the divine policy which is to effect the great end of the prediction of Israel's seers; but it surely cannot be wrong for us to endeavor to promote the happy future by some exertions of our own.

13.

A LOCAL committee was established in Jerusalem to solicit funds for the erection of dwellings for poor Jews outside the old city. Typical of their requests was the letter sent to the Board of Delegates of American Israelites, which had been established in 1859 as the first successful national organization of Jewish congregations in the United States. The text of the request, translated from the German, was published in the board's annual report. Accompanying it was a translation of a Hebrew letter sent at the same time.

Reference: Board of Delegates of American Israelites Papers (I-2), American Jewish Historical Society.

B.

CORRESPONDENCE ON THE SUBJECT OF THE PILGRIM DWELLINGS NEAR JERUSALEM.

(FROM THE GERMAN)

JERUSALEM, *November 12th,* 5629.

ABRAHAM HART, ESQ., PRESIDENT.

DEAR SIR:—

The undersigned local Committee for the erection of dwellings for the poor and pilgrims on Mount Zion, beg to submit the following:

Mr. Selig Hausdorff, formerly appointed as Collector for this purpose in America received the assurance while in New York from the President of the different Congregations and Societies (as we have seen from written documents), that as soon as the then unsettled condition of the country should be terminated by the approaching Presidential election, and a revival of business follow this event, the Officers of the different Israelitish Congregations would make a general collection for the establishment of Poor and Pilgrim Houses on Mount Zion.

This extended charitable enterprise, intended to ameliorate the condition of the poor, as well as to enlarge and beautify the Holy City by rebuilding its ruins, has met the approval of our brethren in Germany, Holland and France, by whose co-operation we have already been enabled to erect upon a lot of 25,000 ells, which we have acquired a substantial building containing twenty-six residences for the poor and pilgrims.

We beg to enclose the accompanying diplomas, appointing you "President for all America," to take charge of collections for the *continued* erection of houses for the poor and pilgrims, hoping you will cause noble collections to be effected by appointing Committees for that purpose in the several American congregations, and erect an eternal monument to yourself by establishing houses for our poor and unprotected brethren in the holy city of Jerusalem, until the Redeemer cometh to Zion, Amen!

Be assured, dear sir, that thousands of your brethren in the holy city, on sacred ground, are praying for the welfare and prosperity of their benefactors and protectors.

We have the honor of signing, dear sir, with the highest esteem,

Your humble servants,
THE LOCAL COMMITTEE
for the erection of Poor and Pilgrim Houses on Mount Zion.
(Signed) SELIG HAUSDORFF,
MALER SCHONBAUM,
J. H. MARCUS,
J. GOLDBURGER,
G. SCHLANK *Secretary.*

(FROM THE ORIGINAL HEBREW.)

"Thus saith the Lord, keep judgment and execute righteousness for my salvation is nigh to come, and my righteousness to be revealed. Seek the welfare of Jerusalem; may thy friends prosper. Let there be peace within thy walls; tranquility in thy palaces."

"There shall rise for you, who fear My Name, a son of righteousness with healing in its wings. They shall return, sit in its shade, they shall revive as the corn, and grow as the vine, the scent thereof shall be as the wine of Lebanon."

May an abundance of peace, and length of days flow from the summit of the eternal hill, and from the everlasting mountains, and descend upon the worthy friend of Zion and Jerusalem that honorable gentleman of universal note, beloved and esteemed by his coreligionists for his exceeding liberality and kindness, Abraham Hart, (whom God may preserve,) a resident of Philadelphia, and President of Delegates of American Israelites. May there be peace in his habitation, and tranquility in his mansion, for ever. *Amen.*

From Mount Zion, our shelter we heard the happy tidings, and a new life was infused into us. Journals and private communications reached the top of this sacred hill, relating with gladness the prominent position attained by our highly-esteemed coreligionist, (whom God exalt still more highly,) and encouraging us by the announcement that you, worthy sir, were chosen as the great chief of American Hebrews. So that now, after you have obtained that lofty position, the tenants of poor and pilgrim houses felt reanimated, because they remembered your former kindness. As at the rising of the sun, everything assumes a bright aspect, and the eye of the beholder delights in gazing on the verdant fields, on the variegated flowers and rich fruits, so did our soul delight in looking from the wall of a building erected as a shelter to the poor and pilgrims, upon you looming at a distance, and appearing in all the glory which was bestowed upon you, and the powers you wield. Blessed be the Lord God of Abraham! for His mercy is favorable unto us; and, since it has been so decreed by God, enjoy your honors and improve them by exercising pious zeal on our behalf, the dwellers of Mount Zion. We inform you, with unutterable satisfaction, that fresh glories have been added to these already proposed by your dear self; for we have appointed you Administrator and Treasurer of the institution for poor and pilgrims' houses, throughout the United States of America, believing that you will represent us, the local committee stationed here and collect all the free will offerings which every man's heart will prompt him to give, to beautify enlarge and firmly establish these *houses on Mount Zion.* Whoever repairs to this place, praises our endeavors, and that which we have accomplished, by the assistance of our brethren; namely, the handsome dwellings, built of large stones, and furnished with windows looking, some towards high mountains on one side of the Jordan, and others towards the ascent of the Mount of Olives, whence a pure air circulates, which are provided also with wells of clear water, sweet to the taste and refreshing. We have likewise an immense space of ground in an eligible location, but for want of means we have hitherto been unable to build thereon; wherefore we humbly entreat that you will assume the charge of furthering our object; for you, dear sir, are wont to offer your aid, and, at all hazards, interest yourself for the benefit of religion, and for giving succor to the seed of Abraham. We entertain no doubt but that you will, in this instance also, gather money in your cities sufficient for our purpose, therefore we addressed you this epistle, for, *no one* who holds you in estimation, *will refuse, when you ask him to give for the sake of Mount Zion.* We trust in the descendants of Abraham that each person will contribute joyfully and readily, and are also certain to be accepted by yourself, in accordance with our wish and that of all the children of Zion. This is a day of gladness to us, when the chosen of the Lord is blessed in our midst by a whole assembled congregation. May this blessing be confirmed by the Lord, and the benediction pronounced at Zion rest upon your head, as it is written: "May the Lord bless thee out of Zion, and may you see the welfare of Jerusalem all the days of thy life," when the Lord returneth unto Zion, may you merit to see the loveliness of the Lord, and seek His temple thrice a year, with a voice of psalmody and joy; which event may speedily happen. May there be fulfilled in you the biblical passage, which says, "The Lord blessed Abraham in all things."

So speak the servants of those who serve the Lord, who sign their names, while offering sincere wishes for your happiness,

THE ADMINISTRATORS AND GUARDIANS
of the Institution for erecting poor and pilgrim houses on Mount Zion, within the city of Jerusalem.

The 12th Adar in the year הר קדשך (thy holy mountain) 5629.

"Cry out and shout, thou inhabitant of Zion, for great is the Holy One of Israel in the midst of thee. For ye shall go forth with joy and be brought in in peace the mountains and the valleys shall burst before you with song. The Lord will command this blessing for thee!"

"The redeemed of the Lord shall return, and come to Zion with song, and an everlasting joy shall be over their heads. For the Lord hath comforted Zion. He hath comforted all her desolations, and made her wilderness like Eden and her desert as the garden of the Lord joy and gladness shall be found therein."

14.

EMMA LAZARUS (1849–1887) was born into a New York Sephardi family. Removed from Jewish concerns in her early years, she awakened to the plight of East European Jewry during the pogroms in the 1880s. She wrote a series of essays in the *American Hebrew* entitled *"An Epistle to the Hebrews,"* a passionate appeal for a return to Zion. Like most supporters of the Return to Zion Movement, Emma Lazarus considered Eretz Yisrael as the only solution for

East European Jewry, for those with no chance of emigrating westward from the lands of persecution.

Reference: Emma Lazarus, *An Epistle to the Hebrews* (New York: Cowen, 1900), pp. 73–74, 77.

My plea for the establishment of a free Jewish State . . . has not the remotest bearing upon the position of American Jews. My sole desire is to arouse in my fellow-citizens a deeper and fuller appreciation of the fact that millions of human beings belonging to the Jewish race and faith are despoiled of their right to justice and freedom, and that it behooves us in our prosperity to assist in alleviating their lot. . . .

The only such measure that has been urged is the Re-Colonization of Palestine which has been ably discussed in the best European periodicals and journals, both Jewish and Christian. The insuperable objections existing against all other propositions heretofore offered make me regard this scheme, despite the tremendous difficulties which it presents, as the only possible issue from a desperate situation. It will be seen that from my point of view it does not affect in any way soever the position of Jews in America, or their loyalty to the flag for which they are to-day ready to sacrifice their lives and which amply protects them against all risk of oppression. If those representatives of the Jewish press, or those private individuals who have so vehemently protested against my advocacy of the movement, and who have themselves so contemptuously repudiated it, will kindly suggest something that offers better chances of relief for the unfortunate Jews of Eastern Europe, I can only say that I will gladly renounce my present position in favor of a less difficult task.

15.

Solomon Schechter (1847–1915), second president of the Jewish Theological Seminary of America came to the United States in 1902. He soon emerged as the foremost scholar-ideologist of the Conservative movement in American Judaism basing his position on the pillars of scholarship, Torah and *Mitzvot,* Zionism and the American center. At a time when Zionism was opposed by many forceful elements in the American Jewish community, Schechter's forthright stand as a Zionist helped turn the tide. He affirmed the Jewish pledge of ages: "Zionism was, and still is the most cherished dream I was worthy of having."

Reference: Solomon Schechter, *Zionism: A Statement* (New York, 1906).

ZIONISM: A STATEMENT

. . . Zionism is an ideal, and as such is indefinable. It is thus subject to various interpretations and susceptive of different aspects. It may appear to one as the rebirth of national Jewish consciousness, to another as a religious revival, whilst to a third it may present itself as a path leading to the goal of Jewish culture; and to a fourth it may take the form of the last and only solution of the Jewish problem. By reason of this variety of aspects, Zionism has been able to unite on its platform the most heterogeneous elements; representing Jews of all countries and exhibiting almost all the different types of culture and thought as only a really great and universal movement could do. That each of its representatives should emphasize the particular aspect most congenial to his way of thinking, and most suitable for his mode of action, is only natural. On one point, however, they all agree, namely, that it is not only desirable, but absolutely necessary that Palestine, the land of our fathers, should be recovered with the purpose of forming a home for at least a portion of the Jews, who would lead there an independent national life. That the language of the leaders was sometimes ambiguous and not quite definite in the declaration of this principle, is owing to the boldness of the proposition and the environments in which these leaders were brought up, where everything distinctly Jewish was in need of an apology, rather than to any doubt about the final aim of Zionism, as conceived in the minds of the great majority of Zionists. Nor was it strange that some backslidings should occur, and that in moments of despair, counsels of despair should prevail, considering the terrible crises through which we have passed during the last few years. The great majority of Zionists remain loyal to the great idea of Zion and Jerusalem, to which history and tradition, and the general Jewish sentiment, point. It is "God's country" in the fullest and truest sense of the words. It is the "Promised Land"—still maintaining its place in every Jewish heart, excepting those, perhaps, with whom Jewish history commences about the year 1830, and Jewish literature is confined to the transactions of the Rabbinical synods of the last century, and the files of Phillipson's *Allgemeine Zeitung des Judenthums.*

To me personally, after long hesitation and careful watching, Zionism recommended itself as the great bulwark against assimilation. By assimilation, I do not understand what is usually understood by Americanization; namely that every Jew should do his best to acquire the English language; that he should study American history and make himself acquainted with the best productions of American literature; that he should be a law-abiding citizen thoroughly appreciating the privilege of being a member of this great commonwealth, and joyfully prepared to discharge the duties of American citizenship. What I understand by assimilation is loss of identity; or that process of disintegration which, passing through various degrees of defiance of all Jewish thought and of disloyalty to Israel's history and its mission, terminates variously in different lands. . . .

It is this kind of assimilation, with the terrible consequences indicated, that I dread most; even more than pogroms. To this form of assimilation, Zionism in the sense defined will prove, and is already proving, a most wholesome check. Whatever faults may be found with its real or self-appointed leaders, Zionism as a whole forms an opposing force against the conception of the destiny of Israel and the interpretation of its mission, the leading thought of which is apparently the well known epigram, "Whosoever shall seek to gain his life shall lose it, but whosoever shall lose his life shall preserve it." Zionism declares boldly to the world that Judaism means to preserve its life by *not* losing its life. It shall be a true and healthy life, with a polity of its own, a religion wholly its own, invigorated by sacred memories and sacred environments, and proving a tower of strength and of unity not only for the remnant gathered within the borders of the Holy Land, but also for those who shall, by choice or necessity, prefer what now constitutes the Galuth.

The term Galuth is here loosely used, expressing as I have often heard it, the despair and helplessness felt in the presence of a great tragedy. And the tragedy is not imaginary. It is real, and it exists everywhere. It *is* a tragedy to see a great ancient people, distinguished for its loyalty to its religion and its devotion to its sacred law, losing thousands every year by the mere process of attrition. It *is* a tragedy to see sacred institutions as ancient as the mountains, to maintain which Israel for thousands of years shrank from no sacrifice, destroyed before our very eyes and exchanged for corresponding institutions borrowed from hostile religions. It *is* a tragedy to see a language held sacred by all the world, in which Holy Writ was composed, and which served as the depository of Israel's greatest and best thought, doomed to oblivion and forced out gradually from the synagogue. It *is* a tragedy to see the descendants of those who revealed revelation to the world and who developed the greatest religious literature in existence, so little familiar with real Jewish thought, and so utterly wanting in all sympathy with it, that they have no other interpretation to offer of Israel's scriptures, Israel's religion, and Israel's ideals and aspirations and hopes, than those suggested by their natural opponents, slavishly following their opinions, copying their phrases, repeating their catchwords, not sparing us even the taunt of tribalism and Orientalism. I am not accusing anybody. I am only stating facts that are the outcome of causes under which we all labor, but for none of which any party in particular can be made responsible, though it cannot be denied that some among us rather made too much virtue of a necessity, and indulged, and are still indulging in experiments in euthanasia. The economic conditions under which we live; the innate desire for comfort; the inherent tendency towards imitation; the natural desire not to appear peculiar; the accessibility of theological systems, possessing all the seductions of "newness and modernity," patronized by fashion and even by potentates, and taught in ever so many universities and condensed in dozens of encyclopedias, are sufficient and weighty enough causes to account for our tragedy. But however natural the causes may be, they do not alter the doom. The effects are bound to be fatal. The fact thus remains that we are helpless spectators in the face of great tragedies, in other words, that we are in Galuth. This may not be the Galuth of the Jews, but it is the Galuth of Judaism, or, as certain mystics expressed it, the Galuth of *Hannephesh,* the Galuth of the Jewish soul wasting away before our very eyes. With a little modification we might repeat here the words of a Jewish Hellenist of the second century who, in his grief, exclaims: "Wherefore is Israel given up as a reproach to the heathen, and for what cause is the people whom thou best loved given over unto ungodly nations, and why is the law of our forefathers brought to naught, and the written covenants come to none effect? And we pass away out of the world as grasshoppers, and our life is astonishment and fear, and we are not worthy to obtain mercy."

The foregoing remarks have made it clear that I belong to that class of Zionists that lay more stress on the religious-national aspects of Zionism than on any other feature peculiar to it. The rebirth of Israel's national consciousness, and the revival of Israel's religion, or, to use a shorter term, the revival of Judaism, are inseparable. When Israel found itself, it found its God. When Israel lost itself, or began to work at its self-effacement, it was sure to deny its God. The selection of Israel, the indestructibility of God's covenant with Israel, the immortality of Israel as a nation, and the final restoration of Israel to Palestine, where the nation will live a holy life on holy ground, with all the wide-reaching consequences of the conversion of humanity and the establishment of the Kingdom of God on earth—all these are the common ideals and the common ideas that permeate the whole of Jewish literature extending over nearly four thousand years. . . .

16.

RICHARD James Horatio Gottheil (1862–1936), born in Manchester, England, studied at Columbia College and later was the first incumbent of the Chair of Semitics at his alma mater. He was a founding member of the Federation of American Zionists, served as its first president, and was a delegate to the first Zionist Congress in 1897. Gottheil's Zionism was rooted in Jewish history and literature as well as in his analysis of the Jewish problem in modern times.

Reference: R. J. H. Gottheil, *Zionism* (Philadelphia: Jewish Publication Society of America, 1914), pp. 198–208.

ZIONISM AND THE WESTERN JEWS

Among the many misconceptions current in regard to Zionism, one of the most popular would confine its function to some particular class of Jews, to some section distinguished either by its economic condition or by its peculiar conception of the Jewish religion, or to those living in a certain part of the great Diaspora. It has been said, and it has been written, that such a concentration of Jews and such a centralization of Jewish efforts as is foreshadowed by the Basel Platform, may be a means for mitigating in part some of the Jewish misery that is only too apparent in Eastern Europe, that it may well prove another outlet for those unfortunate ones who are forced through the Russian and Roumanian mill, that it may relieve the pressure which is so evident in the Ghettos of Galicia, and offer a further means of livelihood to those who are in too active a competition in the great European and American centers. In a word, Zionism, regarded from this angle, has no real message to the emancipated Jew of Western Europe and America, and its sole significance lies in the fact that it is another attempt to heal the wounds inflicted upon the Jews by modern industrial developments.

On the other hand, the assertion is made that Zionism may have a message for those who have remained within the four walls of Orthodox Judaism, and is the logical outcome of the ideas and hopes that have been conserved wherever traditional Judaism has retained its hold, but for those Jews whose trend of thought and whose course of life have led them away from the beaten track, it may be a matter of indifference what the ultimate fate of Palestine is, and a Jewish center has no part in the conception they have of the future of the Jews and no religious worth in their image of the future of the Jewish faith. This is very frankly the attitude of the Reform wing of the Synagogue in Western Europe and in America. For them Zionism has no message, or, if it has any, it is one of despair and an unworthy acquiescence and a somewhat unwilling one at that—in circumstances which we have not religious and moral power enough to overcome. The leaders of American Reform have gone even further than this, and look upon Zionism as the negation of the best hope and promise of Judaism, as a wilful abjuration of the rôle traced for Judaism by the greatest of the prophets. The dissemination and diffusion of the Jews throughout all parts of the world is elevated by them to the position of doctrinal sublimity, and stress is laid upon this dispersion as the means—one might almost say, the only means—for the proper fulfilment of the Jewish "mission."

Now, we may leave out of account any attempt to define the word mission when used of a people. To do so would lead dangerously near to religious speculations and to the discussion of questions which might raise the *odium theologicum.* But the question is pertinent: how is such a mission to be carried out, if in the process the bearers of the mission are bound to succumb? It is true that, until quite modern times, the various communities of Jews maintained their existence in a manner which at first sight seems to defy explanation. Without any visible unity, without any physical or ideal center, at times without much intercommunion, individual bodies of Jews have existed in all corners of the Diaspora. They have succeeded in existing because of the ideal bond that held them together, a common past and a common hope for the future. This bond has remained practically unchanged throughout the ages. Judaism has been surprisingly free from sectarian schisms. With the exception of that of the Karaites, none has come to disturb the unity of practice and aspiration that welded the different communities together into an unseen brotherhood. Living in agglomerations that were usually small in extent, they have been able to keep up a similar communal life by means of a common practice. Territorial distinctions have been disregarded and almost obliterated. In the early Middle Ages there was little difference between the life of the Palestinian and the Babylonian Jew, as little as there was between the Continental and the English. Even the distinction between Sefardic and Ashkenazic Jew was not accentuated until both commenced to live outside the countries from which they derived their nomenclature. An Asher ben Yehiel could become an authority in Spain, a Solomon ben Adret an oracle in Germany. To the great world-movements with which they came in contact they were not insensible. They had a fair share in their development, and were themselves not uninfluenced by the contact. But only in rare instances was this influence allowed to drive deep down into their beings. If Philo was more of a neo-Platonist than he was a Jew, his example was not followed; neither was Spinoza's. From Saadia to Maimonides, it was the non-Jewish systems of philosophy that were put into the strait-jacket of Jewish theology. In most cases the Jews retired from this contact before the harm had become too great. Hellenism is the classic example of the reverse policy, a policy in consequence of which large numbers must have become lost to the Jewish cause.

At the present day, however, the circumstances in which the Jews live are very different. The constitution of European society during the Middle Ages was such as to favor individual groupings. Communities were disjointed from one another; means of intercommunication were undeveloped; news could not spread easily and rapidly; cities were comparatively small, and even in those in which contact with the larger world would have affected adversely Jewish cohesiveness, compensating influences were present in the Ghetto system and in the steady, though scanty, infiltration from country communities. The industrial development of modern times has thoroughly changed conditions. The rise of national feeling has frowned upon other combinations within the state, so that a general leveling process has been at work. Cities have grown to immeasurable proportions. The race to these large centers has been fast and furious. Thus, not only have the Ghetto walls been cast down; the smaller communities outside of the large cities have been greatly depeopled of their Jewish inhabitants. France is a classic example. We think of the flourishing communities in the Midi, in Avignon, Carpentras, Carcassone, etc., where now many of the synagogues are closed, and Jewish centers are on the verge of disappearance, because most of the Jews have gone to Paris, there to be swallowed up in the great army of the unchurched. Italy is another instance. Bari, Otranto, Reggio, Ancona, Pesaro, and many other places that would constitute an "Italia Judaica," have become denuded of Jews, in favor of Rome and Florence. Similar conditions in other countries could easily be cited.

In addition, the language and customs of their surroundings have pressed heavily upon the Jews. In the Middle Ages, documents concerning transactions between Jews and non-Jews were usually drawn up in two languages, of which one was Hebrew. Such documents have come down to us from Spain, from Germany, and from England. There was nothing strange in this; for even among non-Jews a literary tongue, the Latin, was still the language in which official documents of all sorts were drawn up. In modern times, modern languages have displaced the old literary tongue. Latin has been relegated to the store-room of the university, and Hebrew to the study-room of the learned. Custom, social practice, and social life have been unfavorable to the retention of peculiar Jewish observances, which have been largely banished from collective gatherings and from the household. They have been relegated to the synagogue and confined there. But even the synagogue has had to give way to the unifying forces at work to-day. We may think that in many instances, this has gone too far, and an unwarranted desire for assimilation has found a pretext in what is called "the needs of the day." But even where this has not been the case, many concessions have had to be made. There is no doubt that such concessions are bound to increase in the future and in this manner Jewish communities will tend to develop away from each other. The German Jew is not so apt to feel at home in Anglo-Jewish surroundings or in the synagogues of English-speaking countries as he was wont to formerly, nor the Italian Jew in Germany. "Deutsche Staatsbürger jüdischen Glaubens" have commenced to lose touch with their French brethren, and in some circles in the United States we have heard mutterings about an "American Judaism." The points of contact are evidently growing less in number and weaker in strength, and as Jewish unity tends to disappear, a consequent deadening of Jewish consciousness is bound to occur. There is, indeed, evidence that the process has already begun. It is true that at all times such a danger has been more or less present. Many have been lost to the Jewish cause. This enables us to understand the relatively small number of Jews existing at the present day, in spite of the acknowledged fecundity of the race. But the ravages occasioned by modern conditions—active anti-Semitism on the one hand, passive social oppression on the other—are nothing less than alarming. As regards Western Europe and America, this loss has been offset of late years by immigration from Eastern Europe. But such immigration cannot continue indefinitely, and the continued depression of the masses in Eastern Europe is having its effect in making the material with which the reconstructive process in the West is being carried on less worthy of its purpose and less effective in carrying it out. . . .

From the foregoing observations it will be clear that some means are necessary to counteract the corroding influences to which reference has been made. From whatever point of view we regard the situation, the unity of Israel must be restored. A complete reversion to the unity of practice seems impossible, as modern conditions in the Diaspora will continue to increase disfavorably to the Jews. The Jewish hope must be reconstituted upon modern lines. Embodied in a physical center, and that center illumined by a rekindled light, it will serve as a point towards which the thoughts, aspirations and longings of the Diaspora Jews will converge, and from which they will draw, each in his own measure, that sufficiency of moral and religious strength that will better enable them to resist the encroachments of their surroundings. The knowledge that in some one place, in some one country—and that country the most hallowed by its recollections—Jewish life is possible without the unnatural restrictions that naturally hem it in elsewhere, will act as a centripetal force, the very force that is so much needed today.

It may be objected that this will constitute a religious life by delegation to others. But the erection of a Jewish center in Palestine would in no way carry with it the nullification of duties resting upon Jews elsewhere. The Reform Jew, with his ideal of a mission, could carry forward that mission in the future as he has in the past. The theory that Zionism looks for the concentration of all Jews on one spot is a theory of windy unreality, which has loomed large in the minds of those only who do not understand, or who persist in misrepresenting, its basal teaching. For Palestine, even in the broadest definition ever thought of by prophet or singer, is insufficient to contain a large portion of the Jewish population of the world in addition to its present inhabitants. In very fact, a serious stimulus would be given to the spreading of the very mission it is feared will be endangered. The closer Jews are kept within the fold, the greater their interest in Jewish life and Jewish thought, the more propagators there will be for that mission. The early Reformers at least were insistent upon the view that whatever divergence from received practice they favored was not due to a simple love for divergence itself, but was the result of the difficulties experienced in overcoming a situation that demanded a greater sacrifice than their congregants felt able to make. Their spiritual descendants might well welcome any movement calculated to render the Jew more willing to sacrifice than he is today.

17.

Henrietta Szold (1860–1945), eldest daughter of Rabbi Benjamin Szold was born in Baltimore, Maryland. Fortified by Jewish scholarly training and with insights far beyond her years, she devoted herself—to use her own phrase—to the "noble dissatisfactions" of American Jewish life: Zionism and Jewish education.

From her going to Eretz Yisrael for a short stay in 1920 to help cope with the affairs of the American Zionist Medical Unit, Henrietta Szold dedicated the rest of her life to the crucial problems facing the Yishuv in the Holy Land, particularly during the Holocaust and war years.

Reference: Marvin Lowenthal, *Henrietta Szold: Life and Letters* (New York: Viking Press, 1942), pp. 150, 152–53, 165.

October 26, 1920

I may as well confess, since you read it between the lines, that the life here does not make me happy. What else was to have been expected? Again there is a generation of the desert which will have to perish in order to fructify the soil.

First a synthesis of the Jews gathering here from everywhere will have to be brought about, and then we may expect the life here to have some gracious aspects. To what extent the life in Palestine is of a piece with what the whole world is, I don't pretend to be able to tell. To judge from the *Nation,* America is not a marvel of comeliness these days either. Nevertheless, there is no gainsaying the fact that Palestine now is a bundle of problems, and problems are not conducive to happiness. And it isn't conducive to happiness if we keep thinking of the hundreds and hundreds of immigrants in tents while the more fortunate are tightening up every rift and seam to protect themselves against the rains now almost due.

And yet things are not so bad that you must insist upon my coming home. If a woman, asked to guess my age, insists on thirty-eight for me, as happened today, I am not yet a *nebbich.*

November 7, 1920

. . . Incidentally, I had a better opportunity than ever before to come close to the "pioneers." And for the first time I saw one of my hopes connected with Zionism realized. It is not an objective realization—it is not an achievement. We are far removed from any sort of achievement. It is this: I faced a human problem in which Jews are concerned, and alone concerned, and I forgot wholly that they are Jews. And so did they. These "pioneers," a war-bred generation, are living a primitive life, and are grappling with elementary, basic problems of living. I have a strong desire to join them.

Of course, I can't break stones as they do, but I may be able to organize them so that their living conditions are improved. The East

European Jew has idealism and persistence; what he lacks utterly is system and grace. His good qualities are permeated with a stolidity that keeps him from sitting down and thinking out the method whereby his paper plans might be realized bit by bit; or when he lives in communities, he doesn't know that a modicum of social courtesy acts like oil on machinery.

We have at least five hard years of this primitive struggle ahead of us here.

MARCH 13, 1921

. . . If *über hundert und zwanzig Jahren* the Jews possess a homeland, conquered for themselves by work, physical and intellectual, what a testimony it will be to their finer qualities! And I still believe the conquest is possible, though it will be after the long interval implied in the phrase *über hundert und zwanzig Jahren.*

The Jews are ready to work—they are working. Among all my new, vitalizing experiences, none can compare in stupendousness with what I saw and learned in the Jewish road-builders' camps, the labor squads of the halutzim, the pioneers, young men and women from Central and Eastern Europe, who have been preparing themselves for years in language and manual work, for Palestine development. The camps are full of faults of organization, the campers full of faults of temperament, but the movement as a whole is a phenomenon equivalent to a miracle.

And the country? It too is a miracle. Full of faults, like the camp and the campers, but so beautiful. It too must be conquered, its stones, its climate, its swamps, but it is worth, oh! so worth the struggle. I was sent to Galilee on business four weeks ago. It was raining, raining all the week I was away. Neither clouds, nor mist, nor downpour of abundant waters, nor bad roads could obscure the beauty of the land in its spring garb.

The Medical Unit is doing superb work. It too is full of faults and imperfections, and the people, who resent its Americanism, criticize it pitilessly, but it is worth while.

And myself? I am comfortable. Sophia Berger took a house on the outskirts of Jerusalem, its olive-tree garden, with almond trees interspersed, facing the Mount of Olives. Our little house is a dear home. It would be perfect in my eyes if it could be fitted up with steam heat.

Governmental Sources

18–20.

GEORGE Jones Adams, descendant of the renowned Adams family, led in 1866 a group of 157 men, women, and children from Maine to found a colony on the shores of Jaffa. Adams called his sect the Church of the Messiah. He preached that the "End of Days" was near and that the Jews would return from the four corners of the earth to the Holy Land. The Adams Colony was the subject for much intervention by American diplomatic agents in Palestine, Syria, Turkey, and Egypt during 1867–1868, and its survivors troubled the consuls in later years.

Reference for documents 18 and 19: Ms. Var. 849, Manuscript Department of the Jewish National and University Library in Jerusalem.

Hon. W. P. Fessenden
and
Lot. M. Morrill

Jaffa, July 9th 1867

Hon. Sirs:

In accordance with an earnest suggestion and recommendation of Hon. E. Joy Morris Ambassador at Constantinople. We the Undersigned American citizens residing at or near Jaffa (Syria) humbly address you being influential and distinguished representatives of our own native State and Republic: for the purpose of enquiring if it is not possible thay [*sic*] our Government may not, through your liberal kindness and instrumentality, be prevailed upon by legislative or other action, to endeavor to relieve our present terrible situation of bitter want and utter helplessness. While we implore you for succor, we realize that you can never truly feel our distressing destitution: and for this reason, that you may have a thorough knowledge of the details of our Emigration to this land, and its disastrous consequences, we respectfully beg to refer you to documents transmitted to Hon. W. H. Seward Secr'y of State, dated July 4th, 1867. There are many here who doubtless would be able to pay a partial passage home could they successfully dispose of their property here. On the other hand, there are also many who must have immediate relief or they cannot sustain themselves much longer. Everything has been done by our Consuls here that could be done for us, and every exertion is being made for the alleviation of our condition that can possibly be conceived. But we feel that the charity of the people here has been overtaxed and that every project we have adopted to procure means to defray our expenses home through apathy, indifference and want of common sympathy, will prove inadequate and insufficient for that purpose.

Therefore we the Undersigned American citizens entreatingly solicit your kind and earnest efforts to procure a national vessel to convey us (70 persons in all) back to the United States. By our Government Officials here, this is considered as the only practicable method, of obviating an incalculable amount of inevitable distress and suffering. For we are here without employment of any kind, with no schools, destitute of medical advice or assistance, no clothing; and without means, our property being cheated from us through the machinations of the vile imposter [*sic*] Adams, who will have to deal with the God of Heaven, and not with us.

The Undersigned, in conclusion, ardently pray that God may abundantly bless you and your philanthropic exertions to rescue your countrymen—many of whom have chased the bright folds of the Stars and Stripes o'er many a Southern battlefield—from impending starvation. And your memories shall never cease to be cherished and remembered by your grateful, suffering countrymen.

	NO. OF FAMILY			NO. OF FAMILY
Robert F. Emerson	1.		D. J. Watts	4.
J. E. Burns	2.		J. B. Moulton	4.
G. W. Ames	1.		M. T. Wentworth	5.
M. W. Leighton	3.		Z. Alley	3.
B. K. Rogers	7.		R. Floyd	2.
J. B. Ames	2.		J. S. Walker	2.
L. C. Drisko	2.		A. Norton	7.
F. W. Witham	3.		E. K. Emerson	1.
A. Fabet's wife & 2 children	3.		J. A. Drisko	3.
U. Leighton's " " " "	3.		Zimer Ceruso (?)	6.
E. Clark's widow & 3 "	4.		Brought forward . . . (*sic*)	33.
M. Ward and sister	2.	=33.		
			Total. . .	70.

Respectfully, Submitted to the Department for proper transmission to the Honorable Senators W. P. Fessenden and L. M. Morrill of Maine.

Jerusalem, August 12th, 1867
Victor Beauboucher,
Consul

Department of State
Washington, Sept. 23d 1867

My dear Sir:

I have this moment received your letter of the 20th instant, concerning the so-called Jaffa Colonists of Maine.

You are, I think, not unaware that the colonists early divided concerning the probable success of their plantation, and that the division was a very obstinate one. At first, a large majority decided to adhere, and made vehement complaints against the Consul and Vice Consul at Jerusalem, and even The Honorable William Pitt Fessenden, Portland, Maine, demanded their removal on the ground of their supposed distrust of the success of the enterprise. Lately, however, the discontented seem to have come into a majority; but a portion of the colonists are reported as still adhering to the project and its projection.

His excellency Governor Chamberlain of Maine, on the 21st of August, wrote to this Department upon the subject, urging that measures should be taken for the removal of the colonists. I replied to him on the 31st of August, and invited his attention to the fact that information had reached this Department, showing that a new party of colonists were expected to set out from Maine to Jaffa about the end of August to reenforce the Colony; and therefore, I requested him to give me such facts as he might be able to furnish concerning that alleged effort by citizens of Maine to revive and sustain that enterprise. Aware of the importance and urgency of this subject, I further stated to the Governor that I especially desired that the Senators and Representatives of Maine, or some of them, would give this Department information of what may be expected in reference to any movements in that State, either for bringing back the Colonists of Jaffa, or for re-enforcing them or sending them supplies. The information thus called for was rendered necessary by statements coming from the State of Maine, as well as from Syria, which left no doubt that arrangements for such a re-enforcement as was mentioned had already been made and were confidently expected to be carried out. Reports, which, however, are less authentic, are continually reaching the Department that societies of Jews are proposing to re-enforce the Colony from Europe.

I have received no reply to my letter, from the Governor of Maine, and no information from any quarter of the failure of abandonment of the alleged purpose in that state to re-enforce the Colony in Jaffa. It is hardly necessary to observe that it would be very inconvenient for the Executive Government of the United States to engage in bringing away discontented colonists at the same moment when a ship from the State of Maine would be on its way to replace the returning emigrants with new adventurers.

Be assured, my dear sir, that I fully appreciate the gravity of this matter. I pray you now to obtain for me the information which I have asked from the Governor of Maine, and which is so much wanted for the interests of humanity and of good government.

I am, my dear sir,
faithfully yours
William H. Seward

Reference: Record Group 59, Consular Dispatches, Jerusalem, United States National Archives.

United States Consulate at
Jerusalem December 28th 1871

Hon. Second Assistant Secretary of State
Washington D.C.

Sir:

On the 5th of last October I visited Jaffa on business connected with this Consulate, returning to Jerusalem on the 13th of the same month.

The immediate cause of my visit was a suit for slander and defamation of character brought against Rolla Floyd by Mrs. Tabitha Leighton, both parties being citizens of the United States residing at Jaffa.

Both parties demanded my presence, which in the absence of an Agent at Jaffa I could not well refuse. After a careful investigation of the case with the evidence produced I was satisfied that the action could not be sustained, and that the interests of both parties, as well as the good name of all American interests in Palestine, demanded that the case should be dismissed, which I accordingly did after having given the parties to the suit, as well as the other remaining members of the "Adams Colony", who were all more or less mixed up with this affair, some wholesome advice as to their duties to each other, and their unseemly conduct as American citizens, warning them that while I would always protect them in their rights as citizens of the United States, I would at the same time discourage and discountenance all such petty and disgraceful quarrels as this, which only tended to bring their names into bad repute and lower the standard of the American character in the eyes of the natives of Palestine. I think my action and advice was appreciated by most of those present, and I have reasons for believing that their conduct has been more exemplary since. . . .

I am, sir:
Your obedient servant
R. Beardsley
U.S. Consul

21.

DURING the nineteenth century, most U.S. consuls in Jerusalem, especially Frank De Hass (who served from 1873 to 1877) succored protégés, among them disenfranchised East European Jews. The difficulties arising from these efforts are reflected in this dispatch of Consul Selah Merrill, a member of the Congregationalist ministry who served as U.S. consul in Jerusalem 1882–1885, 1891–1893, and 1898–1907.

Reference: Record Group 51, Consular Dispatches, Jerusalem, United States National Archives.

United States Consulate
Jerusalem, Syria,
September 8, 1891

Hon. William F. Wharton
Assistant Secretary of State
Washington, D. C.

Sir:

I have the honor to acknowledge the receipt of your despatch No. 5, dated August 6, 1891, confirming the nomination of Mr. Herbert E. Clark as Vice Consul for Palestine, and Mr. E. Hardegg as consular Agent for Jaffa; also despatch No. 6, same date, respecting the appropriation for interpreter and guards for this consulate for the present fiscal year.

Allow me to call your attention to a very important matter connected with the welfare of this consulate. Owing to peculiar circumstances which make the Jerusalem consulate exceptional if not entirely unique in our consular service, it seems necessary to employ a second dragoman. This has for many years been the custom at this consulate, but for two years past more or less, it has been discontinued. See Consul General Pringle's report to Hon. G. L. Rives, assistant Secretary of State, inclosed in the Department's despatch to this consulate No. 49, February 8, 1889, in which the Consul General advises the discontinuance of unpaid dragomans and "the Department entirely agrees with the Consul General in the belief that the practise should cease."

Some of the peculiar circumstances to which I refer are as follows: A large proportion of the United States' subjects here are naturalized Jews from Russia or Poland. Many of these persons were never in the United States and cannot speak a word of English. To deal with these people there should be connected with the consulate a person who understands not only English, German, and Hebrew, but especially "Jewish Jargon", the barbarous language spoken by most of this class of our American subjects.

The consul is required to keep a register of American citizens and to send a transcript of the same to the Department of State at the close of each calender [*sic*] year. See consular Regulations Paragraph 444. While by the same Article registration cannot be made compulsory, it is certainly implied that the consul will use every reasonable means to make the register as complete as possible. During my former term as consul here I had the list of citizens revised every year. It was always attended with special difficulties and sometimes required three or four weeks of labor before the list could be completed. My successor, Mr. Gillman, gave this matter no attention whatever.

In consequence of this neglect our list of citizens is in great confusion, and it is simply impossible to tell who, or how many, our citizens are, and marriages, deaths, births, removals, new arrivals, date and place of naturalization and other matters which should appear on such a list, are in a jumble. When any citizen applied for registration, however, Mr. Gillman recorded his name and always charged a fee for the same, clearly in violation of Consular Regulation, Paragraph 444, which states that "No fee will be charged for registration nor for any service connected with it."

I called Mr. Gillman's attention to this, and since he left the practise has been discontinued.

For the sake of the good order and discipline of this consulate this register of citizens must be put into proper shape.

This I am already engaged in doing and I am employing to assist me Mr. David Feinstein who has formerly been in the service of this consulate. If the Department is not willing to compensate Mr. Feinstein for his services, then I must do it myself.

The present interpreter on account of the nature of the languages and the character of the people involved, is wholly unable to do this work. Moreover he is occupied with the ordinary duties of the office, and with matters in the Turkish court where the interests of American citizens require his presence. Matters connected with the coming and going of many Jews, their marriages, births, deaths, and divorces, the quarrels which arise among them and which are almost always brought before the consul, make the work connected with this class of our subjects a very important item in this consulate. This work can be neglected, or done in a bungling manner; it can also be done properly by employing a person who is competent to do it.

I respectfully ask, therefore, that I may be allowed to employ Mr. David Feinstein as second dragoman or interpreter in this consulate and to compensate him with the amount of the extra appropriation made for this consulate as reported in your despatch No. 6, herewith acknowledged.

I remain, respectfully,
Your obedient servant
Selah Merrill
U.S. Consul

22.

TOWARD the end of the nineteenth century, American consuls were increasingly called upon to aid—sometimes rather skeptically—enterprising American businessmen. Despite the onerous responsibilities, the love of the Holy Land influenced the decisions of such consuls as Selah Merrill.

Reference: Record Group 59, Consular Dispatches, Jerusalem, United States National Archives.

No. 113

American Consulate
Jerusalem, Syria,
November 12, 1906.

Subject:—Clifford E. Nadaud and his Jordan Water Scheme.

The Honorable
Assistant Secretary of State
Washington, D.C.

Sir.

The rule of sending business reports without accompanying despatches I have felt compelled to depart from in the present instance because it is exceptional. Col. Clifford E. Nadaud came here with such a strong letter from the Embassy at Constantinople as seemed to make it incumbent on this Consulate to show him special attention. We accordingly made his introduction to the Governor and other prominent officials easy, and we secured favorable letters to the Prefect of the Jericho and Jordan District, also to the head of the religious establishment of that region which was very important as he has great influence in those parts, to the railroad and custom house officials, and to the agents of the steamer company that is to transport his great and numerous barrels to New York.

Because of his unfamiliarity with the country, with "Turkish methods" of procedure, and with the natives and their characteristics, Col. Nadaud would have had no end of trouble, worry, and expense had it not been for the Consulate. We told him plainly that we could not be partisans, much less partners; still, without mixing in the matter in any particularly open way we were able to render him most valuable assistance. The importance of our services he fully appreciated and gratefully acknowledged.

This novel scheme scarcely heard of in America, has already filled Palestine with talk and wild rumors and this has made it necessary for us to act with great caution. We think we have acted so carefully in this case that hereafter no one can refer to it as a precedent; for it is certain that if Col. Nadaud's project meets with even meagre success imitators will come forward to create rival companies, and a precedent would embarrass us greatly. For this reason among others, we have felt obliged to caution Col. Nadaud in regard to many things, in any reference he may wish to make to the general assistance rendered by the Consulate, in the use of the Consul's name and the names of the Consular employees, in giving the names of Turkish officials, in describing their activities in his behalf, and in a number of other particulars, and he has promised faithfully to exercise great discretion.

This despatch and my report sent in duplicate, speak for themselves. The only paper that I have given him is a To Whom It May Concern which I have worded so carefully that it cannot possibly be used as a recommendation of his goods. A copy is inclosed which I trust the Department will approve.

I remain respectfully
Your obedient servant
Selah Merrill
Consul

THE RIVER JORDAN WATER COMPANY.

No meagre interest is aroused when one is able to report a new industry connected with the Holy Land. Visitors to this country have always carried away impressions mental or spiritual, and likewise there has always been a desire to take away tangible objects. Its marble steps and columns have been carried to Italy; tons of exquisite shells have been taken from its seashore; loads of its sacred earth have been shipped to Europe and elsewhere; millions upon millions of its lovely flowers have been gathered, pressed, and sent to multitudes of homes in every Christian land; countless photographs of its cities, landscapes, temples, and massive ruins have been sent all over the civilized world; and its antiquities enrich the public and private museums of many countries. For a number of years past the business of collecting and exploring bulbs has been carried on with the result of that some of Palestine's choicest flowers have been nearly exterminated in certain places. This is to be deplored, but there seems no way to prevent it. This land can poorly afford to part with any of the charms of its springtide dress which have so long delighted and charmed the eye. There are two things however which men can never take away from this ancient land, one because they cannot, and the other because they do not want to. The stones that form its hills and mountains and cover its fields are not wanted; and of its unparalleled or rather divine sunlight this country cannot be robbed.

It seems almost a pity to take away water from this country whose people use so little although they need so much. But this is the new industry that has been launched upon the world, carrying thousands of tons of water from the Jordan, Palestine's sacred river, to distant America. America will receive the benefit of this new industry, although perhaps no new opening will thereby be made for American goods.

A company has been formed, incorporated under the laws of the State of New Jersey with the title The International River Jordan Water Company, of which the Hon. Clifford E. Nadaud of Covington, Kentucky, Colonel on the staff of the Governor of that State, is the President. This gentleman has visited Constantinople for the purpose of securing permission from the Turkish Government to act, and of complying with any other formalities that were found to be necessary. In this he had the cordial co-operation of the American Ambassador the Hon. John G. A. Leishman who rendered him important service. The names of the men comprising this Company are not yet made public, but they have been named to me and I know them to be gentlemen of integrity and means, two or three of them being persons of prominence. Hence as to its reliable character there can be no question.

Col. Nadaud has been in Jerusalem and has had made to his order fifty three strong casks which have been most carefully disinfected and cleaned so that the water put into them can have no possible contamination from the casks themselves. These were taken to the Jordan to the traditional place where Christ was baptised, large cauldrons were provided for boiling the water which was first allowed to settle as the river carries a good deal of earthly matter, the water was thoroughly boiled and again purified, and when cool was filtered into the casks.

Each cask contains 600 kilos (a kilo is two and one fifth pounds) making a total of upwards of thirty-four tons of water from the sacred River of the Holy Land. All the casks bear the seal of the American Consulate in Jerusalem, of the Superior of the Convent of St. John near the Jordan who acts by the direction of Damianos the Greek Patriarch of Jerusalem, and of the Turkish governor of the Jericho and Jordan district.

Every precaution has been taken to insure (by evidence) the genuineness of the water now shipped. To the seals mentioned will be added the receipts of the Railroad Company, the Bills of Lading of the steamers, and perhaps also official papers of the Custom House in New York.

The road from Jerusalem to Jericho has a number of very steep gradients and falls 3800 feet in a distance of twenty-two miles. From Jericho to the Jordan the distance is six miles and the difference in level is about one hundred feet. Between these two points there is no made road, wagons go where they can pick their way. Thus the labor of getting the casks to Jerusalem was somewhat formidable. Special carts had to be made and three horses (Palestine horses are not like the great dray horses of America) had all they could do to haul one cask at a time from the river to the railway station in Jerusalem. All these difficulties and many more incident to the country and the people, were overcome and the water is on its way to New York, where it will be stored in the Bonded Warehouse of Baker and Williams of that city, and there bottled by a special commission.

Photographs which are inclosed illustrate the work of preparing the water at the Jordan, of hauling it to Jerusalem and, at the railway station, of some of the casks just before they were loaded on the cars for the seaport at Jaffa.

All this work has required much careful planning, the outlay of much money, and the expenditure of a great amount of perseverance and energy which the gentleman in charge seems to possess in abundance.

Persons who are strangers to this country may not know the character of the Jordan whether its water is filthy or clean. Hence it may be said briefly that few streams of water in the world are freer from contamination than the Jordan. Between the Dead Sea and the Sea of Galilee the distance is 60 miles, but the river by its windings makes a distance of 120 miles. During its entire course there is not a town or village on or near its banks. Jericho is six miles from the river, and besides this place there is no settlement of any kind in the Jordan valley. It is a muddy stream because it flows through alluvial soil, but it is simply impossible that the river should contain any sewage or any impurities of that kind. When allowed to settle it is perfectly sweet, pure and wholesome.

The Company has been well launched by men of character, capital and energy, its purpose is unique, novel, and well becoming American enterprise, and it deserves to succeed. It is not for me to say what degree of prosperity will attend it or the exact amount of returns there will be per dollar of the capital invested.

Selah Merrill
Consul

Jerusalem
November 12, 1906

23.

UNANTICIPATED and discouraging discomforts of travel in the Holy Land are often described in the pilgrimage literature. A novel description of the impact of American technology on the Old World—the first motor car in the Holy Land—is the subject of a report by Consul Thomas R. Wallace (1907–1910).

Reference: Numerical File 13653, Record Group 59, Consular Dispatches, Jerusalem, United States National Archives.

AMERICAN CONSULATE
JERUSALEM APRIL 15th 1908

SUBJECT: THE GLIDDEN MOTOR TOUR IN PALESTINE

The Honorable
Assistant Secretary of State
Washington, D. C.

Sir.

I have the honor to report to you Mr. Charles J. Glidden, the American Motor Tourist, and his wife arrived in Jerusalem on schedule time. I had notified our consular agent at Jaffa to be prepared to render any assistance to Mr. Glidden he might require upon his entrance to that city as it would be the first motor car to enter Jaffa, it was deemed best to notify the people and be at hand in case of need.

The Motor was landed at Haifa and the tour commenced from that point. The landing is difficult at Jaffa and Haifa is the first seaport north. The Journey from Haifa was found the most difficult encountered in their Palestine experience. The roads were impassable in places owing to heavy rains just preceeding [*sic*] their arrival. This road except in the rainy season will be found quite practicable for the Motor Car, but if proper facilities are provided at Jaffa for landing the car this piece of road can be avoided and touring from Jaffa to Jerusalem and from there to other intermediate points can be made without much difficulty at any time of the year.

The road beds except from Haifa are solid with a good foundation, but some of the grades are as high as 20%. It is advised that cars be used with high clearance because large stones are sometimes encountered in the roads and rough places in which ridges appear.

The car used by Mr. Glidden is a 24 horse power gasoline Motor car. Weighing 3500 lbs. 4 Cylindar [*sic*] Engine with high clearance and its capacity is 5 passengers. Gasoline can be obtained at the Sea ports.

Mr. Glidden has fully demonstrated the practicability of touring in Palestine with a Motor car, not a single accident or mishap occured [*sic*] to mar the succes [*sic*]and pleasure of this tour which is a historic event in the annals of Palestine.

The officials informed us that a description of the event would be entered on the records of the City and to the American would be given the honor of first entering the Holy Land in a motor car.

The most surprising part of these tours was the friendly and cordial manner the party was received and treated by the natives at all the points visited. I had made all possible arrangement before the arrival of Mr. Glidden to protect him from annoyance or possible trouble but found these precautions wholly unnecessary. I accompanied him to the old historic city of Hebron, one of the places in Palestine noted for rough treatment some time accorded to tourists, but in this instance the people comported themselves in the most friendly manner.

Although the visit was unexpected large and enthusiastic crowds gathered along the streets and roadways to view the novel vehical [*sic*] all acting in the most orderly manner.

The Mayor and Governor received us most cordially, the former insisting we remain and partake of the festivities of the city, as he expressed it, in honor of the first visit of the motorcar. He and one of his chief officers were given a ride to their evident delight. The native boys both Moslem and Jew chased wildly after the car in a vain endeaver [*sic*] to keep up with it and to remain in view of the wonderful machine.

Mr. Jago the American Missionary at that point says it was the wildest and most enthusiastic time Hebron has experienced since the crowning of King David as King of the Jews.

The Gliddens while here motored in their car to all of the principal points [of] interest usually visited by tourists in the Holy Land. Commencing at Haifa thence to Jaffa, Ramleh, Jerusalem, Bethlehem, Jericho, the Jordan, the Dead Sea, Ramallah, Hebron, Nablous [*sic*] , Nazareth [*sic*] , the Sea of Galile [*sic*] , Damascus, and Beyrout [*sic*] , in all about 750 miles. The ease with which the tour is made far outweighs the small annoyances experienced in their case from Haifa to Jaffa by reason of the rains and if made in the dry season these difficulties are not encountered.

The road to both Jericho and Nablous were represented as not practicable for the Motor both places were reached without difficulty. The Journey to Jericho includes the Jordan and the Dead Sea, usually requires 2 days by carriage or horse and is a wearisome ride. Mr. Glidden started from Jerusalem on this tour at 9 in the morning and was back at 6 in the evening and parties who accompanied him said it was the most pleasant trip they had ever made to these points.

The greatest interest has been aroused throughout the district by these tours in the Motor Car and a number of people are talking of investing in one I am informed. A light strong car with good clearance and sufficient power to make the grades, that is a good hill climber and of medium price, in my judgment, would be the best to meet the demand. While a repair and supply shop would add greatly to the chance for sales of machines in this district.

The tour has opened up a possible market for Motor vehicals [*sic*] not heretofore existing and it was most opportune. A great deal of prejudice existed among Turkish officials and permission must first be obtained from the Imperial Government to this travel through the country. The carefulness and courtesy shown by Mr. Glidden in driving his car has removed this prejudice among the officials here and will render the task of others following less difficult.

It is to be hoped that action will be taken by the Imperial government to remove the restraint now imposed upon the use of the motor car for travel and as free access be permitted as in other lands.

It should be known by dealers who desire to compete for trade in this line of business that there are few very wealthy families in this country, and that the well to do are limited in number, but the latter are increasing, and it would seem that an opportunity is opening for a good business if taken advantage of before the field is occupied by European firms as is too often the case in trade enterprises.

I am Sir
Your obedient servant
Thomas R. Wallace
American Consul

24.

AMONG the numerous unpublished documents on the political aspects of the America–Holy Land relationship are background papers prepared by government officials and agencies to be utilized in discussions and negotiations. The following document, setting forth concrete recommendations, was prepared by the Intelligence Section for President Woodrow Wilson.

Reference: File 185.112-1, *Record Group 258, General Records of the American Commission to Negotiate Peace,* United States National Archives.

OUTLINE OF TENTATIVE REPORT AND RECOMMENDATIONS
PREPARED BY THE INTELLIGENCE SECTION,
IN ACCORDANCE WITH INSTRUCTIONS,
FOR THE PRESIDENT AND THE PLENIPOTENTIARIES
JANUARY 21, 1919.

PALESTINE.

It is recommended:

1) That there be established a separate state of Palestine.

2) That this state be placed under Great Britain as a mandatory of the League of Nations.

3) That the Jews be invited to return to Palestine and settle there, being assured by the Conference of all proper assistance in so doing that may be consistent with the protection of the personal (especially the religious) and the property rights of the non-Jewish population, and being further assured that it will be the policy of the League of Nations to recognize Palestine as a Jewish state as soon as it is a Jewish state in fact.

4) That the holy places and religious rights of all creeds in Palestine be placed under the protection of the League of Nations and its mandatory.

DISCUSSION.

1) It is recommended that there be established a separate state of Palestine.

The separation of the Palestinian area from Syria finds justification in the religious experience of mankind. The Jewish and Christian churches were born in Palestine, and Jerusalem was for long years, at different periods, the capital of each. And while the relation of the Mohammedans to Palestine is not so intimate, from the beginning they have regarded Jerusalem as a holy place. Only by establishing Palestine as a separate state can justice be done to these great facts.

As drawn upon the map, the new state would control its own source of water power and irrigation, on Mount Hermon in the east to the Jordan; a feature of great importance since the success of the new state would depend upon the possibilities of agricultural development.

2) It is recommended that this state be placed under Great Britain as a mandatory of the League of Nations.

Palestine would obviously need wise and firm guidance. Its population is without political experience, is racially composite, and could easily become distracted by fanaticism and bitter religious differences.

The success of Great Britain in dealing with similar situations, her relation to Egypt, and her administrative achievements since General Allenby freed Palestine from the Turk, all indicate her as the logical mandatory.

3) It is recommended that the Jews be invited to return to Palestine and settle there, being assured by the Conference of all proper assistance in so doing that may be consistent with the protection of the personal (especially the religious) and the property rights of the non-Jewish population, and being further assured that it will be the policy of the League of Nations to recognize Palestine as a Jewish state as soon as it is a Jewish state in fact.

It is right that Palestine should become a Jewish state, if the Jews, being given the full opportunity, make it such. It was the cradle and home of their vital race, which has made large spiritual contributions to mankind, and is the only land in which they can hope to find a home of their own; they being in this last respect unique among significant peoples.

At present, however, the Jews form barely a sixth of the total population of 700,000 in Palestine, and whether they are to form a majority, or even a plurality, of the population in the future state remains uncertain. Palestine, in short, is far from being a Jewish country now. England, as mandatory, can be relied on to give the Jews the privileged position they should have without sacrificing the rights of non-Jews.

4) It is recommended that the holy places and religious rights of all creeds in Palestine be placed under the protection of the League of Nations and its mandatory.

The basis for this recommendation is self-evident.

Biblical Place-Names

25.

ALMOST a thousand names of biblical derivation appear on the map of the United States. Not all of them, however, stem from biblical sources. In order to ascertain the origins of these place-names, Lottie K. Davis compiled a master list, collating it with the available official gazetteers, postal guides, state reference maps, WPA guides and studies, local histories, and place-name studies. In addition, a questionnaire was addressed to every village, town, and city on the master list. The following authenticated list of 373 biblical names and their county locations is the first result of this research; every name is based upon a standard source or study.

Reference: Lottie and Moshe Davis, *Guide to Map of Biblical Names in America: Land of our Fathers* (New York: Associated American Artists, 1954).

Alabama

Boaz, Marshall
Goshen, Pike
Jericho, Perry
Joppa, Cullman
Mt. Carmel, Jackson
Mt. Carmel, Montgomery
Mt. Hebron, Greene
Mt. Olive, Jefferson
Pisgah, Jackson
Ruhama, Birmingham

Arizona

Eden, Graham

Arkansas

Bethel, Greene
Damascus, Faulkner
Hebron, Clark
Jericho, Grittenden
Jerusalem, Conway
Mt. Olive, Izard
Shiloh, Clebourne
Zion, Izard

California

Edenvale, Santa Clara
Goshen, Tulare
Havilah, Kern
Jerusalem (Lake)
Joshua, San Bernardino
Mt. Ararat, El Dorado
Mt. Hebron (Peak), Siskiyou
Mt. Hebron (Town), Siskiyou
Mt. Hermon, Santa Cruz
Ophir, Placer
Pisgah, San Bernardino
Pisgah Crater, San Bernardino

Colorado

Ephraim; Manassa, Conejos
Hebron, Jackson
Lebanon, Montezuma

Connecticut

Bethel, Fairfield
Bethlehem, Litchfield
Bozrah, New London
Canaan, Litchfield
Goshen, Litchfield
Hebron, Tolland
Lebanon, New London
Mt. Carmel, New Haven
New Canaan, Fairfield
New Salem, New London
North Canaan, Litchfield
Salem, New London
Sharon, Litchfield

Delaware

Bethel, Sussex
Lebanon, Kent
Mt. Moriah, Kent
Rehoboth, Sussex
Rehoboth Bay, Sussex

Florida

Canaan, Seminole
Lebanon, Levy
Shiloh, Brevard

Georgia

Bethel, Rabun
Bethlehem, Barrow
Hebron, Sanderville
Hephzibah, Richmond
Naomi, Walker

Idaho

Eden, Jerome
Goshen, Bingham
Salem, Madison
Samaria, Oneida

Illinois

Bethel, Clay
Carmi, White

Goshen, Stark
Hebron, McHenry
Joppa, Massac
Jordan, Whiteside
Lebanon, St. Clair
Moriah, Clark
Mt. Carmel, Wabash
Nebo, Pike
New Salem, Menard
Pigsah, Jacksonville
Salem, Marion
Zion, Carroll
Zion City, Lake

Indiana

Bethel, Wayne
Bethlehem, Clark
Canaan, Jefferson
Carmel, Hamilton
Eden, Hancock
Gilead, Miami
Goshen, Elkhart
Hebron, Porter
Lebanon, Boone
Merom, Sullivan
Mt. Carmel, Franklin
Mt. Carmel, Gibson
Nineveh, Johnson
Zoar, Pike

Iowa

Bethel, Van Buren
Bethlehem, Wayne
Egypt, Van Buren
Goshen, Ringgold
Hebron, Adair
Jordan, Harrison
Kedron, Harrison
Lebanon, Van Buren
Mt. Moriah, Van Buren
Mt. Zion, Van Buren
Pisgah, Harrison
Salem, Henry
Sharon, Appanoose
Shiloh, Des Moines
Solomon, Mills
Tabor, Fremont
Zion, Adair
Zion, Van Buren

Kansas

Lebanon, Smith
Sharon, Barber
Sharon Springs, Wallace

Kentucky

Bethel, Bath
Goshen, Oldham
Jericho, Henry
Lebanon, Marion
Mt. Carmel, Fleming
Nebo, Hopkins
Zion, Grant

Louisiana

Ararat, Calcasieu
Ebenezer, Acadia
Eden, La Salle
Nebo, La Salle

Maine

Bethel, Oxford
Carmel, Penobscot
Gilead, Oxford
Hebron, Oxford
Hiram, Oxford

Jerusalem, Franklin
Lebanon, York

Maryland

Bethlehem, Caroline
Damascus, Montgomery
Ebenezer, Cecil
Joppa, Harford
Zion, Cecil

Massachusetts

Goshen, Hampshire
Mt. Horeb, Berkshire
New Salem, Franklin
Rehoboth, Bristol
Salem, Essex
Sharon, Norfolk
Zoar, Franklin

Michigan

Benzonia, Benzie
Bethel, Branch
Eden, Ingham
Gilead, Branch
Sharon, Kalkosha

Minnesota

Aaron (Lake), Douglas
Bethel, Anoka
Eden, Dodge
(and 7 additional names in State)
Hebron, Aitkin
Jordan, Fillmore
Jordan, Scott
Kedron Brook, Fillmore
Mamre, Kandiyohi
Mizpah, Koochiching
Moses (Lake), Douglas
Mt. Nebo, Todd
Nimrod, Wadena
Sharon, Le Sueur
Zion, Stearns

Mississippi

Bethel, Newton
Damascus, Scott
Ebenezer, Holmes
Mt. Zion, Simpson
Pisgah, Charles
Sharon, Madison

Missouri

Bethel, Shelby
Canaan, Gasconade
Jerico Springs, Cedar
New Salem, Newton
Nineveh, Adair
Pisgah, Cooper
Salem, Dent
Zion, Madison

Nebraska

Bethel, Kimball
Elim, Nemaha
Gilead, Thayer
Hebron, Thayer
Lebanon, Red Willow
Salem, Richardson
Zion, Burt

Nevada

Mizpah, Elko

New Hampshire

Bethlehem, Grafton

Canaan, Grafton
Gaza, Belknap
Goshen, Sullivan
Hebron, Grafton
Lebanon, Grafton
Salem, Rockingham

New Jersey

Carmel, Cumberland
Genesis Bay, Cape May
Goshen, Cape May
Jericho, Cumberland
Jericho, Gloucester
Jericho, Salem
Lebanon, Hunterdon
Mizpah, Atlantic
Mt. Bethel, Warren
Mt. Gilboa, Hunterdon
Mt. Hermon, Warren
Mt. Horeb, Somerset
Mt. Nebo, Sussex
Mt. Pisgah, Sussex
Mt. Tabor, Morris
New Egypt, Ocean
New Sharon, Gloucester
New Sharon, Monmouth
Salem, Salem
Siloam, Monmouth
Zarephath, Somerset
Zion, Somerset

New Mexico

Bethel, Roosevelt
Rehoboth, McKinley

New York

Bethel, Dutchess
Bethel, Sullivan
Bethlehem, Albany
Canaan, Columbia
Carmel, Putnam
Eden, Erie
Ephrata, Fulton
Gilboa, Schoharie
Goshen, Orange
Hebron, Washington
Hermon, St. Lawrence
Jericho, Nassau
Lebanon, Onondaga
Moriah, Essex
Nineveh, Broome
Sharon, Schoharie
Shushan, Washington

North Carolina

Ararat, Surry
Bethel, Pitt
Eleazer, Randolph
Mt. Gilead, Montgomery
Mt. Olive, Wayne
Ophir, Montgomery
Pisgah, Randolph
Pisgah Forest, Transylvania
Salem, Forsyth
Salemburg, Sampson
Tabor City, Columbus

North Dakota

Hebron, Morton
Mt. Carmel, Cavalier
New Salem, Morton
Sharon, Steele
Zion, Towner

Ohio

Ai, Fulton
Bethel, Clermont

Canaan, Wayne
Carmel, Highland
Gath, Highland
Gilboa, Putnam
Goshen, Clermont
Hebron, Licking
Lebanon, Warren
Mt. Carmel, Clermont
Mt. Carmel, Sandusky
Rehoboth, Perry
Salem, Columbiana
Sharon, Trumbull
Shiloh, Montgomery
Shiloh, Richland
Sodom, Trumbull
Zoar, Tuscarawas

Oklahoma

Gideon, Cherokee
Jonah, Garfield
Kedron, Cherokee
Lebanon, Marshall
Nebo, Murray
Sharon, Woodward

Oregon

Bethel, Polk
Damascus, Clarkamas
Goshen, Lane
Lebanon, Linn
Mt. Horeb, Marion
Mt. Moriah, Union
Mt. Pisgah, Polk
Mt. Tabor, Multnomah
Ophir, Curry
Salem, Marion
Selah, Marion

Pennsylvania

Ararat, Susquehanna
Bethel, Allegheny
Bethlehem, Northampton
Canaan, Wayne
Damascus, Wayne
Ephrata, Lancaster
Goshen Heights, Chester
Hebron, Potter
Jericho Mt. and Creek, Bucks
Lebanon, Lebanon
Mt. Carmel, Northumberland
Mt. Nebo, Lancaster
New Salem, Fayette
Nineveh, Greene
Sharon, Mercer
Zion, Lucerne

Rhode Island

Eden Park, Providence
Elisha, Little Compton, Newport

South Carolina

Ebenezer, Florence
Mt. Carmel, McCormick
Sharon, York
Shiloh, Sumter
Zion, Marion

South Dakota

Lake Sinai, Brookings
Lebanon, Potter
Salem, McCook
Sinai, Brookings

Tennessee

Joppa, Grainger
Lebanon, Wilson
Mt. Horeb, Jefferson
Sharon, Weakley

Texas

Bethlehem, Hill
Egypt, Wharton
Goshen, Parker
Hebron, Denton
Jonah, Williamson
Joshua, Victoria
Nineveh, Leon
Salem, Johnson

Utah

Eden, Weber
Ephraim, Sanpeter
Goshen, Utah
Jordan, Salt Lake
Mt. Carmel, Kane
North Eden Canyon, Rich
Salem, Utah
South Eden Canyon, Rich
Zion Canyon, Washington
Zion Nat'l Park, Washington

Vermont

Bethel, Windsor
Canaan, Essex
Goshen, Addison
Goshen Corners, Addison
Jericho, Chittenden
Jericho Center, Chittenden

Virginia

Damascus, Washington
Lebanon, Russell
Mt. Carmel, Smyth
Zion, Louisa

Washington

Eden, Wahkiakum
Jericho, Grant
Jerusalem, Stevens
Sharon, Spokane
Tekoa, Whitman

West Virginia

Bethlehem, Ohio
Boaz, Wood
Canaan, Upshur
Damascus, Marshall
Ebenezer, Fayette
Edray, Pocahontas
Gilboa, Nicholas
Hebron, Pleasant
Joppa, Braxton
Kedron, Upshur
Mt. Carmel, Preston
Mt. Nebo, Nicholas
Mt. Pisgah, Clay
Mt. Zion, Calhoun
Nebo, Clay
Pisgah, Preston
Salem, Harrison

Wisconsin

Bethel, Wood
Eden, Fond du Lac
Lebanon, Dodge
Mt. Horeb, Dane
Salem, Kenosha
Siloam, Milwaukee
Sharon, Walworth

Wyoming

Eden, Sweetwater
Goshen County